Other books by Antoinette May

- *Passionate Pilgrim*

- *Witness to War*

- *The Annotated Ramona*

- *Helen Hunt Jackson: A Lonely Voice of Conscience*

- *Psychic Women*

- *Haunted Houses of California*

- *Adventures of a Psychic*

THE
YUCATAN

A Guide to
the Land of Maya Mysteries

plus sacred sites at
BELIZE, TIKAL & COPAN

by Antoinette May

WIDE WORLD PUBLISHING/TETRA

Acknowledgements: This book owes much to the moral and practical assistance of Tommy and Jerisue Thomson of Tropical Travel, David Smith of Select Resorts International, Olga Ayala of Mundo Maya Honduras, Jorge Molanphy of Maya Tropic Tours, Nick and Krys Nocerino, and Ruth Shari; the photography of Vern Appleby and C.J. Marrow; the knowledge of Joan Hallifax, Peter Balin, Brother John and Lola of the Ojai Foundation; the enthusiasm of Ann Shotland and—most specially—to Ann Axtell Morris who provided the spark.

Revised edition 2004.
October 2004 Printing.
Wide World Publishing/Tetra
P.O. Box 476
San Carlos, CA 94070
Printed in the United States of America.
ISBN: 1-884550-33-9

Library of Congress Cataloging-in-Publication Data
May, Antoinette.
        The Yucatan.

            Includes index.   1. Yucatán Peninsula--Description and travel--
1981-
--Guide-books. 2. Maya--Antiquities--Guide-books.
3. Indians of Mexico--Yucatán--Antiquities--
Guide-books. 4. Yucatán Peninsula--Antiquities--
Guide-books. I. Title.
F1376.M43 1988   917.2'604834   86-51427
ISBN 1-884550-33-9 (pbk.)

For my husband,
Charles Herndon

TABLE OF CONTENTS

Columns at Chichen Itza.

INTRODUCTION

There was nothing standing;
Only the calm water, the placid seas,
alone and tranquil.
Nothing existed.

"Then they planned the creation,
And the growth of trees and thickets
and the birth of life.

"Thus let it be done!
Let the emptiness be filled!
Let the water recede and make a void.
Let the earth appear and become solid;
Let it be done, thus they spoke.
Let there be light, let there be dawn in the sky and
on the earth!

Popol Vuh

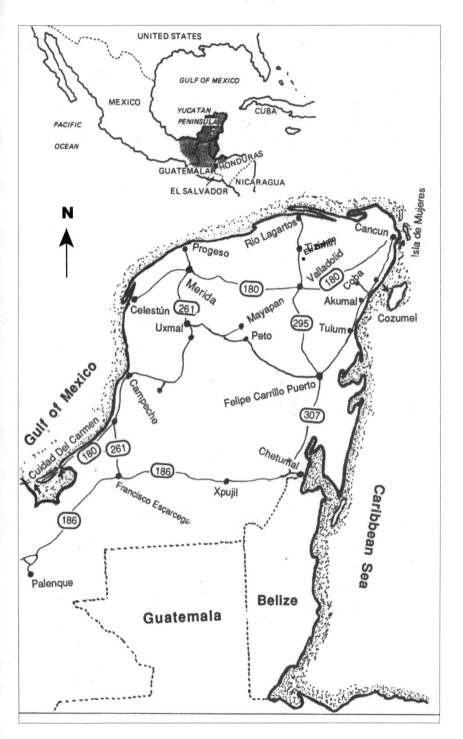

When Atlantis sank, Yucatan rose–and that's just one story. The mysterious Maya have inspired many.

Though the Aztec and Inca civilizations were the dominant ones at the time of the Spaniards arrival, it's the world of the ancient Maya that appeals most to the imagination. All we really know is that the Maya empire, consisting of more than 100 city states, flourished for a millennium. During their ascendency these mysterious people formulated the concept of the zero before the Arabs and devised a calendar more accurate than the one we use today. Then, as mysteriously as it all began, the Maya civilization abruptly ended.

The Maya built great cities, abandoned them, then returned hundreds of years later. Why? Some of their toys had wheels and yet they didn't make use of this basic tool in their labors. Why did this seemingly simple connection elude them?

When the first Europeans set foot on the ancient soil of the "New" World, most of the Maya ceremonial centers had been gobbled up by jungle. Only the tallest buildings still towered above the dense vegetation. Who built these cities only to desert them? they asked, as we do today.

Devout Christians that they were, the Spaniards believed that every human was descended from not just Adam and Eve but Noah and his family, the sole survivors of the great flood. But how could the Indians of the new world claim such descent? Since they couldn't, it meant the Maya Indians weren't quite human. That rationalization helped the conquistadores to justify a lot. Who would blame them for killing or enslaving animals?

The "animals" had to be protected from themselves. One of the most vicious of the protectors was Diego de Landa, first bishop of Yucatan, whose auto-da-fe was intended to–and perhaps did–wipe out the entire Maya history. In his eyes the manuscripts consigned to the flames contained "nothing but superstition and falsehoods of the devil."

Eventually even the conquistadores complained about the extent of de Landa's missionary fervor. The priest was recalled to Spain and imprisoned. With time on his hands, de Landa did an amazing thing. He attempted to replace what he'd destroyed by compiling an account of everything he'd observed about the Maya at the time of the conquest and every story he'd since heard about them. That record, lost and then found 300 years later, constitutes the bulk of what little we know today about the Maya civilization.

While languishing in prison, Landa recalled a story told to him by an old man who said that his ancestors believed themselves descended from a race that had come from the east by way of twelve paths opened through the sea for them by God. From this legend, Landa hypothesized that the Maya must be descended from one of the Lost Tribes of Israel. He was eventually freed and his theory gained popularity throughout the 16th and 17th centuries. It still has proponents which include The New World Archaeological Foundation funded by the Morman church.

As they learned more about the magnificence of the Maya civilization, Europeans simply could not believe these amazing people weren't a transplant from their own world or at least a world with which they were familiar. As a result, the Maya Indians were from time to time identified as descendants of Norse explorers, Phoenician traders, shipwrecked Huns, Romans, Africans, Irishmen, and crew members from the lost fleet of Alexander the Great–or even Alexander himself.

A theory dating from the 16th century which is frequently reintroduced is that the Maya are refugees from the lost continent of Atlantis. According to legend, Atlantis was a great island in the Atlantic that was destroyed by volcanic eruptions, earthquakes and tidal waves. Unproven and frequently derided, the story of this sunken continent lying buried beneath the sea is a myth that refuses to die. It's estimated that some 3000 books have been written about Atlantis in the last 2500 years. If the physical reality remains to be established, the significance of the myth's psychological reality can't be disputed.

Many believe that this lost continent is the ancestral home of both the Egyptians and the Maya. A leading proponent of this theory was the French Abbe Charles Etienne Brasseur de Bourbourg, who became an expert on the Maya language. This brilliant 19th century scholar was responsible for saving many early colonial manuscripts from destruction when the monastic orders were finally suppressed–among them Bishop Landa's lost manuscript. He translated the Popol Vuh, the Maya bible, and other ancient writings, then climaxed a lifetime of research by publishing his premise that the civilizations of Egypt and the Old World came from the New World, where they had previously been brought by colonists from Atlantis.

Augustus Le Plongeon, an archeologist and physician, shared his beliefs. Le Plongeon and his wife, Alice, began their excavation of Chichen Itza in the midst of a minor revolution, settling into a fortified church and walking three miles each day to the ruins. A precursor of Carlos Castaneda, Le Plongeon won the confidence of the Indians who confided to him ancient secrets jealously guarded from the Spanish, secrets for which their ancestors had been tortured or murdered.

Le Plongeon described these revelations as having "a rich living current of occult wisdom and practice, with its sources in an extremely ancient past, far beyond the purview of ordinary historical research." Occasionally, he believed, the mask was lowered sufficiently for him to glimpse "a world of spiritual reality, sometimes of indescribable beauty, again of inexpressible horror."

Some of this was revealed in his book, *Queen Moo and the Egyptian Sphinx*, which draws frequent parallels between the Egyptians and the Maya. Both civilizations had pyramids, hieroglyphic writing, relief sculpture and many common words. The controversy that Le Plongeon unleashed more than 100 years ago continues to this day.

The accepted theory today is that the Maya–like all the Indians of the Americas–migrated from Asia over a long period of years via a land bridge that once spanned the Bering Strait. But if this one seems too ho-hum, consider the another hypothesis: extra terrestrials. The much discussed "Maya obsession with time" takes on new meaning to some who speculate that the early Maya were explorers or refugees from another planet, people desperately calculating just how long their supplies would last. These same theorists insist that there must be some reason why the United States is spending millions of dollars each year on Maya research.

Far out? Literally and assuredly, yet a sarcophagus at Palenque does resemble a man at the controls of a spacecraft, and there's a decided astronaut look about the ubiquitous Descending God. The debate seems likely to stretch into infinity itself.

The best known of all the 19th century explorers fascinated by the Maya mystery was John Lloyd Stephens The fact that Stephens, a prominent New York attorney, had helped to elect President Martin Van Buren didn't hurt a bit when he asked for the position of U.S. Diplomatic Agent to the government of Central America. It was hoped the title might come in handy should an insurrection occur–which it did more than once.

His companion on the journey was the English born artist, Frederick Catherwood who'd traveled and painted extensively in the Near East. Catherwood's fascination with old ruins and exotic cultures was extreme. In order to gain admission to the mosque of Omar where he wished to make detailed architectural drawings, he submitted himself to circumcision.

Serpent sculpture at Chichen Itza.

Undeterred by the grudging welcome they received from the war torn population, Stephens worked for months uncovering the ruins while Catherwood struggled to capture them with pen and ink. Groggy from malaria, their bodies swollen from insect bites, they continued their work until Catherwood collapsed.

When Stephens and Catherwood finally staggered out of the jungle they had the makings of what would be one of the great best sellers of their century. Incidents of Travel in Central America, Chiapas and Yucatan, a two-volume book, revealed a whole new world to the general public and introduced a word that had not appeared in any dictionary. It was Maya. Within three months the book went through ten printings. When Catherwood regained his health, the two returned. The result of the second trip, *Incidents of Travel in Yucatan,* another two volume tome, was an even better seller.

Stephens and Catherwood explored the Yucatan Peninsula nearly 150 years ago hacking their way through almost impenetrable jungle. "We sat down on the very edge of the wall, and strove in vain to fathom the mystery by which we were surrounded," Stephens wrote in 1840. Today, with all our modern innovations and conveniences, the mystery remains the same. Again and again, we ask as he did: "Who were the people who built these cities?"

Like Stephens, we attempt to solve the puzzle, pondering: "In the ruined cities of Egypt, even in the long-lost Petra, the stranger knows the story of the people whose vestiges he finds around him. America, say historians, was peopled by savages; but savages never carved these stones."

And again, like Stephens, we seek answers from the descendants of the Indians who excavated these abandoned masterpieces. Their answer is invariably the same:

"Quien sabe?"

Catherwood's drawing of the Governor's Palace at Uxmal.

Sketch of the Temple of the Magician at Uxmal by Frederick Catherwood.

ROMANCING THE RUINS

*...without the wheel, draft animals or metal
cutting tools, Maya engineers, artisans
and laborers built magnificent cities.*

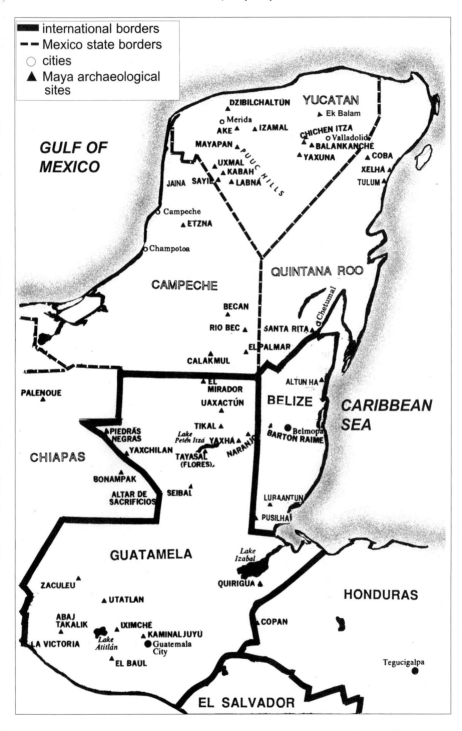

international borders
Mexico state borders
○ cities
▲ Maya archaeological
  sites

GULF OF
MEXICO

YUCATAN

DZIBILCHALTÚN ▲
○ Merida   ▲ Ek Balam
AKE ▲ ▲ IZAMAL
MAYAPAN ▲   CHICHEN ITZA
                ○ Valladolid
▲ UXMAL   ▲ BALANKANCHÉ
▲ KABAH   ▲ YAXUNA   ▲ COBA
JAINA SAYIL ▲ ▲ LABNÁ   XELHA ▲
                              TULUM ▲
PUUC HILLS

○ Campeche
▲ ETZNA

○ Champotoa

CAMPECHE

QUINTANA ROO

BECAN
▲

RIO BEC ▲   ▲ SANTA RITA
            EL PALMAR ▲
▲
CALAKMUL

d Chetumal

PALENQUE
▲

▲ EL
  MIRADOR   ALTUN HA ▲
UAXACTÚN
▲   BELIZE   CARIBBEAN
                           SEA
▲ PIEDRÁS   TIKAL ▲
  NEGRAS   Lake   ● Belmopa
▲ YAXCHILAN   Petén Itzá YAXHÁ ▲ BARTON RAIME
              TAYASAL   NARANJ
CHIAPAS   (FLORES)

BONAMPAK
▲
ALTAR DE   SEIBAL ▲
SACRIFICIOS   LURAANTUN ▲
                           PUSILHA ▲

GUATAMELA   Lake
              Izabal

ZACULEU ▲   QUIRIGUA ▲   HONDURAS

▲ UTATLAN

ABAJ
TAKALIK ▲ IXIMCHÉ   ▲ COPAN
▲ LA VICTORIA Lake
           Atitlán ▲ KAMINALJUYÚ
                    ● Guatemala
                      City   Tegucigalpa
▲ EL BAUL   ●

EL SALVADOR

Any "lost" civilization will inspire a sense of mystery as one ponders the fate of ancient cities covered over by greedy jungles. But an even greater puzzle than the cause of the Maya decline is the question: how did this civilization ever exist in the first place? And, then, by implication, how could it have lasted as long as it did? Most specifically, how it could have existed where it did?

How could the level of social and political organization needed to sustain this civilization be attained in areas of impassable forests, rank vegetation and dangerous animals? Yet it was in just such places that the Maya culture reached its highest level. In many areas the ground is nothing more than porous limestone, the topsoil seldom more than a few inches deep. What little water there is collects in channels below the ground and runs into the sea without ever coming to the surface. How could the greatest civilization in the Western Hemisphere have developed in this hostile environment?

What we know is merely that it did. We also know that without the wheel, draft animals or metal cutting tools, Maya engineers, artisans and laborers built magnificent cities. Around 1500 B.C., the Maya are believed to have migrated from Central America into Yucatan, an area described by de Landa as "the country with the least earth that I have ever seen, since all of it is one living rock and wonderfully little earth."

Why did they abandon a hospitable environment to begin anew in such a hostile one? No one knows.

We do know that this was the beginning of the Preclassic Period which continued until approximately 300 A.D. Bows and arrows yet to be invented, the Maya hunted with snares and spears. They were considerate hunters killing only what was needed. This is still true. Respect for the dignity of the animal and gratitude for its ultimate gift, is demonstrated by the modern Maya hunter when he explains to the animal he has killed, "I have need."

The slash and burn method of agriculture which requires great experience on the farmer's part evolved from this early time and is still in use. A patch of forest is selected and cut down in the late autumn. Then at the end of the dry season the brush is burned. The maize seed is poked into the ash with a stick. This milpa has a life span of only two years. Then the farmer must abandon it for 15 to 20 years and go to another area of the forest and begin again. The everyday life of the Preclassic Maya centered around the rain, sun and wind gods who were—and still are—evoked when the fields are cut, burned and planted, and when the crops are growing.

Then in 500 B.C.– at the same time the ancient
Greek civilization was flourishing—the Maya began
to make great strides. Centuries before the birth of
Christ, the Maya developed what has been called
"one of the brilliant achievements of the human
mind," a system of numeration by position
involving the concept and use of the zero.[1]

The Maya zero symbol.

This is all the more striking when compared with the clumsy Roman
numerical system used in Europe at that time where the zero was unknown.
Why should an agricultural people living in the midst of a jungle bother with
such a highly sophisticated mathematical system? But would the Maya have
invented such a complex order if they hadn't had use for it? What was that
use? These seemingly primitive people measured time in units larger than
23,000,000,000 days. One can only marvel and wonder once again: why?

In the next 800 years–while Jesus was born, preached and was crucified,
Jerusalem was destroyed and the Jewish Diaspora took place, and the Roman
Empire climbed to its zenith and waned–the Maya were developing their
calendar–more accurate than the Gregorian calendar introduced in 582 A.D.,
their beautiful and highly complex hieroglyphic writing, and their architecture.

Then in 300 A.D., while the barbarians were sacking Rome and the Dark
Ages were spreading over Europe, the Maya made a quantum leap into their
Golden Age. What we know today as the Classic Period must have been
grounded in a kind of spiritual awakening. Some mysterious, invigorating
impulse instilled in the Maya a profound sense of the transitory nature of life.
One response was an urgent need to make some kind of enduring mark,
another was to record the passage of worldly events.

Nineteen major cities–that we know of–were built at this time along with
countless minor ones.   Clay mounds gave way to colossal pyramids of cut
stone, majestic temples and palaces adorned with intricately carved facades
and exquisite sculpture. The style was remarkably sophisticated, as intro-
spective as that of Asia and as naturalistic as sculpture found in the
Mediterranean areas.   Maya artists achieved a three dimensional effect by
foreshortening when they chose, but for the most part preferred a flat,
painterly approach. The effect of so much baroque ornamentation is one of
order in complexity. The rigid formality of earlier monuments gave way to a
dynamic imbalance within different parts of the composition which
continues to fascinate while leading the eye restlessly along.

Stelae–great stone monuments —an example of early day public relations celebrating the personal triumphs and grand activities of kings and city states, were commissioned by rulers everywhere. Corbel arches, solar observatories, water reservoirs, all the practical applications of an advanced civilization, appeared.

The finest examples of Maya architecture were conceived and constructed at this time, long before the Gothic style appeared in Europe. How was the creation of these grand cities possible for people without wheels, metal cutting tools or dray animals? How did they transport the giant stones for their temples and pyramids when there was no stone in the area itself? How did they manage to move huge stone heads weighing twenty tons or more through miles of jungle?

Romancing the ruins—Chichen Itza.

The mysteries don't stop here. We know but two things about the Classic Maya civilization. It evolved and then ended. All the rest is pure conjecture. By 900 the Golden Age was over. The sad story is revealed by what wasn't said. One means of measuring time was in batkuns. No commemorative stelae record the opening of Batkun 10 in the ninth century of our era.

What came next is known as the Postclassic Period. Almost over night it seems many of the great ceremonial centers had been abandoned. An epidemic, perhaps? A revolution? Famine? Earthquake? No record or historical indication has ever been found pointing to any of these possibilities. Whatever happened, we know that a few isolated groups stayed on, camping

out in the rooms of forgotten palaces — much like the Lancandon Maya do today — burning copal incense before the likenesses of mortal men who slowly evolved into gods.

Then, in the 11th century, about the time the Normans were conquering England, the Toltecs conquered the Maya. These grim militarists from central Mexico were a new order of men replacing the intellectual leaders of Classic times. The conquest was brutal and violent in the

Maya ruins at various stages—Chichen Itza.

extreme. Warrior gods were introduced, blood sacrifices accelerated. But, like many conquerors, the Toltec were absorbed by their new subjects, becoming essentially latter day Maya.

There were many wars before the big one with the conquistadores and even that was not final. There were also many more cities built, some we have yet to find. In 1840 John Stephens wrote of a city hidden deep in the jungle where chickens were kept underground to prevent anyone from hearing them crow and and where the Maya killed any intruder unlucky enough to happen upon them. Such hidden cities are being discovered to this day, and each time are found to be deserted. How long have they been that way?

Until recent years, scholars unable to read Maya hieroglyphics, tended to idealize the Maya as a peaceful people, intellectuals absorbed primarily with astronomy. Then came the revolutionary discovery of the Bonampak murals, a "true confession" that changed everything. In the past three decades epigraphers such as the late Linda Schele of the University of Texas have broken the code of the faded squiggles and dots to read the bellicose history of monarchical city states where blood was the mortar of society.

Warfare between Maya cities was frequent, and its aim was largely the capture of royalty for torture and sacrifice rather than territorial expansion.

Captives were often pitted against the conquering king in an ancient ball game that was stacked in favor of the king. After the inevitable loss, captives were sacrificed and often decapitated. The Aztecs also had a penchant for human sacrifice, but Yale anthropologist Michael D. Coe points out that "they certainly never inflicted upon their victims the torture and mutilation that were characteristic of Maya sacrifice."

So much for the stereotype of mellow stargazers.

---

1 Although the Babylonians are credited with the earliest development of a positional number system, this does not diminish the achievement of the Maya.

Verdant jungle growth encroaching on ruins.

WHO'S WHO OF THE GODS

Existence depended on a multitude of sacred beings who controlled the universe and everything in it. The cosmos was neutral; its mighty forces neither good nor bad—merely capricious. Like the gods of ancient Greece and Rome, the Maya deities were often childlike creatures subject to fearful tantrums. Because they were dependent on human attention for their welfare, they could be manipulated.

From a Palenque—the lid of a sarcophagus depicting the venerated ceiba tree, and other objects, such as the two headed sky-dragon and celestial birds.

The lush, green Maya cosmos was centered around a giant ceiba tree. Its sacred foliage reached into the heavens, the thrusting roots twisted deep into the underworld. The precious ceiba was the vortex of a kind of compass, each direction having its own colors. The north was white, the south yellow, the east red and the west black. These four directions were the keys to an understanding of religion and magical thinking.

But there was an even more important part to the compass. It was the center. This was the place where man was at any given moment. It stretched as far up as the eye could see as well as deep into the underworld. Its color was green, the green of jade, the most precious of Maya minerals.

Each day the sun began its celestial journey through this cosmos, beginning in the east and climbing into a heaven–arranged in thirteen layers like a pyramid–until it reached the west where it slowly began its descent into the nine layers of the dreaded underworld. The sun's sacred passage through the sky and into the underworld was also symbolic of human life for it is in just this way that man rises, becomes vigorous, weakens and dies.

Life was a dicey business for the Maya, highly transient in contrast with the permanence of the world about them. Existence depended on a multitude of sacred beings who controlled the universe and everything in it. The cosmos was neutral; its mighty forces neither good nor bad–merely capricious. Like the gods of ancient Greece and Rome, the Maya deities were often childlike creatures subject to fearful tantrums. Because they were dependent on human attention for their welfare, they could be manipulated.

Kind, cruel, capricious–the gods of the Maya were just like their human worshippers, in turn bitter, sweet or blankly indifferent. It was dangerous to ignore such moody, frivolous beings, creatures jealous of their power and prominence who constantly expected to be worshiped, celebrated or placated. They had to be housed and cared for, diverted with music and dance and–most importantly–fed.

Each deity could have two aspects or twenty, might appear magnanimous to some, avaricious to others. A single god's duties and attributes could vary according to his mood or the circumstances. Not only could the Maya gods change their function and nature, they could also change form. The same deity might appear as young or old and sometimes even changed sex. Frequently they were known by different names in different circumstances.

In time of drought, Chac, the rain god, would be viewed as aloof or neglectful, withholding his favors for reasons of forgetfulness or even anger; but during periods of abundant rain, he was thought benevolent and generous. In war time, the same god or goddess might be simultaneously regarded as rewarding or punishing–since a victory for one is invariably a defeat for others.

In other words, the triumphs and failures, harvests and famines, victories or defeats of the Maya were directly related to the trenchant moods of some basic personalities. In so much as a "who's who" can be compiled of such chameleons, here it is:

Hunab Ku—the greatest god, the creator of the world, father of the divinities, the one god alive and true, and the deity responsible for the flood that destroyed the four worlds that proceeded that of the Maya. This was the supreme god, but beyond shape and substance so that he could never be represented pictorially.

Itzamna—(Hunab Ku's son) — the sky god, was – for the most part – a benevolent being very like Jupiter in that he presided over the day and the night, and was the sage of all the gods. It was Itzamna who first invented calendars and taught the priests to write. The patron of wisdom and learning, Itzamna–from whom the Itza tribe believed themselves sprung–is depicted as a toothless old man with sunken cheeks, a thin beard and a hooked nose.

Ixchel—Itzamna's wife) –goddess of the moon, prophesy, childbirth, procreation, medicine, shells, and weaving. Though these are associations involving the concept of renewal, Ixchel is frequently portrayed as a capricious crone with a headdress of entwined snakes, a necklace of bones, and jaguar-claw fingernails.

Chac—the rain god, is also the overlord of the gods of the wind who ruled the four corners of the world and held up the sky. Chac controls thunder and lightning and is often attended by toads who serve as his minstrels. In a largely agrarian economy, his importance remains considerable. Months without rain go a long way to explain Chac's survival to this day. His image is ubiquitous in Maya architecture, reaching out from countless friezes everywhere In what appears to be a conscious effort to instill terror, he is invariably portrayed with huge, empty eye-sockets and what looks more like an elephant's trunk than a nose.

Kukulcan—the fabled plumed serpent is the deity of
healing and magical herbs, the lord of hope and the
morning star, a god of spring-time and emergent life.
The major symbol is a serpent wearing the gorgeous
feathers of the quetzal bird, but sometimes he's shown as
a man wearing a special loincloth with a rounded end,
apparently a bag to hold his oversize penis. Though
celibate, he was viewed as the fertilizing breath of life.
His story is the eternal one of sin and redemption, death
and resurrection, the transfiguration of man into god; yet somehow through
the alchemy of time, he changed into a rapacious taskmaster who demanded
blood sacrifices in return for the sun's fertilizing rays.

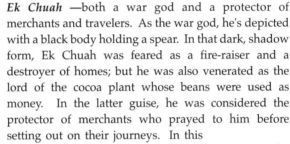

Ek Chuah —both a war god and a protector of
merchants and travelers. As the war god, he's depicted
with a black body holding a spear. In that dark, shadow
form, Ek Chuah was feared as a fire-raiser and a
destroyer of homes; but he was also venerated as the
lord of the cocoa plant whose beans were used as
money. In the latter guise, he was considered the
protector of merchants who prayed to him before
setting out on their journeys. In this
capacity, he's shown as a merchant
with a pack on his shoulders.

Ah Xoc Kin—god of the sun, was the inventor and patron
of both poetry and music. His glyph resembles a St.
Andrew's cross which he's generally pictured wearing on
his clothing or forehead.

Ah Puch—lord of death and the underworld is beyond
question the most terrible god in the Maya pantheon.
Not only does he lie in wait for men and hinder plant
growth, he actively hinders fertility. Ah Puch is usually
depicted as a skeleton or a death's head.

Ixtab—goddess of suicide, is seen hanging
by her neck. She was considered very important, as it was often
necessary to atone to the gods for wrong doing. Suicide was
considered a form of ritual cleansing like hari kari. It was
through Ixtab's assistance that those who took their own lives
were able to find their way to a special paradise in heaven.

Yum Kaax—the handsome, young maize god, personified the ideal of male beauty. He protected not only the maize shoots but young married couples. Yum Kaax is depicted with a headdress of leafy plants and feathers. Maize has always been considered the greatest gift of the gods and is itself venerated. Some present day Maya still address it as "Your Grace." In ancient times a period of abstinence was observed during the planting season and offerings were made in the fields. The Maya never went to war during planting season, maize came before everything.

Xaman Ek—god of the North Star, was particularly important to traders and mariners and assisted architects with the alignment of their buildings. He is portrayed with black flecks and a snub nose.

Chac-Mool—the messenger of the gods. The hearts of sacrificial victims were often placed in basins held by stone replicas of this demi-god.

Are the old gods dead? Not likely. The Lacandon Maya, who live in remote areas, have never accepted Christianity and even in "civilized" areas one finds recent traces of candles and incense before ancient shrines. Shamen using sacred chants and crystals are still sought for their spells and healing techniques. Secret societies continue to exist.

In the four centuries since Catholicism was forcibly introduced, many of the gods have taken on saintly overtones. As an example, the Virgin Mary has fused for many with Ixchel. Kukulcan, wearing a mask and plumed headdress, sometimes replaces Santa Claus at holiday parties or in store windows, once again bringing life and gifts of happiness to the people. Like it or not, the padres admit that the deities of ancient days remain much in evidence.

It can be said that the Maya also worshiped time and cycles of time. The first world cycle was thought to have been destroyed by jaguars representing the earth, the second cycle by air, the third by fire, the fourth by water, a great flood. The fifth cycle, in which we are currently living, is predestined to be destroyed by earthquake.

The Maya believed that this present cycle began in the year 13.0.0.0.0. 4 Ahau 8 Cumku (their calendar) or August 12, 3113 B.C. The ending was predicted for December 24, 2011.

The Maya cyclical pattern is based on multiples of 52. At the end of this Calendar Round cycle (when the solar year and the sacred year calendars coincide), the people extinguished all their fires, lamented and fasted, believing that the world might be destroyed. The end of two of these cycles every 102 years—when solar, sacred and Venus calendars converged— assumed even greater significance.

Of the end of the Great Cycle of 5,200 years there was no doubt. A catastrophe would completely destroy the world as it had on four previous cycles. The duration of these five worlds was thought to total 26,000 years which very closely approximates the known 25,920-year cycle of the precession of the equinoxes.

Bas-relief of victors—next to Ball court, Chichen Itza.

The Plumed Serpent—Chichen Itza

THE PLUMED SERPENT

The human embodiment of divine love and wisdom as well as an able administrator, he united the people and ruled them under one large confederation of tribal groups.

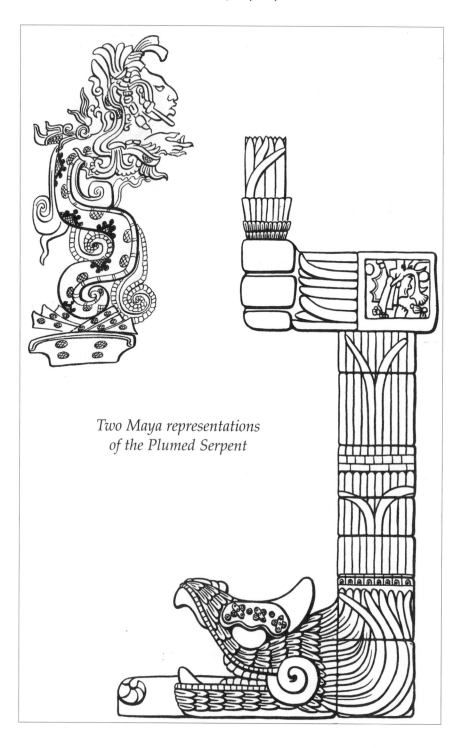

*Two Maya representations
of the Plumed Serpent*

The fabled Kukulcan reaches out to us across the century—a figure of romance, betrayal, illusion and eternal mystery. Who was he? What was he?

Known in other parts of Mexico as Quetzalcoatl, Kukulcan appears much like King Arthur, half man, half myth. Little is known, much is conjectured; and the facts themselves merely add to the puzzle. According to the story, Kukulcan descended from heaven and preceded to introduce the concepts of penitence, love and exemption from the traditional rituals of   blood sacrifice. The human embodiment of divine love and wisdom as well as an able administrator, he united the people and ruled them under one large confederation of tribal groups.

As with the Arthurian Round Table, it was all too good to last. The high priests and warriors didn't take kindly to Kukulcan's substitution of incense, flowers and maize for human sacrifices. There had to be a way of removing him......and, of course, eventually they found it.

Kukulcan was known to be vigorous, sexually potent, and endowed with an enormous penis; yet he vowed to remain celibate, sublimating his considerable energies in good works.   Finally the day came — naturally it would have to be a ceremonial day with an attendant cast of thousands —when the wily priests handed Kukulcan — a drink laced with magic mushrooms. While under the influence of this powerful aphrodisiac, he was tempted by a beautiful woman and made love to her.

Awakening later, he was consumed with guilt. In his own eyes Kukulcan had condemned himself by breaking his self-imposed vows. Leaving behind everything — palaces, kingdom, clothes — he arrived naked on the shores of the Caribbean. After promising to return one day, Kukulcan embarked on a raft of snake skins and sailed eastward until a tremendous heat ignited the boat and, in a burst of flames, his heart arose, flying upward to finally merge with the sun.

Kukulcan's spring time promise is familiar to mythmakers everywhere. He is the martyr who must inevitably suffer, then be driven away or killed before he can return to the kingdom of heaven—and ultimately be born again. This time the self sacrificing god returns as the Morning Star, a symbol of hope and regeneration.

Fact or fantasy? The glyphs in the Vienna Codex record this spectacular astral happening as a solar eclipse, an event verified by the Royal Observatory at Greenwich as having occurred on July 16, AD 750.

The story of Kukulcan's disappearance was told and retold. It was a legend that refused to die, for everyone knew that just as the god had been overthrown in the past, so he would one day return to overthrow his adversaries and usher in a new era of peace and justice. The hope remained for hundreds of years until the early 16th century when history and mythology united to produce a great tragedy.

Gateway at Labna by Frederick Catherwood.

THE WAY IT WAS

"Ci-u-than," their shouted reply, meant simply, "We don't understand you," but the Spaniards believed the words to be the answer to their question. Somehow Ciuthan evolved into Yucatan. Years later a conquistador attempted to set the record straight when he wrote that the Maya "now say their country is called 'Yucatan,' and so it has that name, but in their own language they do not call it by that name." Unfortunately, he neglected to mention exactly what they did call it and now no one knows.

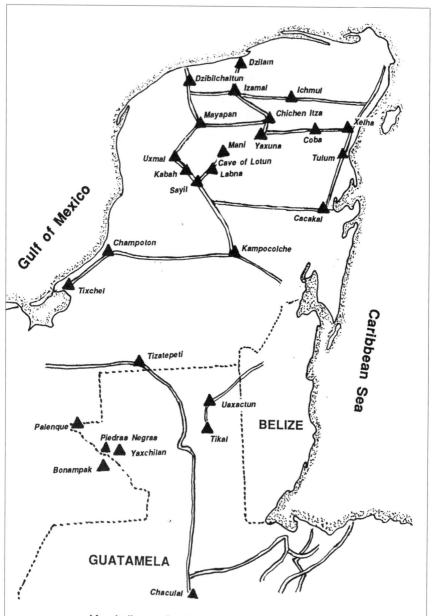

Map indicates the sacbeob (plural of sacbe), which are roads or causeways the Mayas built out of limestone. This map indicates some of the Maya archeological sites located along these roads.

W e don't understaaaaaand yoooooooooooou!"

The words echo eerily down through the centuries. Perhaps this initial communication breakdown explains why the old world believes it not only discovered the new, but invented it as well.

The Spanish explorers studied these new Indians as though taking inventory: strong noses flared slightly at the nostrils, straight black hair, eyes like shining jet buttons under ridged brows, thick, full lips. But there was something else, something more. These mysterious strangers possessed an air of confidence and quiet dignity.

The Indian trading party was leaving now, getting back into an immense dugout canoe. "What do you call yourselves?" the Spanish commander called after the departing boat.

"Ci-u-than," their shouted reply, meant simply, "We don't understand you," but the Spaniards believed the words to be the answer to their question. Somehow Ciuthan evolved into Yucatan. Years later a conquistador attempted to set the record straight when he wrote that the Maya "now say their country is called 'Yucatan,' and so it has that name, but in their own language they do not call it by that name." Unfortunately, he neglected to mention exactly what they did call it and now no one knows.

The Maya, too, were bewildered by the encounter. What manner of thing was this white-winged floating tower? And who were these tall, ungainly men with their white, hairy faces? Before long, word of the meeting had spread across the country all the way to Montezuma in the far northwest.

What would follow was unique in the long, cruel chronicle of exploration and conquest. Two entirely separate worlds were about to collide. Each possessed equally long records of achievement, yet both had been totally oblivious to the existence of the other.

A sense of fate overshadows much of Mexican history. Poor, frightened Montezuma had been waiting for the shoe to drop for several years. From his palace rooftop, the ruler who'd once been a priest searched the skies for portents each day at dawn, sunset and midnight. In 1508 he'd watched with apprehension as a tiny black speck crossed the face of the sun. The last time the planet Venus had transited the sun had been 300 years before. A devastating flood had followed. Now he felt certain that some similar disaster was pending.

When the first man, a lowly peasant, came to him with a strange tale about "a small mountain floating in the midst of the water, moving here and there without touching the shore," Montezuma closed his ears to the account. The trouble maker was thrown into prison for spreading such ridiculous lies. But then messengers arrived from the king of Tulum, deep in the Maya country to the southeast, confirming the report. Two great mountains or towers were, indeed, floating in the sea. Worse yet, they contained tall, light skinned beings with beards and hair that came only to their ears. Montezuma lowered his head. For a time he said nothing as thoughts of the Quetzalcoatl legend returned to plague him. Was the god not tall, fair, bearded?

Quetzalcoatl's return had long been foretold. He'd promised to appear before them again in some Ce Acatl year on the day of his birth, Chiconaui Ehecatl. This combination, which came up every 52 years, was scheduled to occur in the spring of 1519–only a few months away.

In Cuba, Hernando Cortes had never heard of Ce Acatl but hoped that the year 1519 would bring something more rewarding than a job running a small plantation where the Carib Indians had to be watched every minute. (The damn fools would rather commit suicide than work for a Spaniard.) A short, ordinary looking man who walked with a permanent limp since falling from his mistress's balcony, Cortes had big ideas. Even he couldn't have imagined himself as a god incarnate and yet destiny had drafted him for that role.

The 34-year-old adventurer was intrigued by tales of land to the west. Even if there was no gold — as had been rumored — there was at least a native population to enslave. He hoped they'd prove a more tractable bunch than the Caribs. The Governor of Cuba mounted an expedition but was delayed. There was some last minute finagling and Cortes took his place. In the governor's eyes it was to be merely a reconnaissance mission; Cortes envisioned it quite differently.

Meanwhile in Montezuma's palace a great sadness had overtaken the court. The ruler's beloved aunt, Princess Butterfly, fell ill and died. Then three days later the noblewoman astonished everyone by sitting straight up on her bier. The joy that Montezuma felt at her miraculous recovery was quickly shattered. In what appears to have been an out-of-body experience, Princess Butterfly had seen men wearing black stones and riding hornless deer. She went on to describe the capital city in flames, her nephew's murder and the subsequent reign of the most dreadful of the white-faced creatures.

Only a short while later Montezuma received word that men of her description had disembarked from a "winged tower that floated across the sea." The date was April 21, 1519. The Spaniards called it Good Friday, but Montezuma knew that it was Chiconaui Ehecatl, the birthday of Quetzalcoatl in the year called Ce Acatl.

He considered his doom sealed. Who could fight a god? This sense of grim inevitability explains the takeover of a mighty nation by only a few men. By the time that Montezuma realized that they were merely men, it was too late.

It was an initial encounter with the Maya that first stimulated the Spaniards to launch an extensive mission to Mexico; but, for a time, Yucatan was bypassed by the conquistadores.

Cortes didn't get around to dispatching a force to subdue the area until 1527. Then Francisco de Montejo was granted the title, *adelantado*, with permission to exploit Yucatan at his own expense. It's curious to note that the Maya–the first to make contact with the Spaniards–were the least in awe of them.

Perhaps because they'd had ample opportunity to intimately study two shipwrecked Spanish sailors, the Maya had no illusions that their would-be conquerors were gods. They didn't have to fight fate–just men, superior weapons, and smallpox. It took four tries and more than 20 years before the Spaniards succeeded in conquering them–in contrast with two years to completely subdue the Aztecs.

Montejo longed to give up completely. Deeply discouraged, he wrote to the king, "In these provinces there is not a single river, although there are lakes, and the hills are of live rock, dry and waterless. The entire land is covered by thick bush and is so stony that there is not a single square foot of soil. The inhabitants are the most abandoned and treacherous in all the lands discovered to this time. . ."

Despite the fact that the Maya were divided into numerous autonomous provinces, often at war with each other, they still resisted fiercely. Worse yet–from Montejo's point of view–they refused to stay conquered. He lost his entire fortune trying to subjugate the Maya, finally turning the whole venture over to his son.

Spurred on by priests who weren't about to relinquish their power easily, the rebellious Maya planned a massive counter attack for the night of the full moon on November 8, 1546–5 Cimi, 19 Xul, in the Maya calendar, a date designated in their sacred almanac as " Death and the End."

For them, it was the end. But, though the conquest of Yucatan was considered complete by 1547, it continued in a low-key, sporadic way for the next 150 years. The Spaniards actually lost ground as they were forced from time to time to pull back. The Maya, too, pulled back, forming refugee settlements deep in the interior. The Lacandon Maya were never conquered and have changed little to this day.

At first the Maya cyclical view of time helped to facilitate the transition. There's comfort to be found in a world in which history and prophesy intertwine in recurring patterns, events repeating themselves in the same orderly fashion as planets.   "This too shall pass," they believed. All things, both good and bad, have their appointed times to end—if only so that they may be repeated later.

While the conquistadores searched fruitlessly for gold, the missionaries were determined to transform the Maya into idealized Spanish peasants. Here at last was raw material with which to work, subjects that could be molded into standards of sobriety, thrift, industry and propriety unrealized anywhere else.

The resulting introduction of Christianity into Yucatan produced a far more serious crisis in the Maya world than the devastation of military warfare and political domination.   Nothing in their history of conquests could have prepared the Maya for the Spaniard's determination to obliterate their entire culture, but at first they scarcely realized what was happening.

There was nothing unusual about a victorious army introducing a new god. It had happened many times. Not only was it prudent to accept the new pantheon of personalities forced on them, but desirable.   The superior military strength of the Spaniards was reason enough for the pantheistic Maya to recognize that the new Spanish religion was a force to be reckoned with.

The child Jesus was appealing enough, the Mother Mary vaguely reminiscent of Ixchel. The sticking point was the jealous nature of the head god. Accepting this new personage as a sacred being was not the same as accepting him as the only sacred being in the cosmos. The idea that divinity was concentrated in this one remote figure to the exclusion of all the more familiar and intimate deities that permeated their world was incomprehensible to the Maya. The friars could forbid the new converts to worship their old deities but convincing them that such veneration was futile or unnecessary was another matter. The Maya believed that a sacred umbilical cord linked heaven and earth. Nourishment flowed in both directions sustaining men and gods. A ban on ritual could cut this essential cord placing the entire cosmos in jeopardy.

The culture shock that resulted from this assault on the whole nature of the Maya universe is difficult to imagine. Too soon the once willing converts discovered that the missionaries who'd so patiently explained the exemplary qualities of their god could be as cruel and implacable as the soldiers.

Devotions to the old gods were severely punished. The lightest sentence was 100 lashes and interrogation techniques were brutal. The good friars had brought with them from Spain all the refinements of the Inquisition. Many Maya died or were crippled for life. (In a single day, Sebastian Vazquez, His Majesty's Clerk in Merida, recorded that 4,549 men and women were hanged and tortured by the monks.) Others—in the words of the padres— "displayed their cowardice" by committing suicide before the questioning could be completed.

Fray Diego de Landa was the worst of these zealots. In 1552, while serving as Franciscan Provincial, Landa may have forever destroyed the key to Maya civilization by burning every hieroglyphic record he could find along with hundreds of statues, stelae and altar stones. As a result, until fairly recently, all that we knew about the Maya at the time of the conquest or a thousand years before has been filtered through the writings of those appalling padres. Since most of the Spanish priests shared the view of the conquistadores that the Maya were "beasts" or "natural slaves," very little survived.

Eventually the Maya embraced certain aspects of Spanish culture. They built Spanish style houses—though many confessed to finding them less comfortable and healthful than their former ones. They adopted the heavy breeches and tunics, capes, cumbersome shoes and plumed hats, which proved even more unsuitable to the climate. Not surprisingly, they took to swords with far more enthusiasm and discovered a true affinity to European wines and spirits.

The uneasy dominion over the Maya was to last for nearly 300 years; and the ending, when it came, was rooted in events far away.   The wars of independence that overthrew the Spanish Empire in America grew out of Napoleon's occupation of Madrid and the subsequent collapse of Spanish power. Self government was at last literally thrust upon the people, and the taste for it spread from liberals to conservatives, who together achieved independence in 1821.

Because of its isolation, Yucatan had always been controlled directly from Spain rather than Mexico City. Now for a brief glorious period Yucatan was once again autonomous.

In 1823, the Yucatan Peninsula joined with Mexico. It was an uneasy partnership that would explode in less than twenty years.   Meanwhile, the peninsula was a caldron of discontent. One of the chief causes was the change in landholding practices accelerated by independence. With the large scale introduction of sugar cane and henequen cultivation, vast haciendas or landed estates evolved, feudal empires each employing hundreds of Maya who were tricked into virtual slavery.

The hacendados, or land owners, who took pride in their direct lineage back to the conquistadores, realized that the only way to keep the Maya down on the farm was to entice them into debt. When this method didn't net a large enough labor force, a new state constitution was passed in 1825 compelling the Indians who couldn't pay taxes in money to pay them in work. The hacendados and their puppet politicians agreed that once the Indians owed money, they must be kept owing until they were so deeply mired in debt that they could never buy their way out.

The world was rapidly changing and Yucatan with it. The United States and Europe needed rope for shipping. Here was a handy source of supply. The hacendados discovered wealth beyond their avaricious dreams. Ignoring the rest of Mexico as not worth bothering with, they turned to Europe for cultural standards. Children were educated on the Continent and while the Maya worked the land, the hacendados partied in Paris. A way of life was developing, a nobility of style as well as birth that required that one's wealth be produced by the labor of the lower orders.

In 1838 civil war broke out between the liberal federalists who desired more autonomy for the provinces and conservatives who wanted a strong government in Mexico City. It was to culminate in the war between Mexico and the United States in 1846. When Yucatan seceded from Mexico, the same Maya who provided virtual slave labor to the hacienda owners were drafted into the army.

Having been issued arms in order to defend independent Yucatan from Mexico and the United States, the Maya instead turned those guns on their local oppressors. On July 30, 1847 the "War of the Castes" was launched. Valladolid, the most isolated and vulnerable of the Yucatan cities soon fell to the Maya forces. Next Merida was threatened. Appeals for help to Spain, the United States and France went unanswered. Then, just as the governor was preparing to evacuate Merida, the Maya picked up their weapons and walked away.

Vengeance was sweet but corn was the heart's blood of the Maya. When the rains come, the corn must be in the soil. The victorious Maya soldiers turned their backs on certain victory and returned to their fields.

This was just the respite the hacendados needed. Help came at last from Cuba, then the United States sent 1000 "military advisors." Reprisals were merciless. Maya men, women and children were slaughtered whatever their economic or political beliefs. Others were sold to Cuba as slaves. The lucky ones escaped into the jungles of Quintana Roo which remained a literal no-man's land for nearly 100 years. An estimated 300,000 people—half the population of Yucatan—were killed.

What the Maya needed was a rallying point and one day it miraculously appeared. It began with a poor peasant who happened on to a sparkling spring. Water had always been hallowed by his people, so the man carved three crosses on a sacred ceiba tree growing close by. From ancient times the cross had held a special significance for the Maya who saw it as a kind of divine compass.

Gradually word spread that the crosses had come down from heaven in order to make sacred revelations to the fighting Maya. When the crosses suddenly began to speak, a cult sprang up. Of course the voice was generally conceded to be that of a ventriloquist, but there was a precedent for that going back to an oracle on the holy island of Cozumel. People came from all around and built houses near the spring. Their settlement became the village of Chan Santa Cruz; and they, themselves, were known as the Cruzob , or People of the Cross.

It was believed that the words of the cross were divinely inspired. The message was a rallying cry to the Maya soldiers who were back from their planting and ready to go again. After a series of successful skirmishes, the Maya achieved a de facto independence and were recognized by the British who were delighted to sell arms in exchange for timber. Until the end of the 19th century a shaky truce prevailed. The Cruzobs and their talking crosses

ruled the southern Caribbean coast, an isolated jungle kingdom now theirs by default.

Meanwhile, in the northern peninsula the haughty hacendados continued to grow richer and richer while their Maya peasants barely survived. So anxious were they to establish their superiority by setting themselves apart that they passed a law decreeing that women of mixed blood were required to wear huipals, Indian dresses. Augustus Le Plongeon, an archeologist excavating in Chichen Itza during the 1870's, reported that working men on the haciendas were pitilessly and arbitrarily flogged by their overseers, then put in stocks overnight so as not to miss a day's work. Were they, he wrote, to lay their grievances before the owner of the hacienda, their only redress was to receive a double beating for daring to complain. "If they lodged a complaint before a judge as by law they had the right, he is the friend or relative of the planter. He may himself be a planter. On his own plantation he has servants who are treated in a like manner."

It was more than forty years before a new type of politician arose. Felipe Carrillo Puerto was a brave and charismatic leader who gained the support of the peasants and somehow rose to the governorship of Yucatan. Once in power, Puerto organized labor unions and educational centers, then decreed that haciendas not in use be appropriated for the Maya who had once owned all the land.

The growing power of this upstart who refused to see which side his political bread was buttered on was too much for the reigning hacendados. The man had to be stopped and he was. In 1924 Felipe Carrillo Puerto was assassinated along with every male member of his family that could be found.

What was meant to be an object lesson came too late. The winds of change were blowing. A series of sweeping reforms instituted in Mexico City helped to liberalize the social and economic life of Yucatan. President Lazaro Cardenas (1934-40) broke up many of the holdings of the hacendados and distributed parcels to small farmers. In 1936, Cardenas gave half of Quintana Roo, then still a territory to the poor. He also signed a treaty with the still active descendants of the Cruzobs thereby finally putting an end to the conquest of the Maya.

It's a cruel fact of life that Mexico's economic and political burdens are a boon to the tourist and the outside investor. In 1976 the inflation that was affecting the world was literally pricing Mexico out of the market. In an attempt to remedy this critical situation, the peso was allowed to float, finding its own value against the dollar. Response to this legislation brought foreign capital back in a hurry. It was hoped that the influx would create enough jobs to correct the economic condition.

Sunset view at Cancun

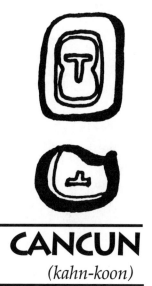

CANCUN
(kahn-koon)

"Like the mist, like a cloud,
And like a cloud of dust was the creation,
When the mountains appeared from the water,
And instantly the mountains grew."
Popol Vuh

And the keys clicked, the data banks gave forth
their sacred information and the
Great Computer spake:
"BUILD THE CITY HERE."

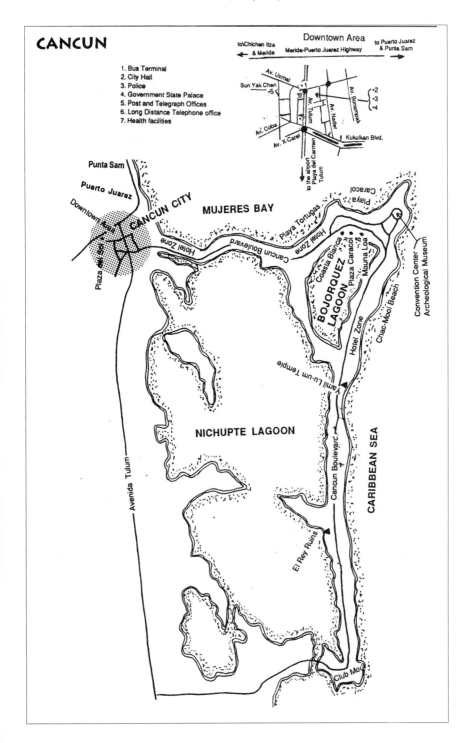

CANCUN

1. Bus Terminal
2. City Hall
3. Police
4. Government State Palace
5. Post and Telegraph Offices
6. Long Distance Telephone office
7. Health facilities

Downtown Area

to\Chichen Itza & Merida ←
Merida-Puerto Juarez Highway
to Puerto Juarez & Punta Sam →

Av. Uxmal
Sun Yak Chen
Av. Tulum
Av. Nader
Av. Bonampak
Av. Coba
Av. X-Caret
Kukulkan Blvd.
to the airport Playa del Carmen Tulum

Punta Sam
Puerto Juarez
Downtown Hotel
Plaza del Sol
CANCUN CITY
Hotel Zone
Cancun Boulevard

MUJERES BAY

Playa Caracol
Playa Tortugas
Hotel Zone

BOJORQUEZ LAGOON
Costa Blanca
Plaza Caracol
Mauna Loa
Hotel Zone
Yamil Lu-um Temple
Chac-Mool Beach
Convention Center
Archeological Museum

NICHUPTE LAGOON

Avenida Tulum

Cancun Boulevard

El Rey Ruins

CARIBBEAN SEA

Club Med

The ancient Maya believed their rain god Chac to be cruel and implacable.

Their modern descendants have little reason to alter that opinion.

The posh, polished resort of Cancun may be the only island in the world to be "discovered" by electronic technology. When the Mexican government sought to create a state of the art tourist mecca in 1967, it collected every scrap of information about what tourists want. When processed by computer, the result was Cancun.

The Popol Vuh, the Maya book of creation, says that only by a miracle, only by magic art were mountains and valleys formed. Then instantly the groves of cypress and pines put forth shoots together on the surface of the earth. Almost as suddenly a vacation paradise emerged seemingly overnight from a tropical wilderness once the domain of macaws and spider monkeys.

It began in 1970 with a small task force. The island had to be connected to the mainland and widened in some places; it was too narrow to even accommodate a coastal road. Since the area was virtually uninhabited, chicleteros were recruited to work on the project. It was a whole new world for these brave men who'd spent most of their lives deep in the neighboring jungles harvesting gum from the chicle tree.

Communication was the next problem, for the workers spoke only Maya and the architects, engineers and planners only Spanish. Three years later the international airport was completed, but there were no lodgings for guests until 1974. Today there are more than 40,000 hotel rooms and a whole network of services to amuse and bemuse the visitor.

The spawn of Mother Nature and Father Computer, has become the VIP of Mexican sun spots, luring one million visitors each year. Shaped like an art nouveau seahorse, the island—connected to the mainland by bridges—is almost fourteen miles long and a quarter of a mile wide. On one side is the Caribbean, on the other placid Nichupte Lagoon. Ixchel, the Maya sea goddess, receives plenty of attention in Cancun. The island's towering hotels gaze out in homage and at the Robert Trent Jones Golf Course one of her temples pops into view on the twelfth hole.

The downtown counterpart is Cancun City, which started out as a minuscule fishing village with 117 inhabitants when the island development began. Today a bustling city of 150,000, it has a variety of restaurants and night spots, some moderately priced hotels, and the Ki-Huic market, filled with Mexican handicrafts. Reasonably priced buses and taxis shuttle back and

Hyatt Caribbe—Cancun

forth constantly between island and city, bicycles and mopeds are readily rentable.

The warm waters surrounding the island offer some of the world's best diving and snorkeling over the four coral reefs between Cancun and Isla Mujeres. Visibility is often to depths of forty feet. Other popular water sports are sailing, waterskiing and windsurfing. Deep sea fishing is outstanding with bluefish, sailfish and mackerel abundant.

A mild climate encourages bike riding or jogging along a six-mile palm-lined, pink-brick path where tropical flowers and exotic wildlife abound. But perhaps the best way to enjoy Cancun's beauty is to spend a relaxing day at the beach. The sea's incredibly blue, the sand like talcum powder and so white that it reflects the sun's heat but remains comfortably cool to the touch. Speaking of the sun—there are 240-plus days of it every year. Miami has 93 and Cancun has less rainfall than either the Bahamas or Nassau.

This is a sophisticated resort with restaurants, outings and night life designed to please every taste. There are quickie bus tours to the ruins of Tulum and Chichen Itza and party cruises to nearby islands. If this is a first trip to Mexico, you'll find comfort in menus printed in English, water you can drink from the tap and the sense that you and your money are much appreciated.

But others will see Cancun primarily as a point of departure. The first hint of more exciting things to come. Across the blue lagoon from the glossy hotels and sleek condos, the mysterious jungle beckons.

GETTING AROUND

Cancun's hotel zone is bordered by Nichupte and Bojorquez Lagoons, the Caribbean Sea and the Bahia de Mujeres (Bay of Women.) Paseo Kukulcan, the beautifully gardened main avenue that traces the hotel zone, finally runs into broad, divided Avendida Tulum, main street of downtown Cancun City.

Paseo Kukulkan Boulevard, the beautifully gardened main avenue, runs the length of the island and connects all the hotels and beaches there with

Cancun City. A public bus system services the entire area on a regular basis at a nominal fee. Taxis from mainland to island are surprisingly reasonable, but it's wise to avoid occasional unpleasant exchanges by establishing the price in advance.

If you're in Cancun for more than a weekend, I can't recommend strongly enough that you rent a car or jeep and get out into the countryside. It's practically impossible to get lost either in town or on the highways–there are so few of the latter. Tulum is very close, Coba and Chichen Itza not so very much farther. Along the way there are fascinating villages and exquisite beaches to explore.

Car rental agencies are abundant, competitive and offer any number of package deals. Maps are readily available and the roads are excellent–but it is important to start off with a full tank, for gas stations aren't as prevalent in Mexico as they are at home.

All the tour buses make a point of visiting Tulum in the morning and Xel-ha in the afternoon. Your enjoyment of both would be enhanced 100 percent if you reversed that order thereby escaping the madding crowd.

WHERE TO STAY

Each new hotel seems to outdo the last in luxury and state-of-the-art amenities — swimming pools encircle the grounds or bedazzle the eye by appearing to drop off into the sea; lobbies are extravagant shopping malls with a wide choice of restaurants.

—PERSONAL FAVORITES —

Camino Real—There are buildings that travel and others that seem to spring from the land. The Camino Real's modified pyramid structure designed by Ricardo Legoretta, Mexico's preeminent architect, is surely of the latter variety. Nothing is borrowed—no pseudo colonial, no Palm Beach deco— the evocative image is of the nearby Maya ruins. Adding to the fantasy feeling is a man made lagoon stocked with large turtles and exotic fish which meanders through the extensive grounds linking the Caribbean to the east with the "real" lagoon on the west. Bordered almost entirely by water, the hotel has the feel of a private island with a sea or lagoon view guaranteed each of it 292 rooms. Telephone number: 1-800-228-3000

Hyatt Regency—Where the action is—within easy walking distance of the Convention Center, archeological museum and the largest concentration of shops, restaurants and nightclubs. When your feet give out, the inner courtyard with its hanging gardens of Babylon architecture is ideal for people watching. Telephone number: 1-800-233-1234

Villas Takul — Is a lovely alternative. Facing the Caribbean Sea on 12 acres of tropical gardens, this delightful inn is close to the Cancun action yet in a tranquil world of its own. Telephone number (1-866-597-9330)

Omni Cancun Hotel—Cancun claims to be the honeymoon capital of the world and of all the elegant hotels this is the prime candidate for that destination. The Omni with its pink stucco walls and tile roofs, a charming blend of colonial and art deco, is most certainly the prettiest and most romantic of all the state-of-the-art hotel complexes. It also has one of the best shops in town—Arodi. Telephone number: 1-800-THE OMNI

Fiesta Americana Condesa Cancun—one of the newest and liveliest on hotel row, this property features three horseshoe-shaped towers surrounded by lush, tropical foliage, cascading waterfalls and swimming pools. The hotel's distinctive architectural design creates an intimate ambience beginning with what must be the largest palapa in Mexico—115 ft. high— shading the expansive lobby to the hotel's extraordinarily beautiful swimming pool with a swim-up bar and restaurant accented by a 135 ft. long waterfall. Telephone number: 1-800-FIESTA-1

Hotel Inter-Continental Cancun—This state-of-the-art high rise offers two swimming pools for laps or lounging, a fully-equipped fitness center with exercise classes and two tennis courts. A thoughtful touch — much appreciated — is the hair dryer in each room. An added dividend is the truly terrific folklorico floor show presented here once weekly. Telephone: 1-800-621-1155

Hyatt Cancun Caribe— A replica of Chac-Mool gazes out to sea here — like any other sunbather.   And why not? All 202 rooms in the crescent shaped high rise have a view of the Caribbean on one side, the lagoon on the other. Telephone number: 1-800-233-1234

Krystal Cancun — No ruins here, but the Krystal is home to two of Cancun's most popular attractions — *Bogart's Casablanca* and the lively disco, *Christine*. Telephone number: 1-800-231-9860

Another with a great beach, lively atmosphere, attractive appointments and moderate (for Cancun) prices is *Plaza Las Glorias*, which serves one of the best breakfasts in town. Telephone number for Plaza Las Glorias: 1-800-342-2644.

Crowne Plaza Cancun— a sophisticated fantasyland that includes one breakfast in bed complete with champagne. Telephone: 1-800-FIESTAS-1.

Radisson Paraiso Cancun — specials include full American breakfast or room service and discounts on excursions. Telephone: 1-800-333-3333.

Le Meridien Cancun Resort & Spa—Bordered by the Caribbean Sea's crystal clear waters and sparkling white beach on one side and the Laguna de Nichupte on the other, this elegant European style hotel and spa is literally the last word. The hotel's *Aioli Restaurant* has an exciting menu that lives up to its promise. Telephone number 1-800-715-1829

CANCUN CITY

The *Parador Hotel* is modern, comfortable and well located with a refreshing oasis-like feeling about the pretty courtyard and pool area.

Hotel America and Hotel Plaza del Sol operate their own shuttle vans to private beach clubs and marinas.

Condominiums Caribe—located in a quiet, tree-shaded neighborhood, these may be the best bargains in town. Attractively furnished one bedroom condos with queen size beds and sofas in the living room that make into twin beds at night rent for half the price of single rooms on hotel row. Contact Caribe Travel Group, 497 Vermont St. San Francisco, CA 94107 or 415 861-8478 for additional information.

All combine the standard amenities with convenient downtown shopping and kind to the pocketbook prices.

WHERE TO EAT

Cancun is seafood heaven. Whatever your preference, with 250 dining options, it's readily available with some innovative nods to current fads and fancies. Lobster, shrimp and a variety of fish are fresh and good here; but since this is a city created for tourists, one needn't be limited to Neptune's garden. Whatever your preference, you'll find it with some innovative nods to current fads and fancies.

Competition is fierce among Mexico's resorts and the city's independent restaurateurs as well as the major hotels contribute substantially to the high standards that keep Cancun in the limelight. Hotels have traditionally been a mere convenience for guests, rarely gourmet enough to warrant outside attention. In Cancun this is rarely the case. Hotel chefs have come into their own; they are upgrade enterprises with a well defined image independent from that of the hotel.

An interesting tendency to specialize; to replace hohum on-site eateries with something creative and unique. A case in point is the *Hyatt Caribe*.

When in Cancun, I do as the Cancunians do—eat Cajun. The best in town is found at the *Blue Bayou* in the Hyatt Caribe. The "blackened" lobster is divine and with it one of the great soups of the world, cream of artichoke with oysters. A special treat is the "Sexy Coffee" after dinner—a warm and sensuous blend flamed at your table. An orchestra plays for dancing; the service is impeccable.

Yes, it's expensive, but worth it.

El Hacienda Mortero is another special favorite. I love the romantic, old hacienda feeling, the colonial elegance, the mariachis, and the delicious food. Paseo Kukulcan Lote 9, Zona Hotelera.

At the *Seafood Market* in the Hyatt Regency, you have the opportunity to select from the delicious seafood and steak display, have your choice weighed on a scale by your host and then cooked according to your directions by the chef. Lobster and shrimp are a specialty. Phone: 883-1234.

I also enjoy the Sunday brunch at *Cilantro*, also in the Hyatt. The chefs will do most anything you ask, but my own favorite is the salmon and caviar omelet. Phone: 83-0966

Henri Charvet, the chef at *Le Basilic*, divides his time between Paris and Cancun. Charvet's Cancun restaurant, located in the *Hotel Fiesta Americana Grand Coral Beach*, combines Old World standards with

Mexican enthusiasm and verve. Inspired by innovative European restaurants, Chef Charvet's avant-garde style unites elements to create a perfect ambiance: soft lights, sea view and French music. *Le Basilic,* honoring its name, utilizes the subtle flavor and delicate aroma of basil in many of its dishes. Watching their preparation is part of the fun. A perfect splurge dinner. Phone: 881-3200.

La Parilla has the best Mexican food in town plus a mariachi band every night. It's lively and fun. You shouldn't miss it. Ave.. Yaxchilan #51. Phone 884-8193.

OK, it's a chain, but don't let that stop you from enjoying everything that the *Outback Steakhouse* has to offer. If you think you know all about *Outbacks,* think again. Cancun's establishment got high marks at the recent Festival Gastronomico. The staff takes pride in what it does and does it well. Try the barbecued duck with smoky plantain and chipotle cream or the lamb chops in mint. The *Outback* is located in the *Flamingo Shopping Center* in the heart of Cancun's hotel district. Phone: 883-3350.

The building approximates a mammoth Maya palapa, the background music is lively but not too loud, the glassed in kitchen immaculate. A colorful menu shows pictures of the native specialties with explanations in English. Two of us spent less than $20 for a dinner that included sopa de lima (lime and chicken soup), poc-chuc (broiled pork meat with tomato, onion, coriander and oranges) served with black beans and tortillas plus three bottles of Carta Blanca. *Avenue Bonampak* at Sayil. Phone: (98)84-0807.

Another downtown favorite is *Du Mexique* on Avenue Coba. This elegant restaurant has an adjacent art gallery ideal for pre-dinner browsing. The dress is casual chic—no shorts. Call 4-10-77 for reservations.

Arrive before the hordes to open-air *Carlos n' Charlie's* (Paseo Kukulcan) which dishes up the best tacos in town as well as good U.S. food, along with pitchers of margaritas.

Dine on grilled selections at *Senor Frog's* (Paseo Kukulcan) and stay to sway to reggae after ten o'clock.

You'll also want to check out the exotic Sergio Bustamante collection at *Zaman Ek.* Two other branches are to be found at *Plaza Flamingos* and *Plaza Kukukan.*

WHAT TO DO

Museo de Arte Popular Mexicano is a tiny gem of a museum that features an exciting collection of Mexican folk art. You'll find traditional masks, regional costumes, nativity scenes, Day of the Dead whimsies, churches, crucifixes, trees of life—everything you can imagine. The good, the bad and the bizarre. Well worth the $10 admission. Daily 11 a.m. to 11 p.m. Blvd. Kukulcan, km 4 in the hotel zone.

Let's face it, Cancun is not a shopper's paradise from an economy standpoint. Prices are often much higher than in surrounding areas. Nevertheless who among us is strong enough to deny ourselves something special on a holiday? And who really wants to be that strong?

Surely the first place to begin a shopping safari is *Plaza Caracol,* the largest and most elaborate of Cancun's shopping malls. I rather particularly coveted the elegant Mexican designer clothes at *Boutique Soqui,* the silver at **Los Castillo** and the brass and copper or enamel belts and jewelry at **Las Palmereas.**

—SHOPPING POSSIBILITIES—

Two good ones in the **El Parian Commercial Center** next to the Convention Center are **Victor** which specializes in high grade Mexican arts and crafts and

Anakena which features original paintings, Maya temple rubbings and hand engraved shells.

At **Artland** in the **Terramar Shopping Center** across from the Fiesta American Hotel, one can find an exciting selection of silk screen work, art prints, black coral jewelry, ironwork, wood carvings and silver.

The **Costa Blanca Shopping Center** in the newly created *Zona Rosa* has two specialty shops well worth checking out. *La Iguana* is a mad menagerie of creatures made from papier-mache or brass and copper. **Mayart** offers reproductions of museum sculpture plus carved masks and temple rubbings.

Masks appearing in
Museo de Arte Popular Mexicano

In most shops prices are established, but bargaining is practiced at the booths at the **Ki-Huic** market downtown and **Coral Negro** by the **Convention**

Center. Store hours are usually from 9 or 10 a.m. to 1 p.m. and from 4 or 5 p.m. to 9 p.m.

I don't think you'll want to miss the art work of Jorge Balcans at the newer *La Isla Shopping Center* on Boulevard Kulkukan Lotes 18-10

Products most native to the area are the *huipil,* a straight muumuu style dress with rich embroidery around the hem and neckline, and hammocks, hats and handbags made from henequen. Despite the abundance of tortoise shell jewelry for sale, this is a no-no with U.S. Customs. The turtle is on the endangered species list.

—ARCHAEOLOGICAL SITES—

Quintana Roo was the home of the ancient Maya, one of the first shores touched by the Spanish conquistadors and a refuge for marauding pirates. To get a sense of this rich cultural history, a visit to the *Museo Arqueologica de Cancun* is a must. The small but well appointed museum is located next to the Convention Center

Maya ruins—Cancun

near Punta Cancun. The hours are from 10 a.m. to 5 p.m. Tuesday through Saturday. Admission is nominal.

El Rey Ruins were named for the skeleton found on top of the pyramid. Archaeologists speculated that he might have been a king since there were other human remains found at the base of the structure. This was a small ceremonial center for Maya fishermen, built very early, then abandoned and resettled near the end of the Postclassic Period, not long before the arrival of the conquistadors. On the west (the lagoon) side of the road, this site is marked by a small wooden sign at the entrance. A dirt road leads to the site which borders the lagoon. Admission is free.

Pok-Ta-Pok was discovered by workmen constructing the 12th hole of the Robert Trent Jones Golf Course. This small ruin from the Postclassic Period is well preserved.

—ON THE SEA—

If you've always wanted to learn or perfect a water sport, Cancun is tailor-made. The clear, year-round warm waters afford perfect conditions. Most hotels have centers where windsurfering, sailboats, kayaks, scuba and snorkeling equipment may be rented and English-speaking instructors are on hand to give fast and easy lessons to those who need them. There's also a wide selection of deep-sea fishing opportunities.

If you like party cruises, the **Fiesta Maya** is available to take you on a five-hour trip to Isla Mujeres. Pirates brandishing swords leap down on unsuspecting passengers for souvenir photos and voluptuous volunteers are selected to mimic the sacrificial rituals in which the hearts of victims were removed. There's an open bar, dancing, loud music and a host who works so hard making it "fun" that some would gladly pay him to take a siesta. Many enjoy this cruise and find it an easy, effortless way to see Isla Mujeres as well as the lagoon and mangrove swamps. Another possibility is the ferry which bypasses the swamps but also the noise.

With much reluctance, I'll share this one. It's so lovely. Tiny Contoy Island is Cancun's hidden treasure. Here is a pristine paradise where one can

Cancun

explore a bird sanctuary and enjoy an exquisite beach in perfect peace. At last, no vendors hawking "silver" bracelets, blankets, tablecloths, etc.

This is the classic "do nothing" get away. Arrangements may be made at your hotel to visit this wild preserve where one can enjoy snorkeling, explore nature trails, see and photograph marine birds. Most trips include a seaside barbecue.

—NIGHT LIFE—

Variety is the spice of Cancun. Every hotel on the island offers its own brand of entertainment ranging from jazz combos to specially arranged "fiestas." *My personal favorites run the gamut.*

The **Ballet Folklorico** is a dinner show rather than a ballet in the theater sense. The evening begins at 7 with an enormous buffet supper possibly weighted more to quantity than quality but there's certainly plenty from which to select. At 8:30 the performance begins. Though not yet the equivalent of the Mexico City extravaganza, the thirty dancers and musicians are good. Two evenings before I'd seen a roadshow production of **Cats** in San Francisco. It seemed a walk through in contrast to this lively, well executed performance. The whole event — food, entertainment, service — works well. Shows are staged in the **Convention Center** auditorium nightly except Sunday.

Mango Tango, a dinner show, accents Caribbean and Latino music with surprises that include a Maya spirit dance and arm-wrestling competitions. The setting is lovely and the seafood fresh and good. Shows are at 8:30 and 10:30 p.m. nightly. Blvd. Kukulcan, km. 14.2, hotel zone. Phone: 885-0303.

Wednesday is nostalgia night in the romantic Atrium Park Lobby of the **Hyatt Regency.** *Moonlight Serenade* is a sentimental journey into the 20's, 30's and 40's. A champagne dinner is served from 6:30 to 10:30 or one may just dance to the big band sounds of the Caribbean Swing Orchestra.

La Boom y Tequila Boom bring you back to the future. Located on Kukulcan Boulevard in the heart of the hotel zone, it's Cancun's primo nightspot. At Tequila Boom, drinks are two for one. It's fun to munch a burger while watching the hot rock 'n roll video, then drift over to **La Boom** to become a part of the disco's state of the art light and lazer extravaganza.

The once tiny village has grown to a city of over 120,000 inhabitants whose round the clock efforts insure a happy holiday.

Ready for the ruins? An evening here should limber you up for the big climb.

View from Presidente Hotel—Isla de Mujeres

ISLA DE MUJERES
(iss-la day moo-hair-es)

The crumbling shrine which threatens to topple into the Caribbean is located on the rocky southern coast of the island. Craggy cliffs and a secluded, seaside setting give the place its very special ambience. A visit in the morning—before the tour boats arrive—can be a mystical experience.

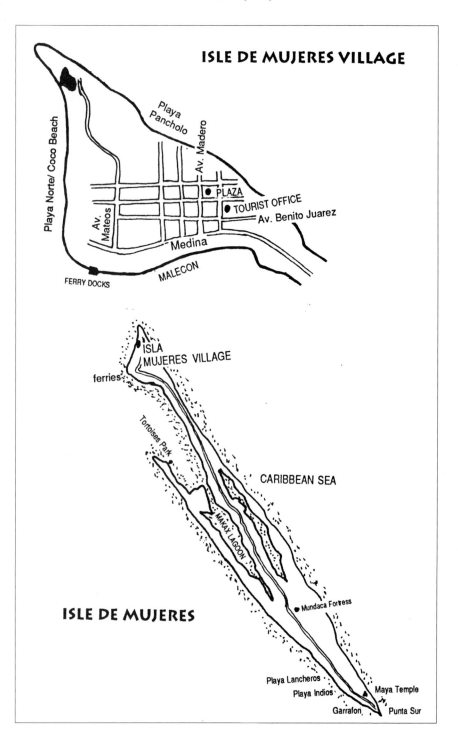

ISLE DE MUJERES VILLAGE

Playa Norte/ Coco Beach

Playa Pancholo

Av. Madero

Av. Mateos

PLAZA

TOURIST OFFICE

Av. Benito Juarez

Medina

MALECON

FERRY DOCKS

ISLA MUJERES VILLAGE

ferries

Tortoises Park

CARIBBEAN SEA

MAKAX LAGOON

Mundaca Fortress

ISLE DE MUJERES

Playa Lancheros

Playa Indios

Garrafon

Maya Temple

Punta Sur

I visited Isla Mujeres for the first time on a "fun" cruise out of Cancun. The attendant hoop-de-doo of chattering, camera clicking tourists rendered the pilgrimage to the temple of Ixchel a study in frustration. I vowed to return alone and did.

The crumbling shrine which threatens to topple into the Caribbean is located on the rocky southern coast of the island. Craggy cliffs and a secluded, seaside setting give the place its very special ambience. A visit in the morning — before the tour boats arrive — can be a mystical experience.

Half hypnotized by the pounding surf and wild grasses rippling in the wind, I meditated on Ixchel, the Maya goddess of creativity. Knowing that this place had once been a temple of divination and prayer, I added a silent supplication of my own. "Let the wisdom and spirit of the Maya flow through me — a fusion of intellect and intuition — onto the keys of my computer and out into the world."

Did she hear me?

How could I know? . . .The caretakers of the shrine sell shells near the road. There was one peachy pearl spiral that I coveted, but the price was far too high. If the woman lowers her price as I pass by her, I speculated. . . .

She did, *drastically,* and with no attempt at bargaining. I considered it a sign. And still do. The shell sits beside me now.

The Plymouth Rock of Mexico, Isla Mujeres was discovered on March 1, 1517 by Hernandez de Cordoba. The expedition had been beset by misfortunes. Lost and adrift for twenty-one days, the seamen at last sighted the island. What greeted them first were statues of Maya goddesses standing watch along the coast. Hence the name: Island of Women.

There's another story about how the island got its name. Pirates once found the place a convenient retreat in which to hang up their cutlasses and stash their women. One particularly romantic buccaneer, Antonio de Mundaca, built a luxurious estate, La Hacienda de la Huerta, for his favorite — La Triguena, a beauty with hair the color of wheat. The remnants of the extensive gardens and the crumbling ruins of the mansion remain to be explored.

Another reminder of a colorful past is Mundaca's tomb, cryptically inscribed: "What I am, you shall be; what you are, I was."

As opposed to Cancun, Isla Mujeres clings tenaciously to its own identity as a fishing village. People marry, give birth, receive communion, die and are buried here as they have been for centuries. Fishermen mend their nets and patch their boats seemingly oblivious to the tourists disgorged daily from Cancun.

Slightly raunchy, down at the heels, quite literally going to the dogs—mutts of every description roam free—the tiny island is a beach town plain and simple.

You reach Isla Mujeres by ferry–if driving, from Punta Sam; otherwise from Punta Juarez, both only a few miles north of Cancun. In either case the price is nominal. The ferries are wonderful, creaky old vessels where you can sunbath on the deck and dream about handsome pirates or their vast treasures still hidden somewhere on Isla Mujeres.

WHERE TO STAY

Posada del Mar, at Avenue Rueda Marina No. 15, is an escapist's paradise. Spacious landscaped grounds provide a tranquil oasis while just beyond the beach beckons. Reservations: (988) 877-0044

This romantic inn has eight ocean view rooms and excellent restaurants. The nucleus is the *Spa Zenter,* an immense facility given the intimate size of the hotel, where ritualistic-style treatments blend holistic, Asian and European techniques. Carr. Al Garragon. L. 8 y 9. US toll-free 1-877-278-8018; Canada toll-free 1-866-818-8342. In Mexico: 988 877-0651

Hotel Na Balam is a perennial favorite. It looks exactly like a tropical getaway ought to look. Zazil-Ha No. 118   Tel. (-998) 877-0279 877-0058.

La Casa de Suenos on Carretera Garafon (phone: (987) 7-06-51) is an intimate and elegant resort hotel with a striking infinity pool with lovely grounds. Each of the nine rooms or suites has a breathtaking ocean view.

Three others to consider are the *Hotel Belmar* (between Madero and Abasolo streets, Phone: (987) 7-04-30) the *Hotel Francis Arlene* (Avenue Guerro No. 7 Phone: (987)7-03-10) and the *Boca Mar* (Calle Nicolas Bravo y Zona Maritima Phone: (987) 7-01-1). All three are conveniently located and reasonable.

WHERE TO EAT

Avenida Hidalgo is lined with restaurants, all much the same. My favorite is *Ciro's.* How could you not like a restaurant that serves lobster prepared in a dozen different ways? I have returned many times to *El Meson del Bucanero* and never been disappointed. I also like *Pizza Rolandi* which offers many other tempting dishes besides the excellent pizza.

WHAT TO DO _____

What to do in Isla Mujeres? We're talking about an island that's only five miles long and in places only one mile wide. You mostly take walks and go to the beach. The ocean extends from white sand in bands of color: first jade, then turquoise, then the blue-green of sub-surface coral reefs and finally the deep marine blue of the open sea.

You can swim through schools of flashing yellow sergeant-majors and parrot fish that flame light gaudy stoplights, but try to get there early before the tourist boats arrive–or most of the fins you see will be made of rubber.

A visit to the national park and marine life refuge, *El Garrafon* is first on most agendas. Swimming and snorkeling are easy even for beginners and there's simple access to the gigantic coral reef and sandy-bottom entry path.

Another must is *Acuarama,* a performance of trained dolphins, seals and an exhibit of elephant seals and a variety of underwater denizens in their natural state. Shows are every hour on the hour every day but Monday.

A few chalky streets have been paved with rosy cement, but La Isla's relaxed pace and small scale simply doesn't change. Savvy snorklers leave crowded Garrafon Beach to the day trippers and head for the wooden pier at the end of Playa Norte.

—SHOPPING POSSIBILITIES—

Though prices here are generally lower than in Cancun, shopping can be frustrating. It's best to plan on paying in pesos. Only a few shopkeepers will take traveler's checks or credit cards and the exchange rate on dollars is poor. No one seems to have change, so paying the exact amount will save you much time and exasperation.

A long midday siesta is observed, stores closing promptly at noon and not opening until four. The most pleasant time to browse is evening.

—NIGHT LIFE—

What to do at night? Not much really–unless you count star gazing.

Be prepared with a long wish list, this is the place to get your priorities straight. Later the surf sings love songs, then lullabies.

Cozumel

COZUMEL
(koh-zoo-mell)

The six mile long Palancar is a massive fortress of coral. Its linear shelf drops steeply from the shallowest level of 10 meters to a depth of 400 meters. This is an ever-changing landscape of towering pinnacles of free standing coral rising as high as 30 meters, arches and tunnels, meandering ravines, blue grottos, dark caves suddenly lit by vivid pink sponges or lacy gorgonia fans. The entire labyrinth is honeycombed with passages leading to sunlit sand flats on the landward side or to a vast electric-blue void on the sea side.

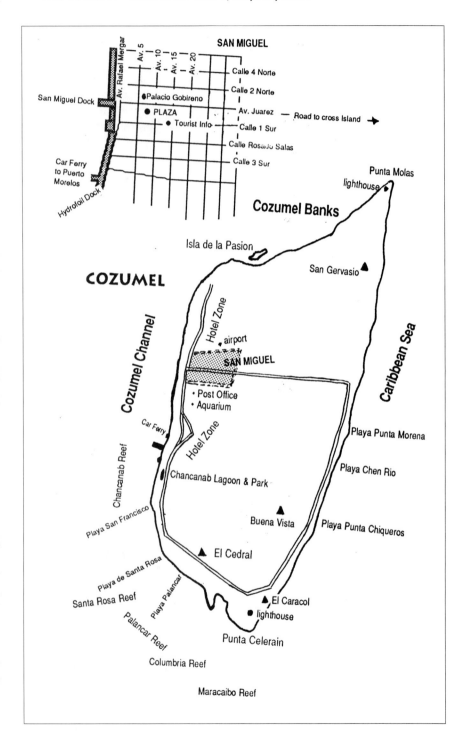

Cozumel, which means "Place of Swallows," was sacred from the very beginning. According to the Chilam Balam chronicles ("Books of the Jaguar Soothsayers") this was the Maya Eden from which the ancients burst forth "like bees from a hive of honey."

Not surprisingly, the whole island was a kind of shrine to Ixchel, goddess of childbirth, fertility, creativity, the sea and the moon. Since the moon rises in the east and appears to be born out of the sea, it all ties together very well. The moon goddess's effect on the tides was easily observable. When the moon would be full or at its beginning, the tides would soon be at their highest, bountifully spilling fish and crabs onto the beach–a lavish feast waiting to harvested. Obviously Ixchel was a deity to be venerated. Fishermen made sacrifices before her shrine before setting out to sea and pilgrims from as far away as Belize, Guatemala, Chiapas and Tabasco came to pay homage.

The mysterious moon goddess also possessed the power of prophesy. Sometimes she employed a medium who worked in the same manner as the oracle at Delphi. A high priest inside a large, hollow idol received her messages and transmitted them to the waiting populace. Pilgrimages from the mainland were considered a holy obligation and were particularly popular with pregnant women or women who wished to become pregnant.

Unfortunately it was this Maya equivalent of Rome or Jerusalem that received the first zealous thrust of Hernan Cortes' idol smashing crusade. In 1519 when the conquistador arrived with his eleven ships and 600 men on their way to conquering all of Mexico, he found an island of some 40,000 inhabitants–twice its present population. Few remnants of Cozumel's former grandeur survived his stay and once the orgy of vandalism was over, the Spaniards lost interest and abandoned the island to less hypocritical predators.

When the pirates arrived there was nothing left to plunder, but Cozumel was so desolate that it provided a convenient hideout similar to Isla Mujeres. Then piracy drifted out of fashion and the island was abandoned once again.

In 1841 when the famous explorer, John L. Stephens, arrived with his artist companion, Frederick Catherwood, Cozumel was a true desert island. "Amid all the devastations that attended the progress of the Spaniards in America, none is more complete than that which has swept over the island of Cozumel," he wrote in his 19th century travel classic, Incidents of Travel in Yucatan. Well, one form of treasure did remain–and fortunately still does. Like many contemporary tourists, Stephens was an avid shell collector. He left the island ladened with Ixchel's jewels.

Today one reaches Cozumel easily by plane or ferry boat navigating between the twin blues of sea and sky. Even from the air the water is so clear that one can see sandbars and coral formations.

Once on land the Caribbean influence is more pronounced than on any other spot in Mexico. Music has a Calypso beat, food a Creole tang, there's a buccaneer flair to place names and souvenirs. (Try traveling with a pirate chest — even a small one —I did. The penalty for temporary insanity is having to carry home the object of your momentary madness. Fortunately there is life after vacation. The wooden chest made a dandy Christmas gift filled with "pieces of eight" candy. The chocolates in their golden foil are long gone, but my friends still display their brass bound "treasure" chest.)

En route to the Palancar Reef

It's been estimated that one out of every six visitors to Cozumel comes for the diving. There are shore dives and night dives, refresher courses for interme-diates and crash courses for beginners, all taught by experienced bi-lingual dive masters. About one kilometer off the southern end of the island is one of the natural wonders of the undersea world, *Palancar Reef,* second only to Australia's Great Barrier Reef in length.

The six mile long Palancar is a massive fortress of coral. Its linear shelf drops steeply from the shallowest level of 10 meters to a depth of 400 meters. This is an ever-changing landscape of towering pinnacles of free standing coral rising as high as 30 meters, arches and tunnels, meandering ravines, blue grottos, dark caves suddenly lit by vivid pink sponges or lacy gorgonia fans. The entire labyrinth is honeycombed with passages leading to sunlit sand flats on the landward side or to a vast electric-blue void on the sea side.

But Palancar—so heart-stopping in its silent immensity—is only one of many coral subdivisions off Cozumel's southwest coast. Snorkeling, too, is also a visual feast and so, for that matter, is swimming. The whole island is literally surrounded by beach. Taxis are reasonable, but jeeps or mopeds are the best ways to explore the island which is roughly 28 miles long and 11 miles wide. It's exciting to roam the solitary beaches and what's left of the ruins. An hour can pass without seeing another person.

San Gervasio ruins, Cozumel.

There are several of the popular Robinson Crusoe Cruises from which to choose. Itineraries and destinations vary but all offer a boat trip, seafood picnic and snorkeling.

Part of the entertainment used to be watching the crew catch the fish and lobster that would later become part of the picnic fare. Now most of the area is an aquatic park so the fish course comes out of the sailboat's refrigerator. Too bad in a way, but at least you don't have to worry about eating that charming spindly-legged coral shrimp or the stunning orange and black angel fish you'd encountered while snorkeling.

Once during the pre-park days, I noticed one of the other passengers boarding the boat with a pretty conch shell she'd picked up from the scrap pile beside the cooking pot. "I wish I'd gotten one of those," I said aloud as the boat slipped out to sea.

A young crew member heard me and dove overboard. Within seconds he'd returned to the surface holding a much larger shell. His friends pulled him aboard and with a gallant bow he presented it to me.

There's a very unpleasant rumor that the U.S. Army Corps of Engineers delivered the coup de grace to Cortes's carnage by plowing under a large Maya city — until then hidden by dense jungle — during the construction of an airstrip. I try not to think about that when I land at what's now the Cozumel airport.

There are 30 surviving ruins—that we know of. San Gervasio is the largest. Located in Cozumel's northern interior, it's easily reachable by car or moped. Travel eastward on Avenue Juarez (hard-packed limestone roadway) then left on a dirt road (watch for the San Gervasio sign) for about 10 kilometers. You're there.

With its century-old Maya structures and temples, **San Gervasio** has been recorded as the second most visited archeological zone in Qunintana Roo. It consists of four distinct historical districts, the first dating from the Early Classic Period (A.D. 300-600) and the last from the Late Post-Classical Period (A.D. 1250-1500.

In recent years, institutions such as the Peabody Museum of the United States and the National Institute of Anthropology and History of Mexico have carried out restorations. A portion of the archaeological zone has been opened to the public.

The Island Foundation of Parks and Museums staffs an information booth and bilingual guides are available to provide narrative tours of the site.

Older yet, probably dating from about 500 A.D., are the ruins at **El Cedral.** They can be easily reached by taking the main highway south out of town past San Francisco Beach. Turn left at the sign and follow a paved road just over 3 kilometers. Surprisingly, this small ruin with a tree sprouting from its roof still bears a few traces of the original paint. The place is a study in contrast. The exposed roots of the living tree hold the ancient stones in a strange embrace and nearby there's a tiny church where one can see among the artifacts evidence of the continuing compromise between Christianity and native religion.

The Maya have endowed the saints with very human attributes. These beings are not unfailingly benevolent. Rather they're neutral like the ancient gods, and can be just as capricious. Not only is deference to their status demanded, but attention to their physical comfort. Garments must be frequently washed and worn ones replaced. Offerings of chocolate and tortillas may often be found before the Virgin and other saintly favorites.

WHERE TO STAY

The *Paradisus Cozumel Melia Mayan* is a first-class all-inclusive hotel. All of the rooms are comfortable and nicely equipped with balconies mostly overlooking the sea. The package includes unlimited food at two pleasant restaurants, brand drinks, horseback riding, kids club, gym, unlimited water sports, taxes, tips, nightly shows and an 18-hole golf course. Carretra Norte Kn58. Reservations: 1-800-359-4827. In Mexico, 987 998 881 1744.

The *Paradisus Cozumel Melia Mayan*

Playa Azul Cozumel is a ten-story, pyramid shaped hotel featuring an impressive Maya–style stone work. A private underpass leads to a small cove with a natural beach. Soak up the sun during the day, then spend a pleasant evening watching stage shows. 1-800-511-4848

Cozumel has an excellent selection of *buget hotels:*

Plaza Las Glorias has a convenient downtown location, its own dive shop and can arrange trips and car rentals. Phone: 987 872-2000. www.cozumel-hotels.net/las -glorias.

Hacienda San Miguel is a charmer with a courtyard edged by spacious rooms with kitchenettes. 987 872-1986. www,gotocozumek.cin,

The *Palma Dorada Inn* by the downtown waterfront has freshly painted rooms with new air conditioners. 987 872 0330. pdinn@prodigy.net.mx.

Fiesta American Dive Resort near Chankanaab Park has good food and a great staff. Nice pool. 987-872-9600.

Iberostar Cozumel is on the southwestern part of the island near Palancar Reef. Wonderful snorkeling, diving, beautiful beach, price all inclusive. 987 29-900. www.iberostar-cozumel.como

WHERE TO EAT_____

Five favorites as different as restaurants can be, but all very, very good:

Casa Denny's—More than 50 years old, Casa Denny's got its start when Miss Juanita took pity on hungry construction workers carving an airstrip out of the jungle and started feeding them. Soon her home kitchen wasn't large enough for everyone who wanted to eat Miss Juanita's food.

The restaurant still takes a casual approach. People drop by in the morning to tell the staff what they'd like to eat that night for dinner. Empanadas are a house specialty, but the seafood's superb. At this writing, $15 will buy an eleven course dinner. Autographed pictures of happy customers include Jackie Onassis and Placido Domingo.

Morgan's (named, of course, for Henry, the pirate, who used to hang out around Cozumel) on the main plaza offers the freshest lobster and the coldest margaritas in town. The bananas flambé is a specialty that definitely lives up to the spectacular promise.

Pizza Rolandion—crazy as it sounds to eat pizza in Mexico, this is a class act operation by any standard any place. The courtyard with its giant shade trees and lush tropical plants is charming. The Four Seasons Pizza is excellent and inexpensive, but so are the other Italian specialties: Serrano ham, cannelloni, lasagna.

Restaurant Las Palmeras near the zocolo is the "real thing," an authentic Mexican restaurant. Breakfast, lunch and dinner are all served here with traditional Mexican favorites, plus guava con queso (guava paste with cheese and crackers)–a pleasant and unexpected touch of the Mexican gourmet.

The ***Blue Cate Cito*** is great for crepes and coffee and La Loncheria Poc Chuc a good choice for green enchiladas.*El Moro* is "where the locals eat" and well worth tracking down. The food's very good, the menu in English, the margaritas excellent. Oh! I want to go back!

You can check or send your e-mails free at ***Tony Rome's Sandcastles.*** Open for breakfast, lunch and dinner. Good seafood and barbecued specialties. On the east side of 5th avenue between Adolfo Rosado Salas and 3rd St. South.

WHAT TO DO_____

The Maya word, Chankanaab — meaning "small sea"— is almost an understatement as a name for the ***Chankanaab Lagoon Park.*** This natural aquarium has more than 60 species of tropical fish, crustaceans and coral foundations. Another attraction is the adjoining botanical garden with 352 species of tropical plants brought from some eleven countries in edition to 417 species of Cozumel's native plants.

Encompassing nearly 450,000 square feet, the park is renowned for its botanical gardens, which showcase more than 350 species of tropical plants. Another park attraction is the Maya zone, where visitors can tour a modern-day reproduction of an ancient village and learn about the Maya culture's building and farming process.

Chankanaab Lagoon is a popular dive site, renowned for its great mounds of coral, called "Bonones." At a depth of 60 to 70 feet, these formations rise from the white sea bed to a height of 25 feet. Enormous yellow sponges, gorgonian fans, and anemones hang from the interior wall of the lagoon, adding splashes of color to the rainbow world. Schools of brightly colored fish dart to and fro through the aquamarine waters as enormous groupers doze lazily in the shadows, providing scuba divers and snorklers with an ever-changing underwater panorama.

Besides snorkeling down below, visitors to Cozumel can now enjoy a "touching" encounter above with playful dolphins at Chankanaab.

Participants in the program are treated to an educational video and instruction from professional trainers prior to actual contact with the dolphins. During their encounter, swimmers work with trainers, performing a variety of exercises with the dolphins before a 10-minute petting session.

Dolphin Discovery is open daily for swims at 9 and 11 a.m. and 1 and 3 p.m. Reservations may be made by calling (987) 2-6604 and (987) 2-2606.

The park, which includes diving areas ranging from 6 to 45 feet deep, a beach, restaurant, dive shop, snack bar, shops, dressing rooms and restrooms is open daily from 9:30 to 5p.m. There is a $2 a day charge.

In Maya art the turtle symbolizes the flat earth surrounded by seas. It was a sacred creature signifying the earth's abundance and fertility. Today the sea turtles are on the decline because of illegal harvesting and the shortage of undisturbed beaches. It doesn't help either that legend says the eggs are an aphrodisiac.

One hope remains. The sea turtle, so terribly devastated by human enemies has at last found friends in the Mexican government and in Pronatura, a private organization. Ecology minded visitors to Cozumel may participate in a hands-on program which is part of the national campaign to save endangered species of turtles. This is one of the few places left in the world where rare and endangered sea turtles come to lay eggs.

The *Cozumel Museum* has introduced field trips enabling visitors to watch the turtles come out of the ocean, crawl up the shore, make nests and lay their eggs. Participants also directly assist in saving the turtles by collecting their eggs and taking them to the local hatchery and by carrying baby turtles who have been in the hatchery 60 days to their natural habitat—the sea.All ages take part in the program which is available through the months of May-September when turtles visit the island.

The event begins with a museum slide show conducted by a biologist who accompanies groups on field trips. Participants then head for uninhabited beaches where turtles--many more than one hundred years old and a yard wide--make their way from the sea. After digging a nest, each turtle deposits her eggs, buries them and returns to the water where her "mate" is waiting.

Participants assist in collecting the eggs (about the size of tennis balls) along with sand from the nest. It's believed that the smell of this sand is what causes turtles to return to their birthplace from spots around the world when they are ready to lay their own eggs.

The field trip continues to the hatchery were biologists demonstrate how to bury the eggs in new, protected nests inside chain-link enclosures. Later newborn hatchings are hand-carried to the sea. Baby sea turtles have a one-in-a-thousand chance of survival.

Arrangements for the *Save the Turtle* tour may be made at Cozumel's charming museum (Avenida Rafael Meiger, between 6th and 8th streets). This little gem is not only a treasure trove of archeological finds and scientific information, but offers one of the best lunches in town, served in a lush tropical garden.

—SHOPPING—

Cozumel has traditionally been known for the excellent Pre-Columbian reproductions sold there. More recently the stock has been varied by whimsical masks and other examples of folk art from the Mexican mainland. For the most part the selections are not only innovative and charming, but also sold at prices very close to those asked in their town or village of origin.

A personal favorite is *El Arca de Noe* at Calle 2, No. 11

The only art form unique to Quintana Roo is handworked jewelry made from black coral. This comes primarily from the reefs around Cozumel. You'll find coral jewelry everywhere. *Mercado de Artesanias* (craft market), just behind the plaza, is a good place to begin your search; but *Van Cleef*, immediately north of the craft market, has the most stunning collection.

Maroma. Photo by Charles Herndon.

THE RIVIERA MAYA

Distances cease to exist as strangely contorted trees, towering plants of emerald green, feathery ferns, spongy fungus all crowd close together. When you can drive no farther, a narrow path snakes its way through the lush foliage dotted by brilliant azure morning glories. Vines writhe their way up through the damp, dark soil. Most look strong enough to support Tarzan.

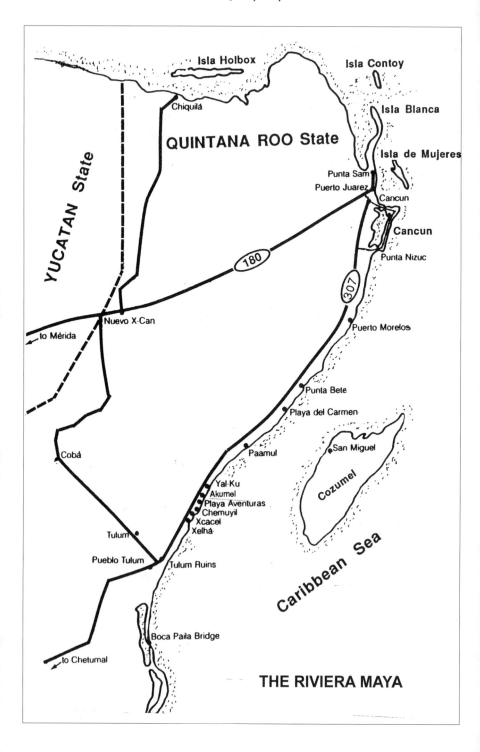

Isla Holbox

Isla Contoy

Chiquilá

Isla Blanca

QUINTANA ROO State

Isla de Mujeres

Punta Sam
Puerto Juarez

Cancun

Cancun

180

Punta Nizuc

to Mérida

Nuevo X-Can

Puerto Morelos

307

YUCATAN State

Punta Bete

Playa del Carmen

San Miguel

Paamul

Cobá

Yal-Ku
Akumel
Playa Aventuras
Chemuyil
Xcacel
Xelhá

Cozumel

Tulum

Pueblo Tulum

Tulum Ruins

Caribbean Sea

Boca Paila Bridge

to Chetumal

THE RIVIERA MAYA

There was nothing standing;
Only the clam water, the placid sea, alone and tranquil.
Nothing existed.

Then they planned the creation,
And the growth of the trees and the tickets and the birth of life.

Thus let it be done!
Let the emptiness be filled!
Let the water recede and make a void.
Let the earth appear and become solid;
Let it be done, thus they spoke.
Let there be light, let there be dawn in the sky and the earth!
                    Popol Vuh

Then the gods concluded their divine dialogue, the jungle was born. It exists now virtually as it did then — a forest primeval. And at its edge laps the eternal sea.

Heading south from Cancun on Highway 307 the road is well paved and arrow straight. On either side is dense, green jungle, enticing to some, vaguely disturbing to others. Who knows what silent, slinking predators watch, listen, wonder at the humans roaring by seemingly oblivious to them.

Once a gathering point for Maya pilgrims on their way to the sacred island of Cozumel, **Xcaret** (pronounced scha-ret), now draws pilgrims of a very different sort. Today's visitors are fun seekers enjoying a unique blend of archaeology, anthropology, sociology, ecology and nearly every kind of water sport.

Okay, so Xcaret (987) 1-40-00) (6 kms south of Playa del Carmen) is Disneyland meets the Maya, but it truly does offer something for absolutely everyone. Plan to arrive early—the park opens at 8:30 a.m.—so that you can book your dolphin swim. Only 36 people a day may enjoy this delightful experience. Reservations are taken in the morning on a first come first serve basis, so once inside, go directly to the *Dophinarium.*

Xcaret is fantasy on the grand scale, an ecological park covering 250 acres of stunning coastline. What to do there? Visit the butterfly pavilion, ride horses through lush tropical foliage, attend a charreda (Mexican rodeo), visit the replica of a Maya village, or watch archaeologists excavate a real one. Check out the turtle, manatee, and bat exhibits, and hear what scientists who're studying them have to say.   Xcaret is justly proud that, as of 2004, 43 Hawksbill turtles were born in the park—the first time in the world that these awesome creatures have reproduced in captivity.

Several Hawksbill males mate with one female. The female then stores the semen of all the males and will mix and fertilize it in her ova. This is known as "multipaternity."

Recently 19 howler monkeys whose lives were threatened by the loss of their rainforest habitat were relocated to Xcaret and are thriving.

What used to be an underground river has been turned into a floating adventure by making openings in the ceiling of an underground cavern to let in light and air. At the entrance of what was once a sacred cenote you'll be given a life jacket. From there you'll float for about 30 minutes for 1,000 feet down river. To me, the float alone is worth the admission.

Outdoor cenote next to Xel-ha.

There are a variety of restaurants in Xcaret—all rather pricey, none bad, but none thrilling. My personal pick is ***Sabores de Puebla***—pretty with good Mexican food. An alternative would be to ask your hotel to pack a picnic lunch as there are a number of really lovely places to stop.

The evening's folkloric extravaganza begins with a candlelit stroll through the reconstructed Maya village—very effective—and ends with a performance by the famed "flying" dancers, Voladores de Papantla. It's quite impressive. Plan to stay for dinner and the presentation. It's worth it. After all, getting into Xcaret is a major investment, so you might as well get your money's worth. The entrance fee is $39 a piece for adults, $24 for children, the dolphin swim is an extra $50. Xcaret is open from 8:30 a.m. until 10 p.m.

To the south of Aventuras Akumel on the left side of the road is *Xel-ha* (shell-ha), probably the largest natural aquarium in the world. It's also the busiest around tour bus time. If you can possibly time your arrival to be in *Xel-ha* when the buses are in Tulum, your enjoyment will be increased immeasurably. But at any hour, this place is not to be missed.

Xel-ha

Xel-ha is a true swimmer's paradise for there's no undertow. A vast labyrinth of underwater caves and tunnels, it covers approximately ten square acres. There are some fifty or so species of fish in every imaginable hue crying out to be admired. Snorkeling equipment can be rented on the spot.

Even if you're not a swimmer, you need only slip into the cool, crystal water and wait for the fish to come to you. It's an incredible experience to feel them. Should you tire of fish and fish stories, lie on the wharf and listen to the gentle lapping of the water.

Only a short distance south of the lagoon on the right hand side of the road are the Maya ruins of *Xel-ha.* Though these begin only a few feet from the highway, passersby rarely see them–a sad omission. Like Xcaret, the lush jungle setting is magical. The ruins are extensive and well preserved, the wall paintings even clearer than the ones at Tulum.

If you're fortunate, the sometime caretaker may come around and show you the way to the cenote. Write your own script, live your own movie, this is the place. We're talking spectacular! The most beautiful outdoor cenote on the Yucatan Peninsula.

SIAN KA'AN

If the traveler were to gaze into the horizon she or he might possibly be able to relive the ancient myth of discovering the subtle line which separates the sky from the sea. Many centuries ago, the Maya discovered this dividing line and called it *Sian Ka'an*: "where the sky is born." They believed it to be in Quintana Roo--where Cancun was eventually born.

Heliconia also known as 'lobster claw'.

Today, with Cancun expanding at the rate of 25 percent a year, that line is apt to be obscured by high rise hotels. At last count there were 200 of them with still more under construction. Despite the promised income, Mexican environmentalists, concerned with the unrestricted development of coastal lands, crusade for more protected spaces such as Sian Ka'an, the state of Quintana Roo's biospheric reserve. They're gambling that low impact visits to such places will provide visitors with memories that will last longer than a suntan.

Located 96 miles south of Cancun, Sian Ka'an is an immense preserve consisting of 72 miles of virgin barrier reef, two of the coast's most fertile bays, pristine lagoons, unspoiled marshlands and tropical forest.   It shelters such diverse species as jaguar, puma, ocelot, boa, tapir, boar, spider and howler monkeys, as well as some 300 species of birds, the endangered tortoise and manatee.

The term biosphere refers to the thin layer of earth inhabited by living things. It's made up of a small section of the lithosphere (the solid part of the earth, composed of rocks and soil), down to where microorganisms and the deepest roots reach; a section of the hydrosphere (the liquid part of the earth, made up of maritime and continental bodies of water) down to where the depth and lack of light make life impossible; and the first eight to ten kilometers of the atmosphere (gaseous part of the earth) where microorganisms float and terrestrial organisms— including man—live.

Jaguar, resident of Xcaret.

A biosphere is, in this sense, a small part of the planet where conservation programs are established, as well as the rational use of natural resources. This concept is part of the scientific co-op program Man and the Biosphere, established by UNESCO in 1971, to deal with man's interaction with the environment.

But none of this really says it. The bays of the Holy Spirit and the Ascension, which partially comprise the reserve are incredibly beautiful. This is a mystic region where absolute silence reigns in complete harmony with the voices of nature. A more beautiful melody does not exist.

Access to Sian Ka'an is from Boca Paila or Punta Allen, seaside, or Chunyache, landside.

WHERE TO STAY_____

The Riviera Maya extends seventy miles south of Cancun's International Airport (twenty miles south of Cancun) and ends in at the village of Punta Allen. For the Maya of the Post Classic era (1000-1550 AD) it was a commercial and religious center. More recently, it used to be the place people went to get away from Cancun. Scrubby jungle still borders Highway 307, but narrow, unpaved roads lead seaward to hotels that resemble everything from Maya temples to Norman castles. Today, sailing, fishing swimming, horseback riding, kayaking and ecotours are the preferred activities of the area. Presently there are nearly 24,000 rooms available in hotels catering to all tastes and budgets. About 100,000 guests, mostly from the U.S., visit the area each year. Go soon before it becomes "Little Miami."

The luxuriously laid-back *El Dorado Royale* offersan all-inclusive getaway for adults. There is nothing not to like. Hot tubs, hammocks, open air showers, all water sports, nightly entertainment. It's a place to do it all or to do nothing. The complex includes five restaurants, eight bars and a state-of-the-art spa. Phone: 1-866-KARISMA or www.karismahotels.com

Casa Caribe, 12 miles south of Cancun in Puerto Morelos, is a small hotel—just six rooms—run by ex-pats, Rick Bryant and Patty Davis. Rooms have tile floors, ceiling fans and lovely sea views. Rates are reasonable and the village nearby. Casa Caribe is a good base camp for forays to the ruins or down the coast. U.S. Phone: 1-763-441-7630; e-mail: casacaribe@modempool.com.

It's easy to miss the turn off from Highway 307 to *Maroma*. There are no signs indicating that you've reached the portals to heaven—just a stucco wall with a bamboo gate manned by a guard. This earthly St. Peter breaks into a bright smile as soon as he knows you're a guest.

The two-kilometer drive through a jungle where armadillos, iguanas, wild turkeys and the occasional jaguar lurk brings you to a hand-hewn stone plaza in front of the hotel entrance which feels like a heritage hacienda.

The 36 small villas, each one a little jewel, are entirely handmade. Mahogany, caroba and ironwood are crafted into chairs, armoires and vanities, hand-painted tiles are used in the bathrooms. Bedspreads and hammocks on the private terraces are made by local artisans.

An added attraction is the hotel restaurant, *La Parilla*. Try the parilla mista (a grilled mixture of lobster, shrimp, chicken and steak.)

A special treat is a sunset couples massage along the water's edge. Maroma is without a doubt one of a handful of the most romantic hotels in Mexico.

Located off hwy 307, 20 miles south of Cancun. Phone: 866-454-9351, locally : 998-87-28200. hchehda@maromahotel.com

Hotel Las Palapas, 35 miles south of Cancun's International Airport and one mile north of the village of Playa del Carmen, is not only a total delight but an excellent value. This charming hotel is nestled within a natural environment of white-sand beaches and lush, tropical gardens. It's small, intimate and lovely with seven thatched roofed, beach-front cabins as well as 48 standard and 20 deluxe garden rooms in one and two-story cottages. Seafood is as fresh as it gets in the resort's two excellent restaurants. Water sports include snorkeling, scuba diving, fishing and sailing. Avenue 34 Norte, between 5a and Zona Federal Maritima. P.O. Box 116, Playa del Carmen, Quintana Roo, 777710, Mexico. Palapas@playadelcarmen.com. 1-800-433-0885, from the U.S. and Canada; from Mexico (9) 873-0584.

Viva Maya , 45 miles south of Cancun on highway 307, is a delightful all inclusive resort planned with kids as well as adults in mind. Everything— food, drinks, diving lessons, theme parties, even water toys—is included in the package. Kids under 12 are free.   Phone: 800-950-1363

La Posada del Captain Lafitte on the Cancun-Tulum road at Punta Bede has a charming ambience. Attractive bungalows with baths and private terraces face the sea. The bar-restaurant is lively, the staff eager, friendly, helpful. "Our knowledge of the ocean is our strength," is the motto. The emphasis is on diving with a staff of professionals, and an ample supply of tanks and boats are available. Phone: 1-800-538-6802.

Kailuum II, successor to the much beloved Kaillum, is a beachfront enclave that consists of a peak-roofed dining room and honor bar, two bathhouses and 31 canvas tents with palapa-roofed, sand-floored terraces. The family style food is excellent. Excursions and car rentals can be arranged and guests share the Lafitte pool, dive shop and other amenities. Thirty miles south of the Cancun airport, off Hwy. 307. (800) 538-6802. www.mexicoholiday.com.

The Hotel Molcas in Playa del Carmen is a romantic hotel with a private beach where a live band plays during lunch. Guests have free and unlimited use of the ferry service between Playa del Carmen and Cozumel. Reservations: 1-800-442-4266.

At *Motel El Crucero*, they're cheap At Motel El Crucero the atmosphere is zero but the prices can't be beaten. The accommodations are clean, adequate and very convenient to the Tulum ruins. El Crucero is located at the junction of Highway 307 and the Tulum access road. Anyone traveling by bus or on a tight budget couldn't do better. There's an adequate, equally inexpensive restaurant with an even better one—*Restaurant El Paisan y El Venado*—just across the street.

Begun as a private residence, the *Shangri-La* has grown into an escapist's fantasy come true. Now 70 rooms and suites share two pools, restaurants, pool room, library and PADI dive shop. The fanciful stucco and thatched cabanas are placed along tropical paths that meander down to the sea. Abundant breakfasts are served and delightful dinners feature lobster tails and seafood pastas. Call 800-555-2220, www.rivieramayadventures.com (from 2001)

If you simply must plug something in like a hairdryer, answering machine, laptop, or razor, better pass *Zamas* by. But if you're looking for something cheap, beautiful and right on the sea, this could be your ticket. Cabanas are roomy, clean and comfortable. Each has a private bathroom with hot solar-powered water, or lukewarm cloud-powered water. The private patios come with the tropical imperative—twin hammocks.

The hotel restaurant, *Que Fresco!*, draws people from miles around. If you've tired of fresh lobster, snapper or grouper, there's wood-fired pizzas, plenty of fresh fruit and vegetables. You're not likely to tire of the margaritas. They're muy fuerte. Call: 800-538-6802; e-mail: zamas@compuserve.com

One of the prettiest places to stay on the Riviera Maya is the *Omni Puerto Aventuras*. The luxurious but intimate 30-room hotel faces the marina on one side and a dazzling white beach on the other. Close by is a state-of-the-art Mexican "village" complete with restaurants and boutiques. An exciting attraction is CEDAM headquarters, an international archaeological organization. A visit to their museum featuring both pre-Columbian relics and sunken treasures from the Spanish main is a must. Telephone: 987- 3-5100

PLAYA DEL CARMEN

Playa Del Carmen: In the mood for bright lights, loud music and tourist shopping? Playa del Carmen, thirty minutes south of Cancun, is the place. Hip, popular with Europeans, the former fishing village has been described as the St. Tropez of the Maya Riviera. Bustling with boutiques and restaurants, Playa del Carmen is as hot as Cancun was ten years ago. Which might be reason enough to make it a one night stop over.

Also consider the **Pelicano Inn**, between Sixth and Eighth streets; 011-52-984 873-0997; Deseo, Fifth Avenue and 12th St., 011-52-984-879-3620, www.hoteldeseo.com; or Hotel Lunata, Fifth Avenue, 011-52-984-873-0884, www.lunata.co.

For a special Playa del Carmen treat, follow Calle 38 to *Cueva de Chango*, where the banana pancakes and papaya shakes are fabulous. (No phone; entrees under $5)

Enjoy the beauty of bareness at the **Hidden Beach Resort**, an all-inclusive au natural club. The 40-acre stretch of white sand beach is located off hwy 307 some 40 miles south of Cancun. A unique architectural feature is a river that meanders across the property connecting all the oceanfront swim-up suites to the main pool and swim-up bar. Km 95 Carretera Cancún   Phone: 984 8757000 or visit 984 875-7000.

"Live large—live free" is the motto of **Freedom Paradise**, a resort designed for those seeking a "size-friendly vacation club." The 3-star hotel is integrated into its ecological environment, has lush gardens and ocean views. Four pools designed for different purposes-- an adult pool, an activities pool, a nocturnal pool and a relaxation pool. The size friendly furniture is sturdy and comfortable. The walk-in showers have grab bars and activities are planned for people of all sizes. Located of hwy 307 61 miles south of Cancun. Phone: 866 548 3995. Locally: 998 887 1101. info@freedomparadise.com

Maya Tulum, once an ashram, still offers yoga, reflexology, massage, and facials—good for the body and soul. Each guest room is a separate building made of stone and stucco. Maya Tulum is solar-powered and lights are turned off from midnight to 6 a.m. Bring a flashlight. Phone 888 515-4580. www.mayatulum.com

Cabanas Ana y Jose has a restaurant, pool, car rental agency and 15 pretty rooms on the beach. Phone: 998-887-5470. www.anajose.com

Amansala, a six-room resort opened by two New York fitness specialists operates as a kind of bikini boot camp. We're talking tough exercise, lean diet, massages and yoga, meditation, sweat lodge and drumming. Phone: 984-1000-805;info@amansala.com.

Accommodations, like everything else, come down to a matter of choices. For more information call Riviera Maya 888-604-6044.

Views of Tulum's famous El Castillo

TULUM
(too-loom)

Mounted on the edge of a cliff, this abandoned city towers above one of the most uniquely beautiful beaches in the world. Yes, it is possible to dodge the crowd, find a quiet corner and meditate on the mysteries of the Mayan world–or one's own world.

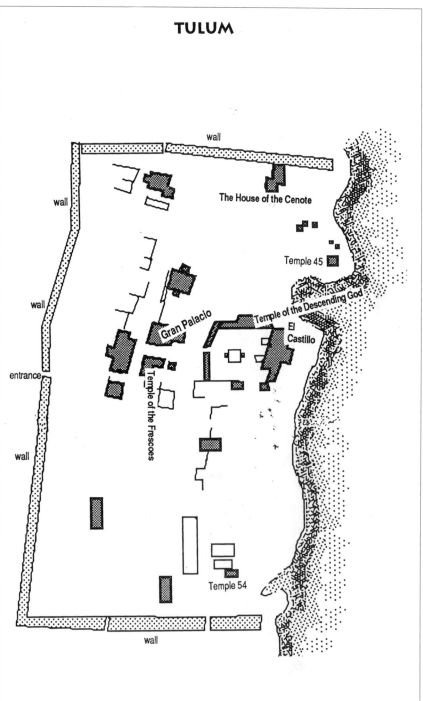

TULUM

wall

wall

wall

entrance

wall

The House of the Cenote

Temple 45

Temple of the Descending God

Gran Palacio

El Castillo

Temple of the Frescoes

Temple 54

wall

Five kilometer south of Akumal on Hwy. 307, a side road leads to Tulum. Here early morning light awakens the "City of the Dawn." Once a mariner's landmark perched high above the opalescent waters of the Caribbean, the fortress city watched over traders gliding by on large dugout canoes ladened with jade, feathers, honey, and the precious cacao beans used for money. Mounted on the summit of a limestone cliff 40 feet high, lashed by waves of open sea, the high, thick fortification walls bespeak local feuds. One of the last strongholds of a dying civilization, Tulum was sighted by the Spaniards in 1517, within 50 years the city lay silent. Today it is the most visited archeological site in the Maya world.

Everybody who was anybody lived in Tulum. This city which reached its apogee between 1000 A.D. and 1600 A.D., during the decline of the Maya civilization, was set aside for nobles and highly esteemed merchants or warriors. Except for slaves serving their masters, the lower classes were kept out.

That rigid selectivity is believed to have been the undoing of the place. Ultimately the peasants who lived outside the walled city revolted. All that remains today of the proud citadel are ruins.

Though the beginnings of Tulum stretch back into earliest time, the majority of its structures are from the Postclassic or "decadent" period. For this reason, Tulum often gets short shrift from classic scholars who tend to write it off as "bourgeois" or even "miserable." This attitude ignores the strength of the architecture–said to have inspired Frank Lloyd Wright himself–and the organizational skill of the people who built these massive structures.

It also overlooks the esthetic and prophetic significance of the seaside setting. Originally called Zama, or "place of the dawning," this was the most important of the strategically located ceremonial centers. It was from the seas beyond the walls that the sun rose each morning and began her sacred dance across the skies, and it was from that same sea that the Spaniards first appeared.

In 1511 a Spanish ship was wrecked off the coast of Jamaica. The survivors drifted ashore at what was by then called Tulum, or walled city, in a small boat. What they saw was a showplace. Every stone was covered with brilliant paintings and carvings–stark white, deep red or vibrant blue back-grounds covered with multi-colored stylized figures. At the top of the largest building–the castillo or castle, as they called it–a beacon fire blazed.

Five of the men including their captain were killed by the wary Maya well aware of an ancient prophecy that warned of bearded men who would come out of the sea to rob them of their land. The two remaining survivors, Gonzalo Guerrero and Jeronimo de Aguilar, had to talk fast to save their lives. Somehow they were able to convince their captors that they were strong and resourceful, an asset to the community.

Aguilar was eventually sold as a slave to a passing trader and taken to Cozumel where he remained until freed by Cortés's invasion. Guerrero went native. Before long he was speaking fluent Maya and moving freely, so freely that he became a military leader and married the daughter of a king.

In 1517 another Spaniard, Juan de Grijalva, sailed by and was so impressed by the sea view of Tulum that he literally wrote home about it: "We sailed a day and a night, and on the following day at sunset, we descried a citadel, or a city, so large that Seville seemed to us neither larger nor better."

Before long a Spanish expedition was sent to pacify and conquer the "islands" of Cozumel and Yucatan. It was Guerrero who incited the Maya to fight fate. He hadn't heard the prophecy and refused to give credence to it. Francisco Herandez de Cordoba was merely a man like himself and could be defeated. Guerrero's battle strategies depended upon surprise attacks, ambushes and cunning. The modern day term guerrilla warfare gets its name from the tactics he introduced.

When the Spaniards were repulsed in Tulum, Cortés offered Guerrero amnesty, sending his old comrade Aguilar with gifts and a promise that the prodigal son would be well received. Guerrero's reply has never been forgotten:

> *"Brother Aguilar, I am a married man, I have three children. They (the Maya) hold me as a chief and a captain during wars. Go with God, for my face is carved and my ears pierced. What would the Spaniards say about me, when they see me in this manner! You have seen my children, how lovely they are. For your life, if for them you'd give me these green beads which you have brought I shall say that my brothers have sent me from my land."*

The three children of Guerrero and his Maya princess are the first recorded mestizos, the first known blending of Indian and Spanish blood.

The fall of Tulum occurred about fifty years after the Spanish invasion of the Yucatan Peninsula but was unrelated to it. The Maya—both triumphant peasants and defeated overlords–left the area. For a time pirates took advantage of the little cove below El Castillo; but by 1842 when John Stephens and Frederick Catherwood arrived, the place was deserted.

The terrain was so desolate that it reminded Stephens "of the witches' gathering place in the Hartz Mountains, as described in *Faust* of Goethe." Later, "an image of a grove sacred to Druidical worship" came to him as he climbed the once grand staircase of El Castillo then overgrown with thick green foliage and looked about at the mysterious buildings that surrounded him.

Years passed. My next trip was by tour bus. When I stepped off the air conditioned vehicle, I discovered that the pirates had returned. They waved and beckoned from small shops pointing out a colorful assortment of blankets, crafts, and jewelry. Once inside the gate I found that the whole site had been cleared. Tulum now looks like a golf course.

Well, so much the better to see, but still a part of me envies Stephens when he wrote:

> "We had undertaken our long journey to this place in utter uncertainty as to what we should meet with; impediments and difficulties had accumulated upon us, but already we felt indemnified for all our labor. We were amid the wildest scenery we had yet found in Yucatan; and, besides the deep and exciting interest in the ruins themselves, we had around us what we wanted in all the other places, the magnificence of nature. Clearing away the platform in front, we looked over an immense forest; walking around the molding of the wall, we looked out upon the boundless ocean, and deep in the clear water at the foot of the cliff we saw gliding quietly a great fish eight or ten feet long."

The party camped in El Castillo and one night when a tropic storm came up Stephens wrote of "the darkness, the howling of the winds, the cracking of branches in the forest, the dashing of angry waves against the cliff. . ." But on another night "the moon was shining magnificently, lighting up the darkness of the forest, and drawing a long silvery line upon the sea. . . " They felt themselves "exalted above the necessity of sleep." Instead he philosophized, "The city no longer keeps watch; the fiat of destruction has gone out against it, and in solitude it rests, the abode of silence and desolation."

There is very little silence or solitude to be had in Tulum at tour time, but the setting is still stunning. Mounted on the edge of a cliff, this abandoned city towers above one of the most uniquely beautiful beaches in the world. Yes, it is possible to dodge the crowd, find a quiet corner and meditate on the mysteries of the Maya world–or one's own world.

El Castillo.. Photo by Charles Herndon.

The city is still effectively enclosed. A veritable barbed wire fence of cactus and other thorny plants covers the cliffs. On the other three sides Tulum is protected by a great wall 3,600 feet in length and averaging 15 to 20 feet in height broken only by five narrow gateways admitting but one person at a time. Beyond the guardhouses stationed at the western end, a solid mass of vegetation extends into the alligator-infested swamps that stretch for miles inland.

The present day Maya say that in ancient times Tulum was connected to Coba, Chichen Itza and Uxmal by means of a skyroad called a cuxan san (living rope). One can only wonder about where this enigmatic fragment fits into the giant Maya puzzle. What we do know is that *sacbes* or stone causeways connected all the ceremonial centers so that traders and supplicants alike could pass easily through the jungle. Tulum's northeast gate was the sallyport to the sacbe that lead to Xelha, six miles away, and that some place close by was a turnoff point westward to Coba and on to Chichen Itza.

Most of the buildings of Tulum share a unique architectural characteristic. The walls are slightly flared upward. This inverted pyramid effect creates areas of light and shadow that not only enhance the sculptured relief but also protect the painted stucco moldings from rain water.

The most dominant building in Tulum was called *El Castillo* by the Spaniards because if it looked like a castle, it must be one. Who knows, perhaps they were right. One thing is certain, El Castillo was one fantastic lighthouse. Researcher Michael Creamer, aided by a National Geographic grant, discovered the long lost secret of this pre-electronic navigational station. He placed a lantern on shelves behind each of two windows located high on the face of El Castillo. At sea where the two beams can be seen at the same time, there's a natural opening in the reef.

Besides its spectacular view of the sea, El Castillo has a mystery to ponder–the red hand prints on its inner wall. Are they the imprint of a living hand? Thinking so brings me closer to the builders of the city. I like to imagine that across the time, the desolation, the stillness and the mystery–another human being reaches out to greet me.

This great temple is made up of three terraced stories, each of which bears a small sanctuary. Its monumental effect is accented by a broad central stairway that rises to the top terrace and leads to the main sanctuary.

Flanking El Castillo are two smaller structures, prosaically designated by archaeologists as *Temples 45 and 54.* Temple 54 is close to the sea and the southern wall. Despite the remoteness of the area and its apparent desolation, Stephens believed this temple was still in use. To the north of El Castillo is Temple 45 which is actually the largest of several offertories. It was here that prayers were offered to Ixchel. Today one can look out as the ancients must have done at the pretty cove below and 400 yards beyond to a "blue hole,"–the sea's equivalent of a cenote.

Adjacent to the eastern gate of the north wall is the *House of the Cenote.* Where there are cenotes, there are invariably nearby temples where offerings were made and gods propitiated by sacrifices and ritual bathing. Here the temple sits above the roof of the cave. It appears to have been built in two different stages. The original building had two chambers with an entrance facing the sea and an altar in the inner room. Later a smaller room was added on the southeastern corner with steps leading into the cave and additional steps running around the mouth of the cenote and down to the bottom of the cavern which is almost at sea level. Unfortunately the cave is full of bats which have an unfortunate effect on the water. It takes a great deal of imagination to visualize what was once a prime source of physical and spiritual well-being.

The *Temple of the Frescoes* is located directly in front of El Castillo on "Main Street." This temple has been added on to many times. The Maya believed that the world came to an end every 52 years (theirs was a 52-year calendar cycle.) The ending was celebrated by canceling debts, the beginning or rebirth by building higher and more elegant structures over the base of older ones. One can easily see the effects of this custom here. First there was a small square single room with a door facing the street, a curved roof rising almost from the floor and an altar on the rear wall. This is now the inner temple of the first floor. The remains of the rich wall murals were preserved by the additions.

Jungle encroaches on Tulum.

A later gallery was added along three sides with four columns on the street side and two on the north and south ends. The walls are covered with greenish blue paintings against a black background. Two of the biggies in the godly pantheon, Ixchel and Chac, are portrayed here along with sacred serpents and more red handprints. These 13th century wall paintings are quite beautiful, but require a flashlight to see to best advantage. The most recent addition is a small upper deck with a single door facing Main Street. There's a small altar here against the rear wall and a curved vaulted roof.

The most intriguing and controversial of all the buildings in Tulum is the *Temple of the Descending God* located to the immediate left of El Castillo. The base of the building is an older structure that's been filled in to support the newer one. A stairway emerges into a single chamber with a window on the sea. On either side are two ceremonial benches. The blue mural represents the night sky with Venus — sacred to the Maya — and other stars combined with mythic serpents. In the center are numerous deities from the Maya pantheon which is as vast as the stars themselves.

But it's the figure above the temple doorway that's most impressive. This is a large carved figure of a deity descending head first. The conventional theory is that the carving depicts Ab Muzen Cab, the Maya bee god. (In Pre Columbian times, as today, honey was a mainstay of the Yucatean diet.)   A more provocative one suggests that the descending god is an extra terrestrial. Could he be in some way connected to the *cuxan san* or the skyway legend?

Iguana at Tulum.

— LAGUNA BACALAR —

Hold your breath, ***Laguna Bacalar***, an off the beaten track hideaway on the outskirts of the sleepy, seaside town of Chetumal, may be the most beautiful spot in all of Mexico. Also known as the Lake of Seven Colors, this is the hidden treasure of the Maya Riviera.

What will lure you there? Its accessibility to Kuhunlich, a ceremonial center occupied between 300 and 1200 A.D. Most of the site is still unexplored, with many mounds still covered by vegetation. The masks found there have human features thought to resemble people who actually existed. Yet the features have super human elements as well. The enormous eyes are related to the sun god, Kinich Ahau, and then there are the jade ears, guarded by monstrous two-headed serpents and the jaguar-like upper face. Who knows....yet. Perhaps one day the archaeologists will tell us.

To get there, continue south to Chetumal, then take highway 186 west 25 miles to Kohunlich.

Bacalar itself is a two-site destination. There's ***Fuerte San Felipe***, a 17th century fort built by the Spaniards as protection from pirates. Once the moat was filled with sharp spikes, today its covered with flowers. The fort and its

Typical tourists—Tulum. Photo by Gary Crall.

museum of pirate artifacts is open daily. The other stop is *Cenote Azul*, a brilliant blue water hole adjacent to a pleasant restaurant.

These are all worthwhile sites where you won't be stumbling over hordes of other visitors all wanting to see and do exactly the same things that you want to do. That's reason enough for coming. But the number one reason is the extraordinary beauty of Laguna Bacalar itself. The majority of this forty mile tropical lagoon is wild and undeveloped.

Rancho Encantado, an eco-resort and retreat center, nestles on the shore surrounded by coconut palms, lush gardens and tropical fruit trees. By day you can enjoy small, customized archaeological tours into the heartland—tours only available by special permit from *Mexico's National Institute of Archaeology*. In the evenings there are spectacular sunsets, cool lagoon waters, excellent food and spa treatments. This lovely place is after the last word. Phone: 1-800-505-MAYA.

Hotel Holiday Inn Chetumal is convenient to the airport for an overnight stay. Phone: 983-2-11-00; faz: 983-2-26-76.

A helpful website that offers a smorgasbord of what's out there waiting to be explored and enjoyed is www.Riviera-maya-touristinformation.com

WHERE TO STAY_____

The Explorean Kohunlich, at 8 km. Carreta a Zona Archaeologica, is a true jungle retreat. Surrounded by lush vegetation and marvelous archeological sites, the hotel combines traditional Maya designs with contemporary luxury and comfort. The accent's on soft adventure with a team of experienced guides to plan exciting tours to ancient Maya sites.

The Explorean Kohunlich includes 40 suites, a sophisticated restaurant, plus a spa and a pool overlooking the vast jungle.

Guests may choose to sail a catamaran on the crystalline waters of *Laguna Bacalar* or venture by kayak to Laguna Palmas where dinner will be served under a starry sky after experiencing nightfall in the middle of a jungle lake.

The ruins at Tulum. Photos by Charles Herndon.

There are excursions to the Maya sites of Dzibanche, Xpuhil, and Chicanna; but, to me, the most exciting and rewarding is to Kohunlich-Explorean's "backyard" site. In the US and Canada, call 1-877-EXPLORA. In Mexico, 1-800-3-66-66-66. Email: contact@explorian.com.

Coba's history is written here.

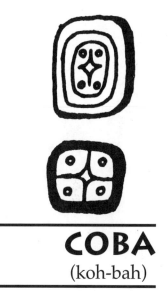

COBA
(koh-bah)

*The canopy of foliage overhead is like a green
cloud cover over the jungle floor. Toucans,
macaws, and turquoise-crested motmots are a
brilliant burst of color against the sacred ceiba
trees hung with Spanish moss. Even at midday
it's a green twilight zone—every growing thing,
even the petals of flowers seem to exude a warm,
moist stickiness that's dense and thick to breathe
like some kind of clear fog. Not too far away
monkeys screech, deer and jaguar slip in and out
of forest shadows. The jungle smells spicy, musky,
ripe and sweet—the odors of rampant
growth rooted in old decay.*

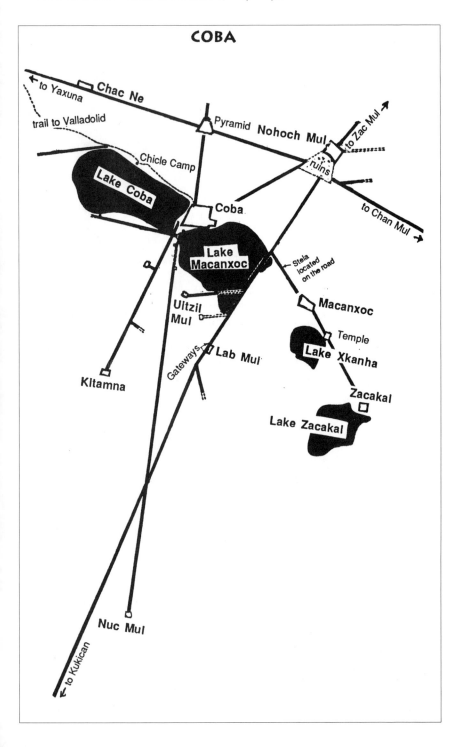

COBA

to Yaxuna
Chac Ne
trail to Valladolid
Pyramid   Nohoch Mul
to Zac Mul
Chicle Camp
ruins
Lake Coba
Coba
to Chan Mul
Lake Macanxoc
Stela located on the road
Ultzil Mul
Macanxoc
Temple
Lab Mul
Lake Xkanha
Gateways
Kitamna
Zacakal
Lake Zacakal
Nuc Mul
to Kukican

It was in *Coba* (koh-bah) that I first learned the true meaning of the expression, "One step at a time." ***Nohoch Mul Pyramid*** has 120 steps and is thought to be the tallest in Mexico. It's a steep climb, the steps narrow and uneven; but once at the top, the view is breathtaking. Of course, what goes up must come down. That was even worse—until I caught onto the jaguar crawl. Think about it.

Walking about Coba would be exciting even without the ruins. The canopy of foliage overhead is like a green cloud cover over the jungle floor. Toucans, macaws, and turquoise-crested motmots are a brilliant burst of color against the sacred ceiba trees hung with Spanish moss. Even at midday it's a green twilight zone–every growing thing, even the petals of flowers seem to exude a warm, moist stickiness that's dense and thick to breathe like some kind of clear fog. Not too far away monkeys screech, deer and jaguar slip in and out of forest shadows. The jungle smells spicy, musky, ripe and sweet–the odors of rampant growth rooted in old decay.

But the ruins do exist—80 square miles of them. An archeological discovery still in progress, Coba, located only 26 miles inland from the coastal ruins of Tulum, (or an hour and a half from Cancun) was one of the largest cities on the Yucatan Peninsula with a population of 500,000. What happened to them, one wonders, looking at the remains of this tumble-down, jungle-covered city spread along the shores of five blue lakes.

As I rested at the top of *Nohoch Mul*, I watched a man slowly toiling his way up. Too macho for the jaguar crawl, he was having a hard time of it. (Going down would prove even worse despite his gallant efforts to appear casual.) Once at the top, he turned panting to survey the scene below. "Wow! It's a jungle out there!" he gasped.

We laughed at the cliche come so literally to life. Below us was a shag rug of rich emerald dotted by five blobs of turquoise — the lakes which once endowed the city with its water supply. Here and there large rocky mounds overgrown with foliage offer the exciting potential of fresh discovery. There are few tourists and one can sit quietly contemplating these treasures in solitude.

Before us stretched Coba, "Water Stirred by the Wind," a ceremonial city and a trade and cultural center built around a group of four shallow lakes. Temples, altars, crumbling walls and yet another pyramid are revealed in the vegetation below—fragments of a civilization that endured six times as long as the Roman Empire.

Coba was a "lost" city until the late 1920s when J. Eric Thompson did some preliminary exploration, but excavations didn't begin until 1973. Very little has been reconstructed or even uncovered of the estimated 6500 structures on the site.

The city is designated as Classic, dating from around 600 to 900 A.D., but there are Preclassic indications on some of the buildings and definite Postclassic additions to the original Classic motifs. The Spaniards never found Coba but for some reason the inhabitants abandoned it. Today the few remaining Maya descendants live resignedly in grass shacks on the outskirts of this vast ghost city. Where did their ancestors go? Why did they go? How did they support themselves in a land where almost nothing grows today? What happened to their vast culture?

So many missing pieces to the Maya puzzle.

One of the features that distinguishes Coba is the prominence of a female figure which frequently appears on the facades of its buildings. Many archaeologists believe that she was a ruler involved in a ritualistic marriage with a high priest from Tikal. This would explain why the ruins are so similar to those found in the Peten region of Guatemala and so unlike anything in Yucatan. Coba will probably prove to be the largest archaeological site in Mexico. *Nohoch Mul Pyramid* alone is built on the grand scale of the Peten pyramids, rising a full twelve stories above the jungle.

One of Coba's beautiful lakes.

Coba is the hub of a complex network of causeways called sacbes that fanned out in at least fifty directions to other Maya cities on the Peninsula.

The longest of these stretches for 62.3 miles through dense jungle with no curves all the way to Chichen Itza. One of them even crosses the arm of one of the lakes. The roads, which were constructed with tollgates, were used as trade and messenger arterials as well ceremonial routes. There were no dray animals or wheels used, so the Maya carried everything on their backs — including their chieftains who were born on litters.

Legend has it that King Ucan unrolled the roads or causeways like a ribbon from a stone on his shoulders. All went smoothly until a beautiful woman appeared to tempt him. When she beckoned seductively, the chaste, workaholic monarch averted his gaze. Though he tried to avoid her, she blocked his way. But xipalaly, or, as they say in English, "boys will be boys." Eventually he dropped his stone and reached for her. Suddenly his magic powers vanished. King Ucan's inability to lift the stone abruptly ended the construction project.

Today the efforts of King Ucan – or somebody – are almost entirely obscured by jungle. These level roads made of local limestone over a rock base are engineering masterpieces, yet a single seed falling into a declivity in the limestone can take root in the jungle atmosphere. Barely discernible, the sacbes remain a marvel.

In the distance, another much newer road beckons anyone with a rental car and the willingness to venture off the well-beaten tourist path.

Hundreds of cars and buses jockey for position on the main highway that brings tourists from Cancun to the ruined fortress of Tulum on the turquoise Caribbean, but during the hour or so that it takes to travel from Tulum to Coba, traffic is sparse.

Along side that road, one sees an occasional village of mud and straw huts identical to the houses depicted on the walls of the abandoned temples. Today's inhabitants are the descendants of the Indians who built this great city more than 1,000 years ago.

Once at Coba, one hears more French or German accents than American. (" Norteamericanos mostly come to Mexico for beach and booze," the bartender at the nearby Villa Archaeologica confided.) As the smartly garbed French women pass (yes, even here they manage to achieve a kind of bush chic), the scent you catch is more apt to be insect repellent than Yves St. Laurent. The "moschetoes" as Stephens called them are very prevalent.

A few yards from the entrance to the site is the Grupo Coba dominated by the 105-step pyramid called the "Church." To the right are several tall structures surrounding a court. One contains an inner chamber with a corbel arch

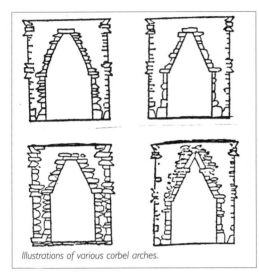
Illustrations of various corbel arches.

roof. The corbel arch with its gracefully upward tapering shape appears again and again in Maya architecture and is considered a unique engineering achievement. Old world structures of the same era were built with a keystone and would have collapsed without it. The Maya had no need for a keystone.

Off to the right of the main road is *Las Pinturas Group*. The main pyramid here is an easier climb. From the temple at the top one can look through the window and see Nohuch Mul framed as though in a picture. The frescoes are still plainly visible, lovely muted shades of red and turquoise.

About a mile further is *Conjunto Macanxoc* where some of the finest stelae — yet discovered — are found. Here as in other stelae (stone slabs generally set in front of prominent structures containing information about the building and/or important people of the era) throughout the site, the theme appears to be that of dominance. One figure, presumably a subject or captive, kneels before an overlord. These stelae are truly magnificent, one rising as high as ten feet. Local tradition has it that a group of people referred to as the pus'ob , or dwarfs, were responsible for the stelae that dot the inner core of the city. The pus'ob are said to have drowned in a self-inflicted deluge that brought an end to the fourth creation of the Maya world.

The most distant and dramatic of the excavated pyramids is the previously mentioned Nohuch Mul. Once you've caught your breath at the top, you'll note three niches over the door of the temple containing descending gods similar to those at Tulum. Bee gods or space cadets? A question to ponder as you look out over the vast expanse of jungle below. The view is particularly spectacular at sunrise or sunset when the shadows accent the myriad mounds of yet unexplored pyramids below.

All along the main trail beguiling paths lure one to new adventures. It's easy to imagine the appeal of archaeology. It's also easy to get lost or at least distracted. There's so much to cover. One could spend a long time at Coba and not see it all.

WHERE TO STAY & WHERE TO EAT

"Accommodations in Coba go from paradise to the pits," a travel agent once told me.

What I subsequently learned from this is that paradise is a very relative thing. The *Villa Arqueologica Coba* isn't my idea of it. Still it's pleasant to find a clean, imaginatively furnished hotel overlooking a placid lake in the midst of a jungle. Rooms are a series of white plastered niches and arches neatly furnished, bathrooms are clean. Common rooms are enhanced by excellent reproductions of Maya sculpture and blow ups of old Pancho Villa photographs. Phone: 1-800-258-2633. Locally: 985-858-1527.

Considering that the place is run by the Club Med, I expected more than I got. The drinks were weak and vastly overpriced. The menu listings make the mouth water but failed to live up to their promise. Guests grumbled. There was talk of taking up a collection to send the chef to Paris for additional training. The next evening I discovered that it would only be necessary to send him half a block away.

El Bocadito, also adjacent to the lake, has delicious food practically for pennies. Five of us ordered five different specialties and shared. It was all extremely good. El Bocadito also has a few rooms for rent. I wouldn't describe them as the pits, but they are spartan–they're also much in demand. If this is your style, get there early as there is no phone.

Coba is a quick, easy drive by car. Proceed south past the Tulum Ruins Junction for 2 kilometers, then turn west on the clearly marked Coba Highway. Coba is 45 kilometers or 26 miles from the main highway. Coba is also reachable by bus from Cancun or Merida, but schedules vary and should be checked and then rechecked.

Villa Archaeologica reservation number: 1-800-528-3100.

Lobby of Hotel El Meson del Marquez.

VALLADOLID
(vie-a-do-lid)

Nowhere in the Americas is there more of a sense of duality than in Mexico. The extremes of night and day, birth and death, plenty and poverty, light and shadow are interwoven into every aspect of the culture.

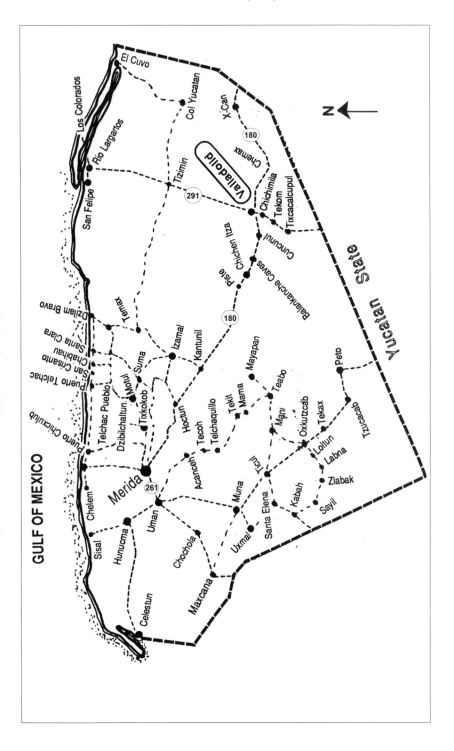

Nowhere in the Americas is there more of a sense of duality than in Mexico. The extremes of night and day, birth and death, plenty and poverty, light and shadow are interwoven into every aspect of the culture.

In ancient times both priest and peasant were painfully aware of the moon goddess's effect upon the tides. *Ixchel* could bring not only fertility and abundance but destruction. From the deep wells of the subconscious came gifts of prophecy and creativity but also dark visions of disaster. With her headdress of twined serpents and jaguar claw fingernails, Ixchel could be the stuff of nightmares.

Twin images of birth and death are equally prevalent today. The tree of life is a perennially popular motif, but so is the skull. Children play with dolls in the likeness of skeletons; confectioners make little skulls of sugar.

Valladolid is a striking manifestation of such duality, its turbulent history rooted in birth, death and inevitable transformation. Today Valladolid is a terrific town with a terrible past. Originally a ceremonial center named for Zaci, its sacred cenote, the name was pre-emptively changed by the conquistadors to honor Valladolid, the Spanish city where Ferdinand and Isabella were married.

Here the Maya fought valiantly to protect their ritual citadel and reprisals against them were particularly brutal. Leading families were forced into their homes and burned alive. Women were hanged with their children suspended from their feet. In one object lesson a virgin and a young bride were slaughtered by a Spanish commander. They were selected simply because they were beautiful. The act was a mixed message. The officer sought to remove temptation from his troops while demonstrating to the Maya that his men weren't interested in their women.

The Maya possess long memories. In 1848 they managed to raise an army of their own and launched the "War of the Castes." The hierarchy of Valladolid was comprised of direct descendants of the Spanish conquerors intensely proud of their heritage. That elitist attitude cost them dearly. Vengeance was savage. Daughters of the grandees were raped, then murdered, their bodies spread-eagled across the grilled windows of their plundered homes.

With vibes like those, small wonder the town is thought to be haunted. Some say the ghost is the very devil himself. I think El Demonico or "talking devil" sounds more like a mischievous poltergeist. Reports have it that he's been known to throw eggs at passersby, talk like a parrot and bombard the rooftops with stones. Some have heard the sounds of mysterious laughter, the strumming of a phantom guitar and the clicking of heels and castanets.

Personally, I like that kind of devil; but apparently the local priests do not. Yes, there have been exorcisms, many of them; but they don't seem to be working.

WHERE TO STAY & WHERE TO EAT_____

The *Hotel El Meson del Marquez* is a delight in every respect. The two gift shops here are at least the equivalent of the best in Merida, not to mention Cancun.

The hotel itself, a survivor of the War of the Castes, is nearly 200 years old. Once the home of a Spanish marquis who got out just in time, the place was purchased in 1854 by an ancestor of the present owner, Mario Ruiz. Ruiz is a kind, thoughtful man with a sense of humor and an excellent command of English, the sort of publican one always hopes to find but rarely does. His hotel is a gem of colonial architecture as well as an oasis with its clear, clean swimming pool. One can eat in the pretty courtyard with its lush greenery, bright bougainvillaea and splashing fountain or in the well appointed dining room. The food is excellent. Phone: 985/6-20-75, Fax: 985/6-22-80

Hotel de la Luz (phone/fax 985-20-710) though not quite as pretty is a bit cheaper. Regardless of your hotel choice, I think you'll want to have dinner at the *Meson de Marquez*. Consider one of the sausage dishes—Valladolid is big on them.

> Valladolid on Highway 180 is conveniently located 60 miles west of Coba and 25 miles east of Chichen Itza. Many economy-minded travelers planning to spend time at the extensive ruins of Chichen Itza stay in Valladolid.

WHAT TO DO _____

—SHOPPING—

If you were born to shop, as I suspect I was, this is the place. It's a paradise for collectors and bargain hunters alike.

If the ghost of John Stephens were ever to return to Valladolid, he wouldn't recognize the place. It was here that the intrepid traveler wasted precious days seeking a shoemaker. Though he'd literally walked through his soles, he was forced to move on without repairs. "There are no shoes ready made and no artist would promise to make a pair in less than a week, which I learned might be interpreted as meaning at least two," he lamented.

Today the indefatigable Stephens would find the town transformed into Sandal City. All sizes, shapes, varieties are available. The tops are covered with beautifully tooled leather, the soles are made from old tires—perfect for cleaving to the rocks, roots and reefs of the Yucatan Peninsula. These are a modern day explorers dream. Don't leave town without them.

Almost all the items on sale in Valladolid are indigenous to the area. Unlike much of the merchandise in major tourist areas, items are as reasonably priced as they are original and appealing. All the stores in and around the pretty plaza are worth exploring, but the *Bazaar Municipal*, a little arcade on the corner, is a good place to begin, particularly if time is limited. I've bought wonderful, whimsical wood carvings from time to time, look for them. Another possibility is Xtabentun, a local liqueur.

—CENOTES—

There's more to Valladolid than shopping. Only three blocks from the main square is the *Cenote Zaci* (Calle 36 between 37 and 39). A winding path meanders its way down under an immense shelf of rock overhanging the pool. Tiny, lacy-winged bats circle endlessly above the moss green water. The effect is slightly hypnotic and strangely beautiful. Adjacent to the cenote is a charming restaurant with subdued music and good food. Close by is a pretty palapa with more shopping possibilities.

Not far from the town on the road to Chichen Itza is the most beautiful cenote in Yucatan. *Dzomit* is not to be missed. Turn off at the sign. A tunnel descends to a cavern lit by a hole in the ceiling reminiscent of a Southwest Indian kiva. The water is a vibrant turquoise. Once you've slipped into those cool, incredibly clear

Cenote Zaci.

waters you can't help but feel a sense of wonder and magic. Cenotes were always thought to be places of visions and prophecy. A dip in this one is like bathing in your own private wishing well.

Ek Balam as seen from the Pyramid. Photo by Charles Herndon.

Ek Balam's exquisite sculpture was preserved inside later pyramids. Photo by Charles Herndon.

EK BALAM
(ec-ba-lam)

Ek Balam is a dream come true. Archaeologists are amazed ...Visitors are delighted ... easy to get to and once at the site guests have this rich archeological treasure to themselves.

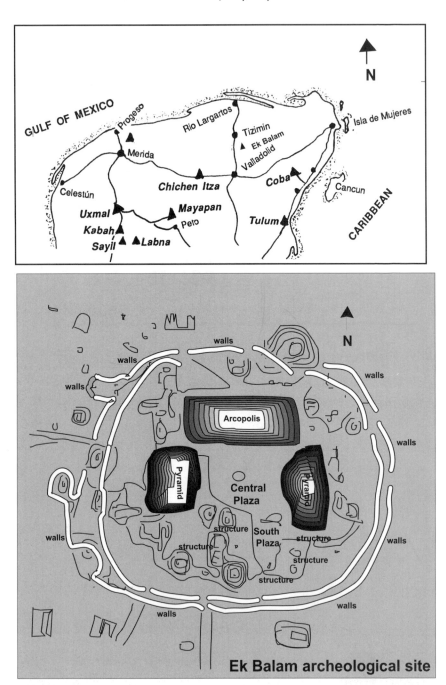

Ek Balam archeological site

Remember *Indiana Jones and the Temple of Doom*? The lush jungle, the lost city, the thrill of high adventure? It was sheer fantasy coming true, unfolding before your very eyes. It was also pretty scary. Maybe you were just as glad that it was all happening on a screen, that nothing could really touch you.

Now—revealed almost overnight—is Ek Balam, a brand "new" ruin thought to stretch back two thousand years. Along with this mysterious Maya ceremonial site comes an opportunity to play like Indie but with no threat of doom.

With its majestic buildings pushing up from great mounds of rubble,

Above, a meandering trail leads to the "lost" treasures of Ek Balam. Below, one of Ek Balam's structures with its corbel arch. Photos by Charles Herndon.

*Construction lines illustrate ongoing excavations &
restorations at Ek Balam.
At right, a stela records the greatness of Ek Balam.
Photos by of Charles Herndon.*

Ek Balam has a sense mystery about
it. The site is a kind of fantasy
dream come true. Archaeologists
are amazed because this is a very
large ruin — no one knows yet just
how large — that appeared
seemingly out of nowhere. Visitors
are delighted because the "lost" city
is so easy to get to and, once at the
site, guests have this rich archeological treasure to themselves — that's
the Indiana Jones part. There are no
roped off areas, no guards blowing
whistles at you, warning you not to
climb, not to enjoy hands on contact
with these wonderful old stones.

Above, a dragon's mouth guards the entrance to a tomb.
Below, much of Ek Balam's elegant sculpture has a comtemplative look.
The thatched roof protects the archeological work under way.
Photos by of Charles Herndon.

Well off the tourist track, Ek Balam (the name means Black Jaguar) is undergoing active excavation and restoration which gives the visitor a wonderful overview of what archeology is all about. Though quite near the colonial city of Valladolid and less than three hours from Playa del Carmen, the marvelous Maya city is relatively unknown and rarely visited. You may very well end up wandering the ruins entirely alone.

The most exciting feature about Ek Balam is its artwork. One can see well preserved wall paintings here unlike any others found thus far. Even more spectacular are large plaster sculptures

Above, The calm stillness of Ek Balam's ball park belles its savage past. Below, Ek Balam's majestic pyramid is one of the largest in the Yucatan. Thatched roofs indicate area where excavations are still taking place. Photos by of Charles Herndon.

that were built inside a pyramid. When the city was abandoned and the jungle encroached, the inner pyramid was protected by rubble for hundreds of years. The incredibly graceful sculptures inside have an elegant, contemplative quality that reminds one of Far Eastern art work.

With its colossal buildings and sculptures unique among Maya sites, Ek Balam feels untouched by time. Archaeologists believe that this art work is certain to alter our concepts of the ancient Maya.

The importance of El Balam in the Maya world is indicated by its lifespan. This was a vigorous community for more than one thousand years—whereas most Maya cities were inhabited for scarcely 500.

Construction began in the Pre-Classic period (about 100 BC) and reached its height between 700 and 900 AD—well into the late Classic time. It is thought that a few people may have still been living there during the Spanish conquest in the 16th century.

Archaeologists believe that Ek Balam was the nerve center for the area's agricultural output and management. Products then, as now, were corn, wax, honey and cotton. Thought to have achieved pivotal status in the public affairs of eastern Yucatan, the settlement's decline may have been due to gradual depopulation caused by political infighting.

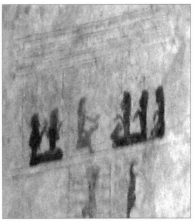

Ek Balam has one of the few surviving frescoes. Photo by Charles Herndon.

When the Maya abandoned Ek Balam, the city went under cover—literally—as the dense jungle engulfed it. Not until 1997 was the site "discovered" and the task of uncovering its abandoned treasures undertaken.

The Acropolis is the largest restored building, measuring 480 feet across, 180 feet wide and 96 feet tall. This palace has six levels where the higher echelons of the city's population lived. You can climb this and see from the top a network of sacbes or roads stretching in all directions, a further indication of El Balam's importance. These well built highways—wide and paved—linked El Balam to Chichen Itza, Coba and Tulum.

Another small structure of Ek Balam illustrates the Maya mastery of the corbel arch. Photo by Charles Herndon.

The sacbes intersected at the entrance to Ek Balam where visitors entered the city through a majestic arch—now beautifully restored. Now, as then, the incoming visitor has an impressive view of the main pyramid—one of the largest in Yucatan—central plaza and ball court.

In Ek Balam, as at other Maya centers, the ball court was seen as the threshold between this world and Xibalba, the underworld dwelling of the gods. The ritualized ballgames played there reenacted the original contest between the gods of death and the Hero Twins Hunahpu (associated with the sun and life) and Xbalanque associated with the moon and death).

Across the plaza is the majestic El Torre, "the tower." The building's magnitude and design is a result of numerous generations of additions— layer upon layer of them. Maya, like many other Mesoamerican cultures, had a tradition of adding a new "shell" of construction, layering temple upon temple. The additions were made at 52 year intervals in keeping with the Maya calendar. Archaeologists have sliced the structure open laying bare the underlying levels of construction in order to examine the building process.

Beneath the outermost layer of the wall, the archaeological team discovered the tomb of the ruler El Balam. Its awesome stucco doorway is made in the shape of a jaguar's mouth with fearsome fangs. Intricately carved from eyebrows to molars, this Chenes style serpent-mouth doorway is the jewel of Ek Balam. To the Maya, it represented a portal to the underworld.

Evidence indicates that blood letting rituals were practiced at Ek Balam. These were self-inflicted by priests and nobles. Some archaeologists believe that one of the human figures depicted above the mouth is a defeated enemy about to be sacrificed, so the tomb may also have been the sight of human sacrifices.

The sculpted works at Ek Balam are both unusual and well preserved. Some figures are winged in a manner reminiscent of angels, others are shown in a meditative "lotus" position, one of the latter sits headless above the monster's mouth. All are beautiful and exquisitely crafted.

A walk around the back of the tower gives an inkling, not only of the vastness of Maya architecture, but the work involved in excavating it. Check out the water reservoirs behind the building. Most cities in the Maya world were built adjacent to cenotes, or wells—their fresh water source in a country with no over ground lakes or rivers. Ek Balam, located a kilometer from the closest cenote, had to figure out a way to store rainwater underground.

Ek Balam is open seven days a week between 8 a.m. and 5 p.m. The entrance fee is about $2—free on Sundays. Though there are no authorized guides, plaques in English, Spanish and Maya give basic information on the major structures. Restrooms are located at the entrance.

Ek Balam is located twenty minutes north of Valladolid and is best reached from that town's main square (El Zocalo). Follow the signs to Tizimin, highway 295. The exit to Ek Balam is well marked.

THE HERO TWINS

Truth be told Hunahpu and Xbalanque were kind of bratty, but since they were such great ball players they got away with a lot. The picture changed drastically when the sound of their bouncing ball vibrated all the way down to Xibalba, the underworld.

Since the underworld gods had already knocked off the twins' father, they weren't adverse to carrying on a tradition and ordered the twins to play in an underworld ball court.

When the twins lost the first match they were required to pay a floral tribute--pretty hard to do since they were imprisoned for the night in the House of Darkness. Fortunately, a colony of sympathetic ants came to the boys' assistance. The following morning, the twins were able to present the gods of Xibalba not only with flowers—but flowers from their very own garden.

After another game, the twins were forced to sleep in the House of Bats. A bat decapitated the unfortunate Hunahpu and the gods decided to use his head for a ball in the next game. Xbalanque made a temporary head for his brother from a pumpkin and enlisted the aid of a rabbit to get Hunahpu's head back. During the game,

Intricate original carvings along the dragon's mouth entrance walls. Photo by Charles Herndon.

the rabbit impersonated the ball and bounced away. This confused the gods and gave Xbalanque the chance to return Hunahpu's head to his body.

Though the twins had defeated the underworld gods, they allowed themselves to be sacrificed. Needless to say, that was not the end. Through supernatural powers, Hunahpu and Xbalancque were reborn and become part of the Maya "overworld." Maya recognize them as the sun and the moon.

Sketch of a relic found at the Balankanche Caves

THE BALANKANCHE CAVES
(bal-ann-kan-chay)

Today, as in ancient times, the Mayans regard their caves as entrances into the underworld and avenues of communication with the gods. It's deep within the earth's inner recesses that the most sacred rituals have traditionally been performed.

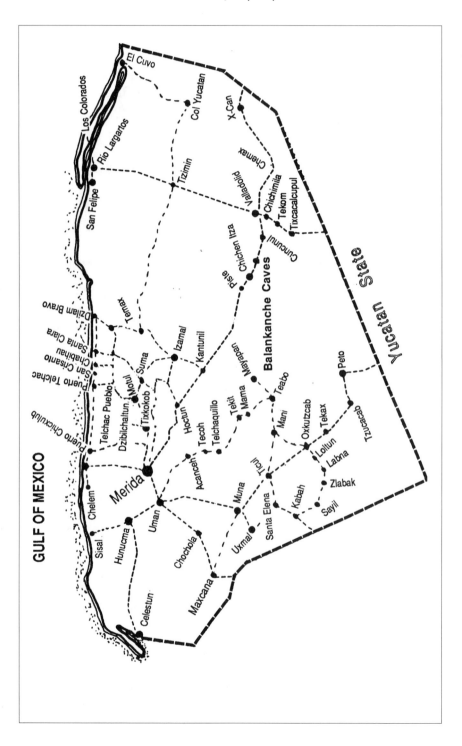

A visit to the ***Balankanche Caves*** is a descent into hell, but it's also an opportunity to slip into sacred space.

Today, as in ancient times, the Maya regard their caves as entrances into the underworld and avenues of communication with the gods. It's deep within the earth's inner recesses that the most sacred rituals have traditionally been performed. Not surprisingly, their whereabouts remain a closely guarded secret whenever possible.

Balankanche (located 3 miles east of Chichen Itza on Highway 180) was no exception. Locals were extremely reluctant to open their secret ceremonial site to the public. It's easy to understand why. This place is very special.

The large network of caverns was well known to natives of the area, but no one knew — or told — just how extensive they actually were or what they contained. Then, in 1959, Jose Humberto Gomez, a tour guide from Merida on a busman's holiday, literally stumbled into a hidden passageway which lead to an underground chamber containing an ancient shrine.

The natives were anything but happy about the discovery and warned that a curse would fall upon those who entered what they knew to be the secret retreat of the rain god, Chac. But the eager archaeologists who quickly converged on the area were not about to be dissuaded. Finally the apprehensive priests decided to conduct a ceremony of appeasement.

Thirteen priests and a small group of children gathered for an all-night rite barred to outsiders. Then in an ancient, but obviously well remembered ritual, animals were sacrificed as Chac's forgiveness was sought for allowing his sanctuary to be profaned by archaeologists and the inevitable visitors who would follow. Apparently the rain god heard their entreaties and was moved as an unseasonable downpour followed drenching the parched countryside.

Today the Balankanche Caves are open for viewing. A guide unlocks the iron gate that prevents curiosity seekers from roaming at will. Only a few people seek out the caves and that's probably just as well. It takes time to navigate the narrow, steep passageways.

Inside the air is damp and earthy, the dimness a startling contrast to the dazzling sunshine outside. Visitors must descend single file as the outside light recedes until it's gone completely. From that point the cramped passageway is lit only by faint–very faint–bulbs suspended from the ceiling.

Finally the tunnel snakes its way past a cenote so clear that it resembles a canyon. In the center, surrounded by water, an image of Chac watches from atop a rough altar. The ceiling is low in places, the ground damp and often uneven. The caverns seem to close in, the effect is eerie, uncomfortable, too far removed from the sunburst outside. And then, at last, the winding maze emerges from the gloom into the ceremonial chamber.

It's immediately obvious why Balankanche means "Throne of the Jaguar" (priest) or the "Hidden Treasure of the Jaguar." Both names are apt. There's a vast array of treasure and a kind of throne in the shape of a magnificent tree formed by a stalactite joined to a stalagmite with thousands of tiny stalactites projecting from the ceiling like leaves. This, the ancients believed, represented the sacred ceiba tree, the Tree of Life, directly connected with their fertility rituals.

Flanking the entrance way are two censors for burning copal. Around the altar-tree are hundreds of ceremonial vessels, spindle whorls and grinding stones positioned exactly as the priests left them; and, unlike artifacts of like vintage exposed for centuries to the sun, these retain their original color.

The effect is overwhelming, the reaction one of awe coupled with a nagging suspicion that somewhere not too far away the old gods still live.

Balankanche is open daily from 9 a.m. to 5 p.m.

Temple of Kukulkan—Chichen Itza.

CHICHEN ITZA
(chee-chen-eet-sa)

Chichen Itza was not only a ceremonial center but a commercial one. It's easy to forget that this monument of cold stone and lost memories was once thronged with vendors hawking condiments, vegetables, jewels and slaves. It's hard to imagine cages of barkless, hairless edible dogs, brightly plumaged birds talking Maya and chattering monkeys, yet we know they existed. There would also have been areas set aside for feather merchants, goldsmiths, curanderos or healers, scribes and story tellers.

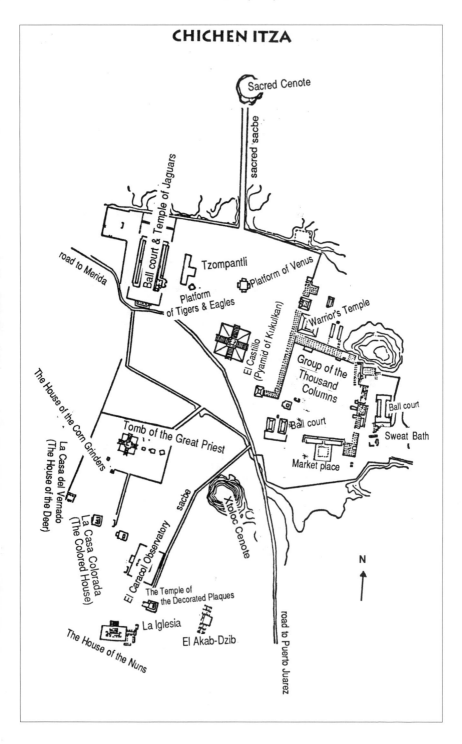

CHICHEN ITZA

Sacred Cenote

sacred sacbe

Ball court & Temple of Jaguars

road to Merida

Tzompantli

Platform of Venus

Platform of Tigers & Eagles

Warrior's Temple

El Castillo (Pyamid of Kukulkan)

Group of the Thousand Columns

Ball court

Tomb of the Great Priest

Ball court

Sweat Bath

The House of the Corn Grinders

Market place

La Casa del Vernado (The House of the Deer)

sacbe

Xtoloc Cenote

La Casa Colorada (The Colored House)

El Caracol Observatory

The Temple of the Decorated Plaques

N

La Iglesia

El Akab-Dzib

The House of the Nuns

road to Puerto Juarez

What was I doing alone in a jungle in the middle of the night? It was a good question, frequently repeated.

First there'd been a ritual ceremony reminiscent of long ago days as a Camp Fire Girl, not a peak experience by any means. Afterwards the others in our group had scattered, most returning to the hotel. Departing with them were the two Maya guides who'd led us to this isolated spot in Old Chichen. They weren't about to spend a night out in the brush far from their homes and hammocks. Neither was our intrepid leader who'd planned this "alone time" in the wilderness.

"My body tells me I should go back," she announced shortly after the chanting and incense burning had ended. (My body would have, too, if accompanied by her new boyfriend.)

The ground was hard, lumpy. After a hot steamy day, the night was surprisingly cold. The two blankets I'd smuggled out of the Mayaland Hotel were totally inadequate and so was my light sweater. I thought wistfully of the Maya guides and particularly of their machetes as I listened to the strange rustling noises all around me. Then I thought of bats, vampire bats. I thought of tarantulas and other more poisonous spiders, some I'd been told were the size of golf balls. I thought of scorpions, of slithering snakes, of prowling jaguars. I didn't have to think of insects. I felt them.

I recalled a story heard only the day before. A photographer had wandered off the trail. When at last a search party found him, all that was left was a skeleton, a camera and the money in his pockets. But that was in Guatemala, not Chichen Itza, I reminded myself, more than once.

Tourists rarely go to Old Chichen. It's well off the beaten track. This was new country to me, the hotel a good two miles away. Trying to mentally retrace my steps, I recalled the overgrown path that led through dense brush. Could I find my way back? My flashlight flickered ominously, dimmed, then gave out completely. I scrapped that idea.

The overnight had been suggested as a vision quest. The Indians, who are big on such things, feel that animal contact is an important part of the ritual. It's supposed to be a very meaningful experience. I hoped fervently that my quest wouldn't include a meaningful experience with a wild boar.

It was going to be a very long night. I tried to relax, seeking a soothing pattern in the rustling leaves. It was cold and I was tired, very, very tired. And then suddenly a form appeared. It was a woman. I could see her clearly in the moonlight She was dressed in a white blouse with a little tie and brown pants tucked into high boots. The hair peeking below a pith helmet was bobbed.

"I'm glad you finally made it," she said to me. "I remember you as a little girl who liked to read about the Maya and longed to be an archaeologist. It's good that you came, you've a job to do here."

I looked at her in amazement, a vague memory faintly stirring. A children's book long, long ago. The writer a young woman archaeologist. I'd idolized her.

"The jungle is a little scary at first," she admitted. "I was afraid in the beginning too. But nothing will harm you, I promise. Why don't you just go to sleep."

And, surprisingly, I did. A month later, home in California, I was able to locate with much effort the book I'd read as a child, *Digging In Yucatan*. There was a picture inside of the pretty author, Ann Axtell Morris. She was dressed as I'd seen her that night in the jungle. What a trickster the subconscious can be. Was it a vision or "merely" a dream? And does it really matter?

The night in the jungle was an empowering experience, one that brought many aspects of my life into sharper focus. Would I do it again? Probably not. It was a crazy thing to do. Would I trade a million dollars for the memory? Absolutely not!

As for the work that Ann spoke of—my task?
Perhaps this book is it.

Some people resent what they view as the "commercialism" of Chichen Itza. Personally, I rather like all this hustle. It seems very appropriate since Ek Chuah, the Maya god of trade, was one of the deities highly venerated here.

Chichen Itza was not only a ceremonial center but a commercial one. It's easy to forget that this monument of cold stone and lost memories was once thronged with vendors hawking condiments, vegetables, jewels and slaves. It's hard to imagine cages of barkless, hairless edible dogs, brightly plumaged birds talking Maya and chattering monkeys, yet we know they existed. There would also have been areas set aside for feather merchants, goldsmiths, *curanderos* or healers, scribes and story tellers.

Jaguar crawl_Temple of Kukulkan.

Too bad that none of the latter are around to tell us what really happened here. We know very little, for this—the most famous of all the Maya cities—was found in an abandoned state. Chichen Itza, which means mouth of the well of the Itza or possibly wizard—since the Itzas were credited with being wizards–flourished during the classic period from 300 to 900 AD. It's believed to have been abandoned, then reinhabited around 1000 AD under Toltec domination.

The synthesis of Toltec and Maya is clearly evident. Quetzalcoatl, the feathered serpent deity, was revered by both the Toltecs and the Aztecs (who probably pushed the Toltecs out of central Mexico into Yucatan.) Representations of this deity–now known as Kukulcan—are seen throughout the site. We also see the Mexican eagle joining the Maya jaguar on wall carvings. Obviously the old Maya order had been overthrown, but Maya priests and noblemen were incorporated into the new establishment. Then, unaccountably, Chichen Itza was abandoned once again in 1250 A.D. —300 years before the arrival of the Spaniards — though it continued to be the site of religious pilgrimages until after the conquest.

Excavations have been going on for more than 100 years, yet archaeologists can still only speculate about what happened here. Only the stones know the true secrets of the Maya, the Itzas or the Toltecs whose cultures are layered in the ruins that visitors see today. The cleared and restored portion of the city is about two miles square, yet it may represent only five percent of the total. South of the road that bisects the site is "old" Chichen Itza where surviving buildings date from 600 to 900 A.D. "New" Chichen Itza, north of the road, was built from 1000 to 1250 A.D.

Today the majestic stone pyramids, temples and palaces towering above the jungle-covered plane hold the same fascination for tourists as they did for the conquistadores more than 400 years ago.

One of the first tourists, John L. Stephens, literally put Chichen Itza on the map with his lucid travel writing.   His account, written in 1842, still captures the magic of the *Well of Sacrifice* for which the city was named:

> "...setting out from the Castillo, at some distance we ascended a wooded elevation, which seemed an artificial causeway leading to the cenote. The cenote was the largest and wildest we had seen; in the midst of a thick forest, an immense circular hole, with cragged perpendicular sides, trees growing out of them and overhanging the brink, and still as if the genius of consummate silence reigned within. A hawk was sailing around it, looking down into the water, but without flapping its wings. The water was of a greenish hue. A mysterious influence seemed to pervade it, in unison with the historical account that the well of Chichen was a place of pilgrimage, and that human victims were thrown into it in sacrifice. In one place on the very brink, were the remains of a stone structure, probably connected with ancient superstitious rites; perhaps the place from which victims were thrown into the dark well beneath."

It was this well, also known as the *Sacred Cenote*, which gave the site its ceremonial significance. The life-sustaining power of water was all important to the Maya, the cenote — a natural well — a gift from the gods. But sometimes it was necessary to propitiate those gods. Human beings—most frequently women — were frequently hurled into the well.

On rare occasions, the victims flung into the jade green depths of the pool survived; and, when they returned to the surface, they were thought to bring with them messages from the gods.

Hunac Ceel, a consummate risk taker and opportunist, used this precarious vehicle to rise from commoner to king. Here was a volunteer victim who not only survived but brought back a prophecy about a new monarch–himself. What could the priests do with a man so divinely inspired but fulfill his destiny?

Edward H. Thompson, some 800 years later, seems to have been cut from the same cloth. He, too, was fated to make waves in the sacred well. Thompson, while still a student at Worcester Polytechnic Institute, wrote an article entitled, "Atlantis Not a Myth," which appeared in *Popular Science Monthly*. His premise, that the mysterious Maya civilization on the Yucatan Peninsula might be a branch of the lost continent of Atlantis, won him friends in high places.

Stephen Salisbury, one of the founders of the American Antiquarian Society, and Charles P. Bowditch, the guiding light of the Peabody Museum of Anthropology, functioned much like high priests. They agreed that Thompson was the very man to investigate Yucatan, an area

Sacred Cenote—Chichen Itza. Photo by Charles Herndon.

that had long fascinated both. With one fell swoop, they insured him both a free hand and a salary by using their political influence to get him appointed U.S. Consul to Yucatan and Campeche. In 1885, Thompson–the youngest consul in U.S. history–set off with his wife and baby daughter to explore Yucatan. It was an adventure that would occupy the next forty years of his life.

Five years later Thompson was able to send a vast array of temple molds for display at the 1890 Chicago World's Fair. Allison V. Armour, the meat magnate, was so impressed that he made Thompson a cash gift that enabled him to purchase the ruins of Chichen Itza. For about $75, the young consul acquired nearly 100 square miles of land which included a Spanish plantation house dating from the 1700's and untold acres of ruins. At that time the outpost area was accessible only by a jungle footpath. On the night he took possession of the place, Thompson stumbled over the remains of the last inhabitant of his new hacienda who'd been murdered by insurrectionists.

Undaunted, Thompson settled in and turned his attention to the legendary cenote. This was and is an oval-shaped opening in the rocky earth crust with a diameter of 180 feet and craggy sides which fall abruptly 60 feet to the rim of the water. Far below the dark green surface is a layer of mud.

Like Hunac Ceel, Thompson had a dream that lured him into that mud. In 1579 the mayor of nearby Valladolid had written to Charles V, "The lords and principal personages of the land had the custom, after sixty days of abstinence and fasting, of arriving by daybreak at the mouth of the Cenote and throwing into it Indian women belonging to each of these lords and personages, at the same time telling these women to ask for their masters a year favorable to their particular needs and desires."

A few women were said to have survived the ordeal. At noon, those that still could, cried out and were pulled up by means of ropes. These survivors told strange tales. Many people of their nation dwelled beneath the waters. These men and women greeted them with heavy blows when they tried to raise their heads. When the victims heads were turned downward they saw "many deeps and hollows, and they the people, responded to their queries concerning the good or bad year that was in store for their masters."

Of less melodrama and more interest to Thompson was mention of treasure being thrown into the sacred well along with the maidens.

Thompson made friends with the *H'Menes*, or Maya wisemen, who initiated him into the *Sh'Tol Brothers*, a sacred society that had escaped the Spaniards. The H'Menes confirmed the legend and pointed out to him the area of the cenote beneath which the rain god had his palace.

It remained only for Thompson to take the plunge. Holding a torch with a submarine telephone in one hand, the young archaeologist shook hands with the other. It was obvious that his awestruck assistants were certain that he would never return. Then he was lowered to the cenote surface on a pontoon from which he dove into the depth. Feeling only slightly more secure than the sacrificial victims, Thompson groped his way down sixty feet into the ooze. Though his diving gear may have been considered state of the art for 1904, it was still very primitive. One must marvel at courage only slightly less than Hunac Ceel's. Several of these early dives were very nearly fatal; one resulted in a ruptured eardrum.

Day after day passed, then week after week. Once Thompson floated up to the surface by accident without warning and struck the bottom of the pontoon with a loud thump. His terrified helpers ran off screaming, certain that it was Chac rising in righteous anger at this invasion of his sacred sanctum. Load after load of mud was brought up and examined. Hours of heartbreaking anxiety and backbreaking efforts netted nothing more than rotting leaves, decayed twigs and fallen trees.

Then one day two white balls of something turned up in the muck. Thompson pounced on them, felt them, smelled them, tore one open   and touched a match to its heart. As a long spiral of sweet-scented smoke curled upward, he recalled the words of one of the H' Men:

"In ancient times our fathers burned the sacred resin and by the fragrant smoke their prayers were wafted to their god whose home was in the sun."

Thompson shouted and danced like a child, realizing that the two small balls were copal which the Maya used for incense. For him, it was the scent of victory. He knew now that he was close. A few days later he raised   the skeletons of three women. Soon after gold discs were uncovered, then jade, precious ornaments, jewelry —hundreds of priceless artifacts of all kinds. Most of these relics were discreetly smuggled out of the country to his Boston sponsors.

So there was Hunac Ceel diving into the Well of Sacrifice in search of fame and fortune, followed by Edward Thompson hoping to extract a bit of the same. Unfortunately Thompson wasn't as lucky as his predecessor. Success was followed by disaster. Alma Reed, *New York Times* reporter persuaded him to disclose his forty year secret. Her article revealing that more than $2 million dollars worth of treasure had been smuggled out of the country in a diplomatic pouch and were now being held by the Peabody Museum in Boston didn't sit well with the Mexican authorities. A fifty peso lien was slapped onto Thompson's Chichen Itza property.

In the midst of the ensuring litigation, a local revolution erupted, and his hacienda was burned by rebels, the crops destroyed and cattle driven off. The most tragic loss was Thompson's priceless library. From the depth of his depression, he wrote, "Much of the fruit of my long life of studies went up in a whirlwind of smoke and ashes," he wrote out of the depth of his depression. It was a crushing blow; but Thompson, now well into his sixties, rallied.

In an effort to recoup some of his losses, he rebuilt the hacienda, hoping to turn it into a hotel. The idea was later realized by others, but at the time Thompson's legal and financial difficulties made it impossible. Eventually a deal was struck whereby the Carnegie Institution took over the hacienda and continued his work. Disheartened, the explorer of the the Well of Sacrifice left the only home of his adult life and his beloved ruins, returning to the United States.

More recent dives with modern equipment have netted startling findings. According to legend, the victims were virgins. This fine point can't be determined, but it does seem certain that at least some of the women didn't go willingly. Heads showed evidence of severe blows and one woman suffered a fractured nose. This new evidence also calls to mind the enigmatic story of the pugilistic people who dwell beneath the waters.

The peak of the sacrificial cult was reached after the decline of Toltec Chichen (by 1250 AD) and continued beyond Colonial times–far beyond. A doll was hauled up from the depth wrapped in rayon cloth.

The well has changed little since Thompson's day–or Hunac Ceel's for that matter. Visitors almost tiptoe to the edge, gaze wonderingly into the murky depths with a sort of fearful curiosity, then draw back to talk in instinctively lowered tones. A sense of mystery, even of horror, pervades, surviving the lapse of centuries.

CENOTES

Cenotes (a Spanish corruption of the Maya word for sinkhole, dzonot) are formed when rainwater eats away at the limestone bedrock, creating an underground cave. Eventually the cave roof collapses, exposing subterranean water sources.

Cenotes were thought to be the home of the rain god Chac. To insure that rains would come, Chac had to propitiate with gifts. Great cities like Chichen Itza depended on cenotes as their primary water source, small villages in the hinterland still rely on them. There are 2500 known cenotes in the state of Yucatan.

The most impressive and intriguing structure in Chichen Itza is the *Temple of Kukulkan*, sometimes referred to as El Castillo because the Spanish conquistador, Francisco de Montejo set up his headquarters there. Whatever one calls it, this construction is as fascinating for architects as it is to archaeologists and astronomers. It took Frank Lloyd Wright, whose revolutionary use of geometric form in architectural design was generations ahead of his time, to point out the perspective of each of the staircases. As you face them head-on, they appear as wide at the top as at the bottom. Looking more carefully, it becomes apparent that the steps widen gradually, giving the illusion of symmetry as they get farther away.

That isn't all. Besides being an architectural triumph, the Temple of Kukulcan is a kind of time machine.

First of all there are four stairways (four creatures held up the world) with 91 steps, comprising a total of 364; plus a platform which totals 365–as in days of the year. The 52 panels on each side represent the 52-year cycle of the Maya calendar (the **Calendar Round**) with nine terraces (nine regions of the Maya underworld) on each side of the stairways– a total of 18 terraces to represent the 18-month ceremonial calendar.

THE ROAD TO LIFE
—THE MAYA CALENDAR —

In a world regulated by clock radios, parking meters and time tables, it's difficult to understand the Maya fascination with the slow, dignified ritual progression of long periods of time.

This was a system of cycles moving within cycles in an endlessly rotating wheel. "Progress," as we know it, had no part in it. Not surprisingly, the Maya were fatalists. The movements of the heavenly bodies weren't thought of as revolutions but as events that repeated themselves in a given pattern as time itself was repeating. It's as if all the secrets of the universe were contained in these calculations with the lives of the Maya people rigidly governed by calendars and their portents.

The Maya scientists, often mind boggling in their brilliance, had little interest in pure science for its own sake. Astronomy and mathematics were merely a means of divination and regulation of religious ritual. When the Maya recorded their history they also

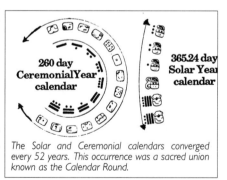

The Solar and Ceremonial calendars converged every 52 years. This occurrence was a sacred union known as the Calendar Round.

foretold the future in terms of the past. In putting together astronomical calculations and ritual cycles, they developed the most sophisticated calendar in history. The ancient Greeks had something like it. They called it the "zodiac," or road of life.

First there was the *Solar Calendar,* which was precisely measured and consisted of 365.24 days. This was a measure of eighteen "months" of twenty days plus an extra five. Those five days weren't really considered days, but rather a necessary gap between one year's last month and the next year's first. At this season the sun was generally pale and cool and hung low in the sky. It was thought that the gods dozed and no sensible person would do anything to risk annoyance by disturbing them.

During these five "lifeless" days it was considered fruitless, even rash or hazardous to do anything. All avoidable activities ceased. Couples refrained from sexual connections less they conceive a child and children born during this period were considered highly unlucky. Crowds were avoided, cooking fires extinguished; people stayed indoors, occupying themselves with trivial pursuits such as mending fish nets or tools. Mostly they sat about contemplating the awful possibility that the world might end at any moment.

The days of the month in this secular calendar are numbered O Pop, 1 Pop, 2 Pop, etc., through 19 Pop, when one then goes on to the next month.

The *Ceremonial Calendar,* completely different from the solar one, operated concurrently. It, too, had twenty days, each with a definite character, some auspicious, others malevolent. All were named for gods, beginning with Imix, the earth god. These days were attached to numbers, 1 through 13. At the end of the 13th day, the numbers started anew. In this way 260 days–13 times 20–passed before the same name was again accompanied by the same number. (Imix and 1, for instance.)

Priest-historians used this calendar for recording such significant events as wars, the length of a ruler's reign and — most importantly — foretelling the future. This was divinatory almanac or *Book of Good and Bad Days*, a Book of Fate rather than a calendar dependent on seasons. The primary function of priests was to be the guardians of this astronomical and calendrical data, using it to pro-pitiate the gods, to tell the people when to cut and burn their fields, to plant and to celebrate.

The sacred and secular calendars mesh, so that a significant day can be read today on a stela– such as 2 Imix, 4 Pop. The two calendars, one with a cycle of 365.24 days and the other with 260, converge every 52 years. This occurrence was a sacred union known as the **Calendar Round.** For most, it was a once in a lifetime experience.

To these calendars was added a third, The **Venus Calendar,** based on the transits* of the planet Venus. Sometimes Venus served as the after blossom that blazed immediately following sunset. At other times it moved on to the other side of the sky where it would be the last star visible as the sun rose and washed away all the others. Lovely as all this star-talk sounds, astroarchaeologists now believe that the Venus transits and calendar data had a direct bearing on war strategy.

And yes, the Venus Calendar was also linked to the other two. The length of the Venus synodical revolution in the heavens varies between 580 and 588 days over a span of five revolutions, giving an average length of 583.92 days. The Maya made it 584 so that five Venus "years" equated with eight solar years of 365 days. The discrepancy between 584 and the actual length of the Venus revolution was made up by corrections amounting to 24 days in the course of 301 revolutions, which reduced to an error of one day in every 6000 years. These machinations were necessary to also reconcile the Venus Calendar with the ceremonial one.

Convoluted as all this sounds, the Maya chronological system based on names and numbers for days and months enabled the priests to designate a particular date which could not be mistaken for any other through thousands of years.

And here's one more bit of intrigue to ponder. This complex system is known to have begun on August 12, 3113 BC. This cycle–in which we are currently living–will end, if the Maya priests are correct, with the destruction of the world on December 24, 2011.

The pyramid was built over an earlier structure undoubtedly at the end of some long ago 52-year cycle. Inside, a narrow, claustrophobic stairway ascends to a sacrificial altar-throne encrusted with jade–thought to be Chinese in origin. How did it get there?

Equally intriguing is the shadow of a giant snake which descends from the Temple of Kukulkan twice a year–always at the spring and fall equinoxes. On the 21st of March and again on the 21st of September, the shadowy reptile slithers its way along the balustrade disappearing in the direction of the sacred cenote just as the sun sets. For 34 minutes, the snake created by a play of light and shadow moves from the top of the pyramid to its base. For the ancients it must have been the ultimate fertility symbol. The golden sun god had penetrated the earth. It was time to plant.

Dr. Clemency Coggins of the Peabody Museum at Harvard University believes that the pyramid and the snake were the core of a new ceremonial center established in Chichen Itza to mark the year 830 AD which united the Maya with the Toltec arrivals from central Mexico. This was the year, she believes, that a major Maya time period ended, and the year when the Toltecs had to rekindle their fires.

The new fire ritual took place every 52 years. To commemorate the occasion a captive was sacrificed, and a new fire kindled in the victim's recently vacated heart cavity. Such measures were necessary in order to prevent the sun from abandoning the earth completely. Both priest and peasant knew that the sun required nourishment to remain strong and diligent in its daily labors. What could be more re-vitalizing than the very life energy the sun itself gave? It all makes perfect sense, except whatever happened to Kukulcan's original message of peace?

The ruling priests would undoubtedly have marked the approach of this sacred date decades in advance and planned the new ceremonial center to commemorate it. Coggins speculates that the pyramid would have been completed the previous year, so that the serpent's shadow would move down the stairway for the first time on March 21, 830.

Clap your hands in front of the pyramid and an odd echo replies. It's a quick, descending tone that some guides say echoes the screams of sacrificial virgins being tossed into the sacred well. Some scientists have another theory. They say it's a re-creation of the cry of the quetzal bird.

The fast-disappearing quetzal lives in in the shrinking rainforest of Central America and Mexico hundreds of miles from the Temple of Kukulkan. Yet its long blue-green tail feathers adorned the helmets and robes of Maya kings across a region stretching from present day El Salvador through the state of Tabasco in Mexico.

David Lubman, an acoustics consultant based in Westminster, Calif., theorizes that the ancient Maya knowingly planned the building to echo with

The Observatory—Chichen Itza.

a quetzalchirp as a way of paying homage to the revered bird. Lumban suggests this may be the world's oldest known sound recording. He and other acoustics specialists agree that a cascade of reflections from the temple's 92 stone steps generates the echo's sliding pitch. He believes this was intentional.

Lubman got the idea after reading that the quetzal was considered the messenger of the gods. At the October 1998 meeting of the Acoustical Society of America in Norfolk, VA., he played recordings of the bird's call and the echo while displaying their sonograms which are curiously alike. The pitches of both sounds fall at the same rate from a frequency of about 1,500 hertz to less than 1,000 hertz. In effect, he believes that the stairs' echo is a 1,000 year old recording of a quetzal call—a reminder to the people of the sacred bird's spiritual nearness.

The genius that made this magic trick possible was fostered on the other side of Chichen Itza in a building called *El Caracol* by the Spaniards. The "snail" name comes from its twisting interior staircase. The building is now known to have been an observatory–the only one in Mayaland. It is the oldest Toltec building on the site and the greatest achievement.

The circular superstructure consists of a lower story with radial shafts emerging from its center. The platforms, doorways and shafts were aligned in accordance with the cycles of the Sun, the stars, and the planet Venus.

It's no simple matter to make accurate observations of sunrises and sunsets, eclipses, and planetary transits in a country of frequent tropical rainfalls, yet that's exactly what was going on in this extraordinary building. Night after night Maya priests using only their eyes marked the heavens with remarkable sophistication. They were particularly fascinated by the planet Venus.

Limited by what they could see, the Maya had no idea of the solar system's planets revolving around the sun, but they knew that Venus appeared and disappeared on the western and eastern horizons at different times of the year and that it took 584 days to complete the cycle. They also knew, as has been previously explained, that five of these Venus cycles equaled eight solar years. Venus, then, appeared at northerly and southerly extremes every eight years. Several aspects of El Caracol's alignments point to these southerly and northerly Venus extremes. The Venus combinations come up again and again in Maya almanacs or astrological handbooks indicating that this planet had a role in all aspects of Maya life.

Obviously the Maya priests were well rewarded for their brilliance. The rich ceremonial life of the people centered around their calendars and observations. Imagine the effect upon the people when the priests predicted an eclipse and that eclipse occurred on schedule. Imagine the power of one who contained all the secrets of the universe in his calculations.

Here was a science that sought to explain and connect every aspect of human affairs, relating celestial movements to war, agriculture, politics and environment. To write it off because of the non-technological basis or the astrological/ religious roots would be shortsighted. This was a science that developed in an environment devoid of technology, and this was a science that worked.

Nothing comparable to the magnificent Temple of the Warriors has ever been found in the Americas. When Ann Axtell Morris and other archaeologists from the Carnegie Institution happened on it in 1924, there was only a great mound thickly covered with thorn bushes. Tops of columns showed above the tangle, many more lay sprawling in the thick brambles. The archaeologists began to count them–800, 900; then just before rounding back to the starting place, the grand total of 1000. And so the place received the other name for which it is frequently known, the ***Temple of the Thousand Columns.***

It would take them four years of excavation to lay bare the vast complex of buildings piled upon buildings, pyramids within pyramids, hidden paintings, grotesque sculpture, buried sacrificial treasure and tunneled passages. In the midst of a series of major and minor revolutions, with admitted bandidos for workmen, the archaeological team preceded to uncover and restore one of the most impressive and beautiful structures anywhere in the world.

Today the approach through impressive files of square columns is like a huge foyer. Each colonnade is decorated on all four faces with reliefs of Toltec officers. Originally their eyes were inlaid with white shells, the pupils painted in pitch — consider the effect. These stone colonnades originally constituted the substructure of the temple and helped hold up the heavy beamed roofs that collapsed long ago.

Inside is a pyramid with four terraces rising to a height of 37 feet. Two statues of standard bearers guard the top of the stairs leading to the last terrace where Chac-Mool gazes out upon the main plaza. This is a stony reminder that countless numbers of sacrificial victims died on a nearby altar,

The temple of a Thousand Columns.

bodies arched backwards, chests thrust forward as if eager for the blade. Here the priest sliced open the chest of the victim, tearing loose the still beating heart from its enlargement of blood vessels. It was thought that the heart donor lived long enough to see his still throbbing heart held triumphantly aloft by the priest, then placed in Chac Mool's sacred basin. It was also believed that sacrificial victims–as well as women who died in childbirth–lived out their after lives in a very special paradise.

The entrance to the temple itself is flanked by two feathered serpents and beyond them is the principal sanctuary with its altar supported by Atlantean Toltec warriors. All interior walls had been frescoed with lively scenes related to the Toltec conquest of Yucatan. Intriguingly, some of the Maya are pictured with blond hair.

After two years of excavations–when the end of their labors seemed in sight–the archaeologists discovered the vestiges of still another structure, now called the *Temple of Chac-Mool*. This one seems to have been almost a model for the later more impressive structure. Among the rubble the remains of a giant Chac-Mool was found, which must once have towered above the temple entrance in awesome grandeur.

Architecturally at least, Chichen Itza went out with a bang, not a whimper. Built in 1250 A.D., The Temple of the Warriors was very likely the last building constructed, an eloquent final statement.

The saying, "Good guys don't win ball games," could very well have originated in Chichen Itza, where ball teams literally played for keeps. Most Maya ceremonial centers had ball courts, but the "Olympics" —the Maya Ball Games were well established in the New World about 500 years before the Greeks founded the Olympic Games during the first century B.C. — must have been played on the gigantic *Sacred Ballcourt* opposite the Temple of the Warriors.

The playing field proper is 309 feet long and 114 feet wide. Two walls 26 feet high flank its entire length. At the field's center two large stone hoops are positioned near the top of each wall–23 feet above the ground. Spectators sat on the two long terraces that run along the base of the walls.

This was a savage, ritualistic game played with knees, hips and elbows. The use of hands and feet was against the rules. The idea was to get the rubber ball through the stone hoops—obviously a rare occurrence. The winning team was far more apt to be the one that committed the fewest errors: hitting the ball with the hands, allowing it to touch the ground or go out of bounds.

On the night before the game, the two teams prayed. Players asked the gods for blessings for themselves and their equipment (helmets, kneepads, shoulder pads, mallets.) There's no question that they needed all the help they could get. The bas-reliefs bordering the eastern terrace below the great stone serpent are grimly explicit. Seven players of each team are shown gathered around a ball decorated with a human skull. Two large spirals rise out of the skull's jaws symbolizing death.

In the central scene the first player on the team holds in his right hand a sacrificial knife; in his left hand is the head of the presumed captain of the opposing team, the losers. The torso of the decapitated man is on its knees, and from his bleeding neck seven serpents writhe–the central

Bas-relief of a jaguar—Chichen Itza.

snake in the shape of a luxuriant plant full of flowers and fruit.

Here we have seven players, seven serpents. The number seven symbolized maize—life itself to the Maya. In some way this, too, must have been a fertility sacrifice. The ball perhaps represented the course of the sun, with the result of the match, or the sacrifice involved, fertilizing the earth. Very likely the winning team carried out prescribed rituals involving the use of the losing group as sacrificial victims.

Whatever the rationale, the heads of the losers adorned the rack on the adjoining skull platform, or *Tzompantli*. Carvings of skulls encircle the platform today. Another interesting bas-relief adjacent to the ball court is a reminder that this grisly stuff was the gift of the conquering Toltecs. It shows the Toltec eagle holding a sacrificial heart, positioned next to the Maya jaguar now also doing the same. The inference being the acceptance of a new, more militaristic culture.

Perhaps the *Sweat Baths* were once used for ceremonial purposes —possibly by the ball players. Today one can see the remains of a waiting room, a steam room, the oven and underground drainage canals.

Among the most intricate and beautiful carvings at the site are those found on the walls of the *Nunnery,* an excellent example of Late Classic architecture. The original purpose of the Nunnery is unknown, but the Spaniards put it to practical use during the conquest.

The Maya put up a stiff fight for their sacred city, forcing the Spaniards back until they finally sought refuge in the tower atop the Nunnery. At first this seemed good strategy. The foundation of the building was high with straight

The Atlantean Columns—Chichen Itza.

walls and staircases so steep that it seemed a simple matter to defend the building from attack.

The Maya agreed, so they simply fell back. No fight, no contest. Theirs would be a waiting game. Sooner or later the Spaniards would need a drink of water badly enough to come down and get it.

Before long the Spaniards did get thirsty, and hungry too. Finally there was only a little food left. That night their leader played a desperate game with it. A hungry Maya dog was lured up the stairs with offers of meat, then grabbed and tied to a bell. Meat was placed all around him just beyond reach. All night long the dog pulled in one direction then another, setting off a frantic clamor.

Thinking this signified an attack, the Maya massed around the stairway and readied themselves for battle. The noise continued all night long. When dawn broke the Maya began to cautiously ascend the stairs. At the top they found a deserted fort held only by their own miserable dog. The Spaniards had all escaped by sliding down a rope on the back side of the building.

The Nunnery had another use in the 1880's when the English scholar, Alfred Maudslay, camped out there. Maudslay and his companion, Miss Annie Hunter, had hardly arrived before they each came down with malaria. A peculiarity of the disease is that it frequently strikes on alternate days. On one day the patient may have a high fever, while on the next he's tired but normal. As it turned out, Alfred and Annie were afflicted on opposite days, so they were able to care for each other in shifts. It couldn't have been easy, the nearest water was a mile round trip up and down a precarious trail. Somehow the intrepid team put in six months in this fashion, all the while mapping, drawing and photographing the ruins.

Another remarkable pair were Alice and Augustis Le Plongeon, who despite a revolution going on around them, took more than 500 photographs of Chichen Itza and made 20 careful sheets of mural drawings. The couple ventured deep into the jungle, encountering natives who practiced mesmerism, induced clairvoyance, and used "magic mirrors" to predict the future.

From a 150-year old Maya, Le Plongeon learned that men still existed who could decipher some of mysterious hieroglyphs scattered about the area. As he himself mastered these hieroglyphs, Le Plongeon came to believe that a strong link existed between the Maya and the lost continent of Atlantis.

More practically, he was the first of the archaeologists to sense that the Maya might be building one pyramid on top of the other. There was only one way to prove his hunch. It was drastic, but Le Plongeon bit the bullet–almost literally. He dynamited the building, only to reveal yet another hidden within. Today you can see evidence of his daring, which paved the way for other more sophisticated means of exploration.

There are many more smaller, but equally interesting buildings waiting to be explored. Some are mere piles of rock and stone crying out for rescue from the death grip of the jungle. These are located in the area known as Old Chichen.

To reach them, continue down the road to the south, away from the main ruins and past the *Hotel Hacienda Chichen*, the original hacienda which Edward Thompson once bought for $75. Follow the trail to the right. It isn't well marked, but that adds to the adventure. Most who venture here agree that the experience is worth the effort. After a half hour or so with the madding crowd far behind, you begin to have some sense of the mystery that has drawn so many explorers to this remarkable area.

Soon you'll see two Atlantean figures supporting a door lintel which contains a hieroglyphic of the year 879 A.D., the only proven date in Chichen Itza. Beyond this is the *Temple of the Phalli*. The unknown sculptor of the objects protruding from the temple walls leaves little doubt about what he had in mind. Since, as a rule, the Maya didn't go in for erotic art, it's believed that this was a temple dedicated to fertility. Some believe that couples who wished to have children may have come to this sanctuary.

Other temples reclaimed by jungle include the **Temple of the Little Heads,** **Temple of the Four Lintels, Temple of the Jaguar, Temple of the Turtle,** and **Temple of the Sculptured Door Jambs.** All are named for the remnants of carvings found on the walls, or for outstanding architectural features. All about you is verdant jungle for unbroken miles. Continuing on through the brush, you'll come to two Atlantean columns beneath which this writer spent one very long night.

WHERE TO STAY

The Hotel Hacienda, formerly Thompson's Hacienda.

No matter what the season, Chichen Itza will be hot at midday. This is the time to enjoy a leisurely margarita or splash in a pool, not clamber up pyramids. It's best to plan on spending at least one night at Chichen Itza. This will enable you to explore in the morning when it's cool and in the late afternoon when the Sun God turns benevolent showering the temples with burnished gold.

There are any number of tours that can arrange this for you, or you can rent a car or hop a bus in Merida or Cancun. Once at Chichen Itza, there are three hotel possibilities immediately adjacent to the ruins.

The **Hotel Hacienda Chichen** (tel: 1-800/624-8451; fax: 99/24-50-11: website: www.haciendachichen.com) is so pretty and so historic that it's hard to imagine staying anywhere else. Dating from the early 17th century, the hacienda was the residence of Francisco de Montejo, conqueror of Yucatan. Many stones from Chichen Itza were used in its construction and priceless carvings are imbedded in the walls. Later the hacienda was the home of American diplomat and archaeologist Edward Thompson. In 1923, the property became the headquarters of the Carnegie Institution's research team. Each cottage on the grounds is named for an early archaeologist who worked at Chichen Itza.

The *Mayaland Hotel* (tel: 1-800/235-4079; fax: 985/1-01-291) is closest to the ruins, kid friendly, and still retains much of its original 1920s charm. The grounds, literally a botanical garden, are dotted with cottages built like Maya bungalows. Be sure to ask for one toward the back—a snorting tour bus is not a pretty sound. The grounds have three pools and 100 acres of botanical gardens to explore. Maya dancers entertain every afternoon.

Another possibility is the *Villa Archeologica* (1-800/258-2633) (fax 98/51-00-18) which has the best food in the area. Not as pretty as the Hacienda or the Mayaland, it's equally convenient. Though run by the Club Med, don't expect a landlocked Love Boat. This place is quiet. Oh, well, you need your energy for climbing pyramids.

For more than eighty years the village of Piste (2.5 km. west of Chichen Itza) has maintained a proud tradition of providing the work force for the site's archaeological digs. Now Piste's growing up. The *Hotel Mision Chichen* (1-800/223-4084) and *Pyramide Inn Hotel* (1-800/262-9696) are mainstays. but new hotels and restaurants seem to be springing up every month as more and more tourists are drawn to the area.

WHERE TO EAT

You go to Chichen Itza to get into the ambience of the ruins and the country and that's about it. All the hotels have restaurants with adequate to excellent food–depending on who's in the kitchen at the time. Each hotel has an attractive shop. There are also a few "curio" stores in Piste and a number of restaurants to sample. A guide recommended his brother-in-law's restaurant, insisting that it was the best in town. I thought "Oh, sure it is," but was glad I tried it. He was right, it is! Try *Restaurant Xaybe*. Another one of those "X-words", it's pronounced shabe.

WHAT TO DO

Night time entertainment narrows down to the Sound and Light Show— reserve your English language audio in the afternoon, as they tend to run out, or strolling about Piste where there are always promenaders and often dancers in the square. Cap either with a bit of stargazing. After all, that's what Chichen Itza is all about.

Merida—the white city.

MERIDA
(may-ree-dah)

Merida has a very special flavor totally unlike any other city in Mexico. One could easily spend hours people watching while sitting on one of the lacy, wrought iron benches that line the plaza.

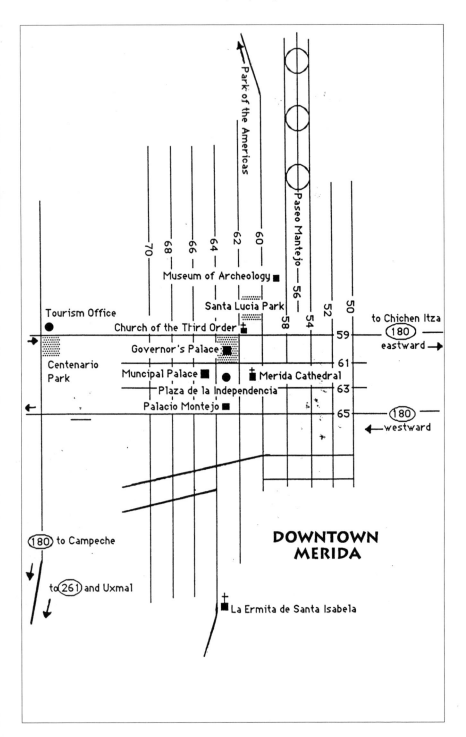

Park of the Americas

Paseo Montejo

70 68 66 64 62 60 56

Museum of Archeology ■

Santa Lucia Park

58 54 52 50

Tourism Office ●

Church of the Third Order †

to Chichen Itza

180

eastward →

Governor's Palace ■

Centenario Park

59

Muncipal Palace ■ ●

Merida Cathedral

61

Plaza de la Independencia

63

Palacio Montejo ■

65

180

← westward

180 to Campeche

DOWNTOWN MERIDA

to 261 and Uxmal

■ La Ermita de Santa Isabela

THE ROAD TO MERIDA

Izamal, possibly the prettiest small colonial city in Mexico, lies just off the Chichen Itza/Merida highway. Do it! Go there! About mid point between the two destinations is Isamal (turn north at Kantunil).

A slumbering charmer, Izamal caused a brief blip on the world's consciousness when Pope John Paul II visited during his 1993 trip to Mexico. The walls are kept a rich gold by city ordinance that enhances a sense of life in another century. At its center is the impressive 16th century monastery of St. Anthony de Padua, perched on—and built from—the remains of a pyramid devoted to Itzamma, god of the heavens. The convent's atrium is truly remarkable, a lawn enclosed by 75 arches and said to be the largest churchyard in the world—second only to St. Peter's in Rome. The modern city of some 25,000 clusters about the church and monastery begun in 1553 by Diego de Landa, a fanatical Spanish cleric, using stones plundered from a Maya temple. Landa, who first arrived in Yucatan in 1549 at age 25 as a Catholic priest, later became a bishop. Izamal became his headquarters. Behind his church stands a massive 56-foot-high, 600 foot-square Maya ceremonial platform toppled with a pyramid from which, according to Landa, "the eye can reach easily down to the sea." That may have been true when he arrived, but so much stone was stolen to build the church that the surviving pyramid is quite modest.

Pony carriages surround the town's large square, which fronts the cathedral. Why not take one to **Kinich Kakmo,** the pyramid survivor of the Maya city that once flourished there. Named for the Maya sun god, Kinich Kakmo is only a few blocks from the monastery.

Izamal. Photo courtesy of Marian Sanders.

There's another Kinich Kakmo you surely won't want to miss. It's a delightful garden restaurant at 299 Calle 27. Try the poc-chuk, a Yucatecan specialty of sliced pork marinated in sour orange juice and served with pickled onions and cilantro-tomato salsa.

A cool, clean place to stay in Izamal is the ***Green River Hotel,*** Avenida, Zamna No. 342. Phone: (995) 04-03-37. Fax (995) 4-03-37.

To continue on to Merida. hang a left to the tiny village of Citilcum, and then turn south (left again) to Hoctun and the Merida-Cancun highway.

Hacienda Katanchel. Photo courtesy of Marian Sanders.

Hacienda Katanchel (26 kms. East of Merida, off the Merida-Cancun Highway. Phone: 999 910 4617 or website: w w w . h a c i e n d a - katanchel. Beyond the tourist meccas of Cancun and Chichen Itza, Yucatan reveals itself with striking architecture and mys- terious ruins. One of the best vantage points from which to explore it all is from a hacienda—a country hotel created from a former plantation mansion. One of the loveliest is Hacienda Katanchel.

In the beginning there were the Maya. Their word, Katanchel, means "Where the Milky Way passes over." At night the constellations were (and remain) so incredibly clear that priests chose this corner of the jungle for an observatory to track the heavenly progress of the gods. Hundreds of years later the Spaniards came along and built a ranch there. Later, in the 19th century, the rancheros turned to the lucrative business of growing and processing sisal—a fiber derived from agave plans, used principally in making twine, and named for the Yucatecan port from which it was shipped. Then along came man made fibers and sisal bottomed out.

Hacienda Katanchel fell into disrepair and was abandoned for forty years. Not until 1995, when architect Anibal Gonzalez and his botanist - archaeologist wife, Monica Hernandez bought the crumbling manor house, did a new incarnation take place.

In the process of clearing the jungle, they discovered thirty-three out- buildings, most of them workers' bungalows, scattered around the property. The couple renovated them along with the main house and an old general store. Today the 17th century hacienda has been splendidly transformed into a deluxe hotel surrounded by 240 secluded acres of jungle. Guest rooms are small pavilions along a garden walkway—each with its own very, very private mini pool. The grounds, complete with sweeping lawns, lush gardens, fountains and an enormous swimming pool fed with organically purified water, are gorgeous.

Inside the thick, adobe walls, the atmosphere's a bit like an elegant ashram. The owners have fashioned a retreat for the soul as well as the body. Along with the idyllic environment and upscale refinements, there's an emphasis on holistic healing, Maya wisdom and a strong connection to Mother Earth.

Though Katanchel omits the treadmills, exercycles and weight lifting machines considered de rigueur at most hotel/spas, there's an Olympic size pool, plus 740 acres of botanical gardens and encircling jungle to explore-an area that includes pre-Classic Maya ruins and a cenote, or natural well, long venerated as a source of energy and spirituality.

The spa treatments combine organically grown herbs and flowers with both modern and ancient scientific techniques.

The Honey Body Mask with Flower Petal Treatment is a kind of pre-history beauty ritual. Carolina Martinez Guzman, the curandera, or medicine woman, wears a jade necklace, which, like the treatment itself, is a legacy from her Maya ancestors.

The hacienda's centerpiece is the former casa de maquinas, once the sisal processing center, now a sitting room, cocktail patio and elegant dining room. Guests can enjoy organic greens and vegetables grown in the hacienda's gardens, fresh baked bread brought in from Tixkokob—a neighboring village where Maya is heard as often as Spanish—and fish from the coastal village of Telchac just twenty-five miles to the north. The food is wonderful. Try the chilled sour orange soup made from a recipe known to be at east 100 years old and quail in X'Tabentun.

Side trips to ruins, cenotes, working sisal plants and tiny villages can be arranged for those who come from Merida by taxi.

Built in a "tropical colonial" style, **Hacienda San Jose** is a fantasy of arched rooms surrounding a leafy courtyard. This blue-and-white oasis in the center of a jungle brush has 15 rooms, each furnished with museum-quality antiques. Charming gardens with a pool, lounge, bar and restaurant. Phone: (999) 910 4617; website: www.luxurycollection.com.

Hacienda Teya, km. 12 Carretera Merida-Cancun, (phone: 999 228 5000; fax: 999 224 5853) is another once-grand plantation house that fell to ruin when the sisal industry was displaced by nylon. Now it's been transformed into an inviting 10-room inn with an excellent restaurant. The historic home, built in 1683, is an inviting enclave with lovely gardens and a large pool. Located only 12 miles from Merida, this is a tranquil spot to stay—or stop for lunch-- within easy driving distance to the city, ruins and picturesque villages.

Cenote at Katanchel.

MERIDA

Once there was a beautiful American journalist who came to Mexico by special invitation in recognition of an investigative series written in defense of the California Chicanos long years before that term came into vogue.

In the course of her travels, she caught the eye of the handsome governor of the war torn state of Yucatan. The governor wrote a love song for her. There were flowers, serenades, rides about the main square in a horse drawn calesa. He told her about the immense land reforms that he'd undertaken in an effort to give the Indians a share in the vast wealth that land owners were amassing at their expense. Obviously the two were made for each other.

He proposed; she accepted. The journalist was sailing to New York to buy her trousseau when she received word that her lover had been murdered by a cabal of land owners. She never married, choosing instead to devote the rest of her life to the fostering of Mexican culture.

The love song was *La Peregrina*. The governor was Felipe Carrillo Puerto, who was executed January 3, 1924. The journalist was Alma Reed who died in 1968. Reed's last wish was that she be buried beside Felipe and that's where she rests today.

The place was Merida.

Traces of a romantic past are very much a part of its lively present. Calesas still clop their way around the plaza and down the broad Paseo de Montejo. One can hear **La Peregrina** sung most any night. There's even a restaurant named for it.

The ghosts of Alma and Felipe walk the streets and others do as well. You feel them at night when the white city turns to antique ivory in the lamplight. First there are the restless shades of the Maya. The stone buildings of the 6th century ceremonial center of T'ho reminded the conquering Spaniards of the Roman ruins in Merida, Spain, so they leveled the Maya stronghold and changed its name to Merida.

Francisco de Montejo had been trying for 15 years to conquer the inhabitants of the area. He celebrated his victory by "founding" Merida on January 6, 1542. The Maya Indians were subsequently enslaved and put to work building the churches, mansions and government buildings with limestone snatched pre-cut from the ruins of their temples and palaces. Naturally one of the first residences constructed was Montejo's. Fifty-eight generations of the conquistador's descendants lived on in the grand mansion until it was sold to Banamex in 1980. Today you can cash your checks here–Banamex seems to give the best rates in town–while admiring the sweeping stairway, enormous courtyard and floors made of Carrara marble once brought from Italy as ballast by sea captains who returned home with the much prized palo de tinte or logwood. Outside you see the Montejo family crest, a foot planted firmly on the head of a Maya slave, repeated the length of the building. One would hope the ghost of this arrogant conquistador would be an uneasy one.

As the hub of the giant "thumb" that comprises the Yucatan Peninsula, Merida was—until the advent of Cancun–the traditional gateway to the Maya country. It remains a principal tourist headquarters and hotel oasis. With a population of 500,000, Merida is the largest Mexican city east of Veracruz. With all of this, it has a very special flavor totally unlike any other city in Mexico. One could easily spend hours people watching while sitting on one of the lacy, wrought iron benches that line the plaza. With its low-rise colonial buildings and wrought-iron balconies, the city looks a bit like New Orleans.

With no through highway from Mexico City until 1961 (and no railway until 1965), the Meridians frequently felt themselves more culturally linked to Europe than Mexico. It was easy for them to travel by ship to Spain, France, England, or Germany and easy for European colonists to reach them. Many young people were and are educated in Europe. When independence was finally won from Spain, Yucatecans were drawn to the total autonomy achieved by fellow Maya in their newly established country of Guatemala. Permanent alliance with Mexico wasn't easily achieved. Yucatecos still consider themselves special and are. Quick, witty, independent, Meridians, in particular, look and act different from their not so near neighbors.

One obvious difference is their clothing. The guayabera, an open necked, handsomely pleated shirt, is worn everywhere. For women, the huipil has been the choice for centuries and still is often seen on the streets. This loose fitting white shift is richly embroidered in an opulent flower pattern at the square neckline and hemline and is worn over a lace trimmed petticoat. An accompaniment is the rebozo de Santa Maria, a stole of woven silk which can be tied in any number of attractive variations.

But clothing is only one small difference that distinguishes Meridians. The others become quickly apparent as the wonderful montage of diverse cultural influences comprising the city become apparent. Merida is an unusually easy city to explore because of the way the streets are numbered. Even numbered calles, or streets, run north to south, odd numbered streets run east to west. All down town streets are one way. The main plaza, which remains the heart of town, is bordered by streets 60, 61, 62 and 63.

WHERE TO STAY

Among the downtown hotels, you really can't beat the *Casa de Balam* on Calle 60, #488. (1-800-624-8451) (fax: 99/245-011) "The House of the Jaguar" is within a block of concerts, shops and excellent restaurants. After a day of sightseeing, the lush, tropical courtyard is a delightful oasis. The staff is pleasant and helpful, and there's an excellent travel agency in the building. Check out the sumptuous bridal suite—it's surprisingly reasonable, well worth considering. The room is truly lovely with its spectacular antique bed, mahogany furnishings and intimate balcony overlooking a private garden.

An alternative is the *Gran Hotel,* Calle 60 #469. (tel: 999 924 7730; website: www.granhotelmerida.com.mx). A turn of the century charmer, with its Art Nouveau courtyard, Greek columns and sweeping mahogany stairways, the Gran is a delight. Rooms overlook a pretty park.

La Mision de Fray Diego is an elegant residence dating from the 17th century now converted to a small luxury hotel just one block from Merida's historic center, theaters, museums and shops. Calle 61, 524. US and Canada (1-888) 903-9512.

All the comforts of home happily relocated in a setting reminiscent of a colonial mansion may be enjoyed at the *Merida Holiday Inn,* Avenida Colon 498 at the corner of Calle 60 (Phone: 1-800-465-4329). It is nice after a long day of exploring and/or shopping to settle in beside the mini-bar and before the TV set to rest up before the evening's entertainment. And that evening could include the excitement of dancing at the hotel's lively L'Disco. Located at Avenida Colon just off Montejo Blvd., the area is blessedly quiet at night and has easy accessibility to smart new suburban shops and restaurants.

The *Montejo Palace* (Phone: 99-24-76-44) faces on the broad boulevard Paseo de Montejeo which some have likened to the Champs Elysees. It has a lively nightclub and a charming sidewalk cafe which spills out from the elegant veranda. From there it's fun to watch a passing scene that includes both old and new. One of the best offerings is the "sweet" man who strolls by balancing a tray on his head. My first day in town, I'd opted for a margarita and a seafood cocktail. But how could I resist that marvelous praline-like thing from amidst the beguiling assortment he offered? I couldn't. The maitre'd in passing remarked, "We have a saying, "One who takes a sweet with a drink is a very sweet drunk." We agreed that it probably lost something in translation.

Two biggies that try hard to project the mellow old Merida ambience are the *Fiesta Americana* and the *Hyatt Recency Merida*. The former, at Avenida Colon 451 (Phone: 1-800-FIESTA 1), a luxurious add on to a colonial mansion, has all the amenities. The Hyatt Regency Merida at Ave. Colon at Calle 6 (Phone 1-800-233-1234), not only the newest kid in town but the tallest, a regular rascacielos or skyscraper, has everything you could possibly imagine.

Very different, but also very charming *Casa Exilio*, Calle 68#495. (Phone: 1-800 538-6802) is a bed and breakfast celebrating the tradition of Old Mexico. There are ten rooms some with tropical gardens or sun decks, each restored to something beyond its original elegance.

Luz En Yucatan, Calle 55 #499, is an urban retreat for weight loss and wellness. Guests usually come for a week, enjoy walks, a variety of exercises, sight seeing and excellent low calorie meals. (Phone: 99-24-00-35) (email: lunenyucatan@yahoo.com)

WHERE TO EAT

Portico del Peregrino, at 501 Calle 57 (Phone: 99/28-6163), named for the song, is the kind of place that Alma and Felipe would have loved, a romantic restaurant with arched courtyards and delicious food.

But I think they would also have frequented *Pancho Villa's Follies*, at 509 Calle 59 (Phone:99/23-09042). The food is equally outstanding. (Lobster thermador practically for pennies.) The decor is Maya funk, beaded lamps, a blaze of hot pink draperies, clashing happily with striped table cloths. How could you not love a place where the bandido waiters wear crossed cartridges and sombreros? These guys are friendly, funny, nice and that marvel in Mexico–fast. The music's lively, the ambience upbeat.

There's nothing particularly romantic about *Soberanis* at 503 Calle 60 (facing the main plaza) The ambience is zero but the seafood's the tastiest in town and the prices are unbelievably cheap. Just thinking about it makes me want to fly down for an oyster fix.

Restaurant Amaro, corner of calles 59 and 60, offers a slice of history along with its excellent food. The patriot, Quintana Roo was born in this charming colonial building with its arched courtyard. In addition to Mexican and American cuisine, the restaurant offers tasty vegetarian dishes.

WHAT TO DO

In the center of of town the zocolo or Plaza de la Indepencia is the perfect place to orient oneself. Prior to the conquest, the zocolo was the site of the great temple of H-Chum-caaan, surrounded on all sides by other temples and pyramids. Today the only trace of them can be seen in the walls of the most prominent building on the plaza, *Catedral de San Ildefonso.*

Despite the busy world that borders it, the plaza retains its colonial charm. The S-shaped just-the-two-of-you stone love seats look like lacy valentines and above them the India laurel trees have a story of their own to tell. Two hundred years ago they were seedlings bound for Havana when a storm came up and sank the boat. Merida reaped the wild wind.

Facing the plaza on the east is the lemon colored cathedral begun in 1561. The building is massive–more massive than Merida merited in the eyes of the Spaniards, but by the time they dis-covered their mistake........It

Street scene in Merida. Photo courtesy of Marian Sanders.

seems that the plans for a small cathedral originally slated for Merida were substituted accidentally for the more grandiose design meant for the cathedral in Lima. (Where the gold was.) Maybe this explains why the twin towers of Merida's cathedral are so dinky, seemingly out of scale with the rest of the building. Perhaps, it was at this point that they realized their mistake.

The *Casa de Montejo*, on the south edge of the central plaza, was once the home of Yucatan's conqueror, Francisco de Montejo. Considered one the New World's most important works in the flamboyant 16th century-style known as Plateresque, the building was erected in 1542 using talented Maya slaves and stones pulled from their temples. The extraordinary sculpted façade of sword wielding conquistadors, their feet planted firmly on the heads of the Maya remains in place today. Thirteen generations of Montejos resided in the mansion until 1980 when the mansion was sold to Banamex. The bank takes up the entire structure. You can see the enormous patio during business hours (weekdays 9 a.m. to 5 p.m. and Saturday 9 a.m to 1:30 p.m.) What a place to cash your travelers checks!

Though the cathedral, finally finished in 1599, was built in the fortress style with wall slits to place firearms in case of an Indian attack, this feature didn't save it from being sacked during the 1917 revolution. A startling contrast to the churchly opulence seen in other parts of Mexico, this cathedral has a stark, stripped down look. It's one highlight sounds like the patron of footsore tourists–Christ of the Blisters. Actually the statue is reputed to be carved from a tree that burned all night without being destroyed. The statue was then placed in a church that caught fire. The next day the statue was found blistered but not burned and was transferred to the mother church in Merida.

The *Government Palace*, lined with murals by Yucatan's leading artist, Fernando Castro Pacheco, is a must-see. On the second floor is the hall of history filled with murals that depict the birth of the Maya, their trials and tribulations, their gods, heroes, villains, the whole grand sweep of events on the Yucatan Peninsula from ancient times up until the 20th century. You can even see Felipe Carrillo Puerto, but not, unfortunately, Alma Reed.

The *Santa Lucia Square* on 60th Street, a block up from the Casa Balam, was once a stage stop for those arriving and departing the city. The 22 hooks where the horses were tied are still visible. Across the street is another poignant memory, a small stone chapel dappled and gray was built some 400 years ago for the use of the mulattoes and blacks brought to Yucatan as slaves by the Spanish conquistadores.

Happier memories are recreated on Thursday evenings when the place comes alive again. An orchestra of guitars and brass begins to play. Women in huipils and men in white cotton suits appear before the floodlit wedding cake facade of white arches that partially enclose the square. They dance with trays of glasses balanced on their heads, they dance as matadors and bulls, they dance with woven ribbons around a maypole, they dance with baskets of fruit and colored shawls. It's very pretty and colorful; a wonderful place to catch the flavor of Meridian life as it was and still remains. Santa Lucia Square is also notable on Sundays as a flea market.

The *Regional Museum of Archaeology* is a delight on several levels. As one of the finest provincial museums in Mexico, it brings into focus the history, culture and lifestyle of the Maya. The building itself is an architectural gem, one of the most beautiful of the many mansions built along the Paseo Montejo by the henequen barons who became millionaires during the 19th and early 20th centuries when the sisal fields of Yucatan furnished the world with ropes and fibers. It's possible to see exhibits here that no longer exist at the sites themselves–displays of artifacts, reconstructed plans of old cities and an excellent explanation of how the people actually lived. Here in this opulent wedding cake of a mansion is an easy to digest overview of the ruins that exist in the area and beyond.

—SHOPPING—

Merida's a good shopping town with opportunities literally everywhere. Many of the charming exhibits at the *Museum of Popular Art* are for sale.

Both shoppers or non-shoppers will be equally fascinated by the *Mercado Municipal*, a great, huge barnlike structure where everything from howler monkeys to gold jewelry can be obtained. You can find the pretty stoles called rebozos de Santa Maria   here as well as huipils and richly embroidered blouses. You can also buy sandals, machetes, birds, birdcages, baskets, copal, gold encrusted bugs–anything you can imagine and more. If you like to bargain, this is certainly the place; but do   inspect your treasures very carefully. What you buy may be slightly cheaper but often isn't as well made as the merchandise back in the high rent district. Whether you buy or not, the ambience of this place is not to be missed.

A DREAM TRIP

Once in a while an itinerary comes together that really has it all. My friend, Tommy Thompson, Tropical Travels maven, and his partner Augustin Ortiz, a Meridian otherwise known as "Mr. Yucatan," tailored this one to my fantasies. Unlike many plans that evolve over moonlight and margaritas, this trip is very doable.

Day 1 - ARRIVAL IN MERIDA, MEXICO —Depart immediately by van for Chichen Itza where travelers will stay at the Hacienda Chichen, an inn dating from the 17th century. A guide will point up the fine points of this most historic of all the Maya sites. Guests will enjoy a welcome dinner.

Day 2 – CHICHEN ITZA, MERIDA — Travelers will have an opportunity to enjoy this site in the cool of the morning when there are few others about. Lunch at Hacienda Teya is next on the agenda. A plantation house dating from the X1X century, Teya reincarnated as a charming restaurant with French and Spanish architectural touches. Continuing on to Merida, guests will check into the romantically elegant Grand Hotel, a treasure trove of art and antiques dating from the XIX century. There's a little time for shopping before dinner at the hotel.

Day 3 - MERIDA — The day begins with a sightseeing tour of Mérida, a unique colonial city with strong French influence. After lunch at the Cenacolo Restaurant, a Victorian mansion on the Apse Montejo, one of the most beautiful avenues in Mexico, it's on to Conkol. Though hardly more than a village, Conkol has an extraordinary museum of religious art and an onsite lecturer, Maureen Ransom--the anthropologist who designed it. Returning to Mérida for an evening walk in the Central Square, guests will enjoy the music of the trovadores who serenade each night.

Day 4 – UXMAL, KABAH, LABNA— Many consider Uxmal to be the most beautiful ceremonial center in Mexico. A morning tour of the site will be followed by lunch at Hacienda Uxmal, once the headquarters of the archaeologists who excavated it. The unique and impressive sites of Kabah and Labná will be visited next on a scenic loop drive through the Puuc hills. The day's final destination is the lovely and historic Hacienda Blanca Flor where a fascinating conference will be held on the history of Yucatan's haciendas and the sisal boom that spawned them. Dinner will be served in the hacienda's historic dining room.

Day 5 – HECELCHAKAN, JAINA, CAMPECHE — Besides being the most historic hacienda on the Yucatan Peninsula, Blanca Flor is a birder's delight. After breakfast in the lush gardens, the road beckons to Isla of Jaina, a sanctuary only recently opened to the public. Possibly the most important Maya ceramic pieces ever discovered were excavated here. There'll be a stop in the tiny village of Hecelchakan to visit an impressive museum filled with treasures from Jaina before lunch in Campeche. A tour of the fortresses and colonial buildings that have made Campeche an international landmark will be enjoyed before returning to Blanca Flor for the night.

Day 6 – PALENQUE —In the heart of the Chiapas jungle, Palenque is without a doubt the most beautiful ruin in Mexico. It's many temples and palaces are beyond belief. An overnight at Chan Kah Resort is a delightful capper to an exciting day at the site.

Day 7 - AGUA AZUL—The waterfalls of Agua Azul are among the most dramatic sites in Mexico. The color of the water varies with the season, but it's always spectacular. After a swim, its on to the lush Rio Bec Region and an overnight at the Chicanná Ecovillage Resort.

Day 8 – CALAKMUL, CHICANNA, XPUJIL, BACALAR —The day begins with an exploration of the Calakmul Biosphere Reserve continuing on to the site of Chicanná. After a refreshing splash in the pool, travelers will continue on to Laguna Bacalar, stopping enroute at the small citadel of Xpujil. Dinner and an overnight stay will be at the exciting Explorean Hotel in the heart of the jungle.

Day 9 – OXTANKAH, PLAYA DEL CARMEN— The day begins with a visit to the citadel of Oxtankah, a place associated with the romantic union of the Spaniard, Guerrrero and his Maya princess. Their children were the first recorded mestizos, a blending of Indian and Spanish blood. The route then leads north along the Riviera Maya to Playa del Carmen and the hotel Maroma on the shores of the Caribbean.

Day 10 - PLAYA DEL CARMEN —Guests will enjoy the facilities of one of the prettiest and most romantic hotels in Mexico.

Day 11 - DEPART PLAYA DEL CARMEN — Depending on flight schedules, there may be time to visit the town's enticing shops before transferring to Cancun's airport for the flight home.

Check out the adventure for yourself on www.themayantraveler.com or by talking with Tommy Thompson at 1-800-451-8017.

An arresting bas-relief at Mayapan.

MAYAPAN
(my-ah-pahn)

This was the last great Maya stronghold and,
for a time, the most important city in Yucatan.
Today it's virtually forgotten.

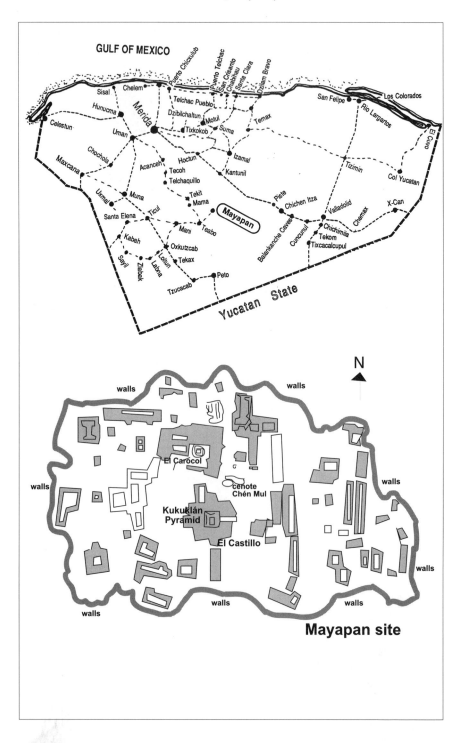

Mayapan site

Hunac Ceel was one of those take charge people who made his own luck. He was tired of the way things were going within the Triple Alliance, an organization of city states comprising Mayapan, Chichen Itza and Uxmal. As far as he was concerned, Chichen Itza was getting far too uppity; but as a commoner, there was nothing that he could do about it.

Well aware that under the strict cultural rules of the hierarchy he had no chance of ruling, Hunac Ceel decided to take both his own life and the destiny of his people into his hands. His big chance came when the authorities of Mayapan organized a pilgrimage to the sacred cenote at Chichen Itza. On this occasion many people were thrown into the well in the hope that at least one would return to the surface with a message from the gods concerning Mayapan's administration.

A collective sigh of disappointment arose from the crowd gathered about the rim of the well. The waters were ominously still, not one person had emerged from the depth. It was the moment for which Hunac Ceel — who'd secretly taught himself to swim — had been waiting. Suddenly he bounded forward and dove into the cenote.

The people gasped in astonishment as he disappeared into the blue-green waters and then cheered as he re-emerged. "I have spoken to the gods," Hunac Ceel cried out. The crowd was stunned into speechlessness when he revealed the full extent of the divine message. The gods had announced that he was to be king of the entire Yucatan peninsula.

Pulled from the well, Hunac Ceel was proclaimed Lord of Mayapan as well as all the cities of Yucatan. A man unwilling to leave anything to chance, he insured Mayapan's supremacy by calling on Mexican mercenaries known as ah canuls or "protectors" to assist him. The ah canuls were expert archers credited with introducing the bow and arrow to Yucatan. The Cocom dynasty founded by the resourceful Hunac Ceel is believed to have lasted for 250 years.

Then in 1441 a gathering storm broke. The Mexican mercenaries were understandably unpopular from the beginning, and the Cocoms, as their patrons, were increasingly resented. The old angers smoldered until inevitably a boiling point was reached. Under the leadership of the Xius, the surrounding countryside rose up against Mayapan. The fortress city was destroyed, the Cocoms slaughtered with the exception of one son who was away.

The hated Ah canuls were driven from the area, some taking refuge in Tulum. After their victory over Mayapan, the Xius founded the city of Mani

which means "it is past." Unfortunately this was just so much wishful thinking. Bygones refused to remain bygones. The surviving prince returned and founded the city of Tibulon which means "we are betrayed." The rest of Mayapan was split into a dozen or so small, angry communities. No one forgot anything.

This was the condition of things when the Spaniards arrived on the scene. Despite their lack of unity, the Maya were able to repulse the invaders twice, literally pushing them from the land, but then the old enmity flared again. In 1536 the Xius undertook a pilgrimage to Chichen Itza and asked the Cocoms for safe conduct through their land. They were surprised by a warm welcome. For four days and nights the visitors were feted. It appeared that the old feuds were at last at an end.

It appeared wrong. The grandson of the slaughtered Mayapan king wasn't about to let this opportunity pass. The seeming hospitality was merely a ruse. On the fifth day the Cocoms fell on the unsuspecting Xius and massacred all of them.

Rendition of stela 1 at Mayapan.

This was the final nail in the coffin of unity. When the Spaniards returned for another try in 1540, they found a strife-torn land exhausted by civil war. The Maya could no longer resist the invaders with their superior arms and fearsome diseases. The country fell. In 1546 and again in 1547, the Maya rose against the conquerors but by then it was too late.

The sense of loss, of devastation, is more apparent in Mayapan than any other site. This was the last great Maya stronghold and, for a time, the most important city in Yucatan. Today it's virtually forgotten. Nineteen miles away in Merida, a bus leaves the main terminal every hour. It stops at Mayapan, but hardly anyone gets off. Too bad, the guide, obviously eager for company, is very helpful.

Wandering about the deserted ruins, one finds an ample base from which to speculate. The structures cover a vast area and have, for the most part, been left in their original state of decay. An air of lonely quiet pervades the site.

Archaeological excavations serve only to emphasize Mayapan's architectural mediocrity, yet for well over two centuries this center dominated the entire Yucatan peninsula.

Unlike ruins in other areas of Yucatan, we know what happened in Mayapan. This was a city destroyed by war. In 1950, archaeologists found skeletons with flint spear points protruding from their bones. Today we can still detect burned beams and broken altars.

Unlike the other Maya sites—primarily ceremonial centers–this was a real city. Its inhabitants were very like the ancient Romans, far more involved with military strength, empire building and administration than in esthetics or religion. Mayapan was a political city and a fortress. Very few of its buildings were temples, and those that existed were shabby, clumsy affairs, mute testimony to the cultural poverty of a military regime.

Ten thousand or so residents lived within walls, but in the end these barricades proved no protection. The tombs of the leaders tell a grisly story of massacres that must have taken place in the midst of funeral rites. In one tomb, 41 skeletons surround one skeleton, who appears to have been their master in life.

Here was a government primarily occupied with power and war. Its obsession ultimately resulted in oblivion.

The site is open between 8 a.m. and 5 p.m. and a small admission fee is charged.

The crumbling ruins at Mayapan.

Xlacah cenote is a fine swimming hole.

DZIBILCHALTUN
(tzee-bee-eel-chahlt-toon)

Hundreds of structures have been uncovered in this major metropolis and archaeologists estimate that there may be at least 8000 more. Its size and the fact that it wasn't periodically deserted as were most of the other cities, have lead to speculation that Dzibilchaltun may have literally been the capital of Mayadom.

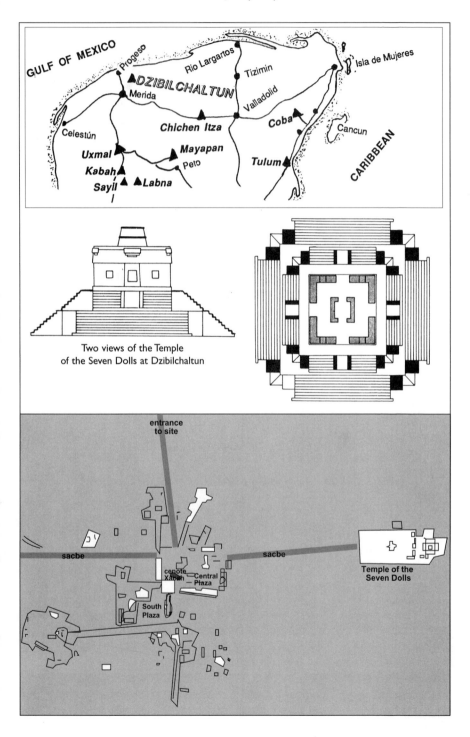

Two views of the Temple
of the Seven Dolls at Dzibilchaltun

The tree-ringed cenote, a limestone sinkhole at the ancient city of *Dzibilchaltun*(tzee-Beel-chal-hl-toon), holds secrets of the past. On March 21, the spring equinox, the rising sun beams directly through the opening of the Temple of the Seven Dolls providing yet another spectacle of Maya exactitude. The equinox 'event' at Chichen Itza is at sunset, so one can actually see both in one day. While the equinox phenomenon can be viewed in Chichen Itza for three days, in Dzibilchatun, it can only be seen on the exact day - March 21 at sunrise.

Dzibilichaltun is located 8 km. North of Merida on the Progresso road. The turn-off is well marked on the right and continues for 4.6 km. To the ruin. The site is open from 8 to 5 and the museum from 8 to 4. On the spring equinox the site opens at 5:30 a.m. to allow visitors to see the sunrise.

It also holds potential pleasure for the present. Pilgrims to this seemingly forgotten–yet easily accessible–Maya stronghold should bring their bathing suits.

Dzibilchaltun, "the place where there are symbols inscribed on flat stones," is the oldest Maya city continuously in use. This vast site–dating from 2000 B.C. until after the Spanish conquest–is spread over an estimated 25 square miles. Hundreds of structures have been uncovered in this major metropolis and archaeologists estimate that there may be at least 8000 more. Its size and the fact that it wasn't periodically deserted as were most of the other cities, have lead to speculation that Dzibilchaltun may have literally been the capital of Mayadom.

Despite all this, Dzibilchaltun is a kind of stepchild. First, of course, there were the Spaniards. The conquistadores razed many of the structures to build the inevitable church. You can see this edifice as you approach the site. It stands out immediately because of the very broad arch. (The Maya utilized only the narrow corbel, or "false" arch.) Today that monument to arrogance and bigotry is merely another ruin.

Unfortunately the plundering didn't end there. Over the years local builders continued the tradition, blithely destroying temples whenever they needed building materials. Archaeological digs sponsored by Tulane University and the National Geographic Society begun in the 1950s may have put an end to the devastation, but Dzibilchaltun is still virtually ignored, a place somehow lost in time.

Located just off the Progreso Road, the site is easy to reach by bus or car. There's a small museum just outside the ruins and a minimal entrance fee.

Usually you can have this extensive site to yourself. It's a wonderful place to spend the day wandering at will, picnicking and swimming.

Xlacah, the sacred cenote, is a wonderful swimming hole. Bathing's permitted, the water's sparkling clear, water lilies grow toward the shallow end, the deep end descends to 55 meters at least 100 feet farther than the better known well at Chichen Itza. Some of the bones and other artifacts found here are on display at the museum.

The *Temple of the Seven Dolls,* reached at the end of a 500-yard sacbe leading from the large central area, seems small and unimposing from a distance but has been beautifully restored. It's unusual because of its square plan, two windows in the sides of the main structure—Maya builders apparently didn't do windows!—and the pyramid form in the roof comb. All of these are considered unique in Maya architecture. The temple has been carbon dated as a fifth century structure which places it in the Classic period. Each of the seven terra cotta figures found inside portray a different physical defect. Were they a kind of voodoo doll? Or possibly a healing tool? Ponder their use in the museum as you leave.

WHERE TO STAY

About a mile north of Dzibilchaltun on the Progreso Road, is *Hacienda Xcanatun*—newly morphed into the Casa de Piedra Hotel. (Km 12 Carretera Merida/Progreso. Phone: 999 941 0213; website: www.hacienda@ xcanatun.com. *Hacienda Xcanatun* is a classic example of the lavish constructions of the 17th century, initially dedicated to agriculture and livestock, and later to the production of sisal (henequen) fiber, during the "Green Gold Era."

Hacienda Xcanatun— Dzilbilchaltun.

Rooms are charmingly decorated with antiques and have jacuzzis and private verandas looking out over tropical gardens. Hotel guests will see the former House of Machinery now reborn into a restaurant where they can enjoy Mexican, Caribbean and international cuisine. The former chapel has been transformed into a library-sitting room. The spacious grounds also include two swimming pools, a spa, health and beauty center.

_____NUEVO YUCATAN_____

Continuing north on the Progreso Road, you'll be rewarded by a beach where you can walk "forever" and not see another person. Hurry! It can't last.

Less than an hour's drive from Merida, on Mexico's Gulf Coast, a new area is being developed. It's called Neuvo Yucatan and thus far it's so nuevo that there's only one resort in place—the **Reef Club.** (Phone 1-877 733 3258; e-mail: reservations@interclubresorts.com)

The club's all-inclusive policy covers three meals a day, snacks and beverages (including alcoholic), nightly entertainment and water sports. The ambience reminds you of what a Catskill resort must have been like in the old "Dirty Dancing" days. Staff members double as entertainers and they're good. Lots of amusing skits and lively dance routines.

Rates are low and children under 12 are admitted free. A professionally staffed child center complete with mini theater, pool snack bar and plenty of activities keeps them happy and entertained.

Nearby are the ruins of **Xcambo** and the **Uaymitan Flamingo Preserve**. Also, don't miss the opportunity for lunch at **Moctezuma's** (Calle 19 #48) in nearby Chicxulub. They just may have the best sea food in Mexico!

Nuevo Yucatan.

Temple of the Magician—Uxmal.

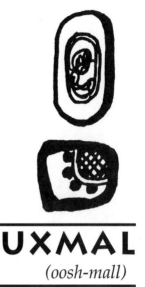

UXMAL
(oosh-mall)

The city of Uxmal (600-1000 AD) is a stunning example of Classic Maya architecture, visually the most dramatic site in the Puuc "highlands" and, some believe, in all of Yucatan. Grouped as they are on a broad plateau, the buildings appear almost unreal.

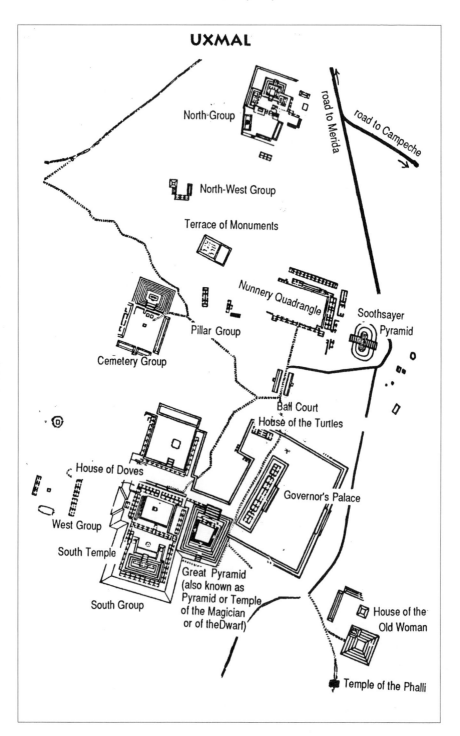

UXMAL

North Group

road to Merida

road to Campeche

North-West Group

Terrace of Monuments

Nunnery Quadrangle

Soothsayer
Pyramid

Pillar Group

Cemetery Group

Ball Court

House of the Turtles

House of Doves

Governor's Palace

West Group

South Temple

Great Pyramid
(also known as
Pyramid or Temple
of the Magician
or of the Dwarf)

South Group

House of the
Old Woman

Temple of the Phalli

That the architecture of Uxmal should be frequently likened to the Acropolis seems appropriate for a ghost town haunted by parallels to both Hercules and Helen of Troy.

According to legend, Uxmal was founded by a dwarf. Obviously the dwarf lacked the physical attributes of the Greek super hero, but he was more than Hercules's equal in luck, cunning and chutzpah. Both were assigned seemingly impossible tasks, both succeeded and received rich rewards achieving a kind of demi-god status.

The story of the miraculous dwarf begins with the kind of prophecy we've heard many times. A king is warned that his kingdom must be forfeited when a magic cymbal is struck by a man not born of woman. The improbability of it all insures the king's complacency.

In this story the king's domain was a small, insignificant one, his palace only a white house; but his was the only game in town and he liked it that way. Naturally it was all too good to last.

In a tiny hut on the edge of town lived an old woman skilled in sorcery, a woman with strange friends in mysterious places. Some rightly called her a witch for she did many marvelous things like concoct midnight potions that could both cause and cure illness. (It's said that the ancestors of the present day curanderos, or witch doctors, learned their skills from her.)

One morning the woman woke feeling old. What I need to cheer me is a child, she decided. That night the witch went to the dark caves in the hills where the hunchbacked ones live. There one of her colleagues gave her a great egg. The witch brought the egg home and secretly buried it in the earth to hatch. A few days later out popped a boy with the face of a man. To avoid embarrassment (a baby at her age!), the old woman introduced him as her grandson.

The child was unusually precocious — he could talk from birth—but his physical growth stopped when he was only 7 hands high. The bright boy was aware almost from the beginning that his grandmother was no ordinary lady. Soon he was snooping about the hut trying to learn her secrets. The dwarf was certain that there was something buried under the hearth. Finally this bratty kid tricked the witch by puncturing her water jar so that she would remain at the well a long, long time.

During her absence, he dug into the ashes and pulled out a golden cymbal and a little rod. Of course the dwarf struck the cymbal, but even he was surprised by the results. The sound was like thunder, the earth trembled, and there was a great uproar as people ran out of their houses.

The king heard the mighty roar and shuddered. The words of the forgotten prophecy came back to him: The mighty city of Uxmal will appear in the place that bears that name. Whatever man may be seated on the throne let him prepare to leave it for no one can resist the king who is coming.

The incumbent had no intention of bowing to the inevitable. He ordered his warriors to find the person who'd struck the cymbal and to bring him back. When they returned with the tiny dwarf everyone laughed and the king breathed a sigh of relief.

"So you're the one who would be king," he greeted the boy. "That's all very well, but first you must prove yourself. There are three tests. To begin with you must prove that you have more wisdom than I. Tell me without omitting a single berry how many fruits hang in the branches of the sacred ceiba tree?"

Without blinking an eye, the young dwarf replied: "One hundred thousand twice 60 and 3 times 3 and if you don't believe me, count them one by one."

As the king looked at the tree uncertain of what to do next, a great bat swooped down and whispered in his ear: "The boy spoke the truth."

The king turned pale and bowed his head, but raised it again. Power was sweet and not to be relinquished easily. "Tonight let us each make a statue in our own image and tomorrow we shall compare which is the most beautiful and durable."

The boy agreed . That night he constructed not only a statue but–with the help of his witch patron and her hunchback friends–a broad white sacbe. The next day he and the witch returned to town on it. Behind them followed a procession of townspeople who no longer considered the dwarf a laughing matter.

The king's statue was attractive enough but made of wood. When put to a test, it burned; but the dwarf's statue was made of wet clay and the fire baked it fine and hard.

People began to crowd about the dwarf congratulating him, their allegiance clearly shifting. There'll be one more test," the king insisted.

"I shall command a scaffold to be built tonight," he told the boy. "Tomorrow the executioner shall break open thy head with a mallet of steel. If you can survive that, you will be king."

Once more the boy agreed, but added, "If I come out alive will you submit to the same test?" And the king who should have known better said, "Yes."

"Spend the night here with me in my house," he then suggested to the contender. The boy refused. The king's little white house was simply not up to his standards of what a palace should be, so overnight the dwarf and his magical helpers constructed a new one.

The following morning the crafty kid went smiling to the scaffold. He was still smiling when he knelt before the executioner and even when he rose again — the witch had hidden a copper plate under his hair which deflected the mallet blow. Now it was the king's turn and he did not survive the test.

On the next night the small village was transformed into the great city of Uxmal —temples, palaces, courtyards. It's the same magnificent city that we see today with the *Temple of the Dwarf* (more frequently called the *Temple of the Magician*) dominating the scene.

Uxmal thrived for hundreds of years and part of its success was due to a triple alliance with Chichen Itza and Mayapan which the canny dwarf-magician was said to have founded. The Triple Alliance was all well and good until it turned into a triangle......and that's another story.

Princess Sac-Nicte was beautiful. Canek, the young king of Chichen Itza, was handsome. When they met by chance it was love at first sight. Unfortunately there was one major drawback, the lovely daughter of Hunac Ceel, the Lord of Mayapan, was engaged to the King of Uxmal.

Perhaps Sac-Nicte pleaded with her father. But her romantic preferences were of little importance to him. As the daughter of a king, hers was a marriage of state. The agreement had been made, a slight to the King of Uxmal unthinkable. The wedding plans continued.

At last the day came when Hunac Ceel brought his daughter to Uxmal for the nuptial ceremony. People bearing lavish gifts flocked to the great city from all corners of the Triple Alliance. Then a murmur arose. Where was King Canek's tribute? Where, for that matter, was King Canek? Could such a strange behavior go ignored?

The three day marriage ceremony began, one day of festivities, then a second day. Princess Sac-Nicte walked through the rituals as though in a trance. Then on the third day King Canek arrived with a large army and literally swept her off her feet. In the confusion, the lovers disappeared leaving the three armies of Uxmal, Mayapan and Chichen Itza to slug it out among themselves.

While Sac-Nicte and Canek were settling into married life in Peten–their chosen lovenest — the forces of Chichen Itza were devastated by the combined armies of Mayapan and Uxmal. The survivors are then said to have abandoned Chichen Itza, scattering into fragments which would one day rally to overthrow the descendants of Hunac Ceel and his hated mercenaries.

These legends make as much sense as what we actually know about Uxmal, for it, too, was ultimately abandoned. Why?

We know it was rebuilt as many as five times. Why again? Why was it built even once? There is almost no water in the area. Yucatan is one vast limestone slab with rivers running underground. In some places the rock has caved in, forming great natural wells of water which are called cenotes. These are prominent at other ruins, but there are none at Uxmal. Here the Maya builders carved giant reservoirs, but surely there were years when there was no rain. It's easy to understand the prevalence of Chac, the elephant nosed rain god, on so many of the buildings.

WHAT TO SEE_____

The city of Uxmal (600-1000 AD) is a stunning example of Classic Maya architecture, visually the most dramatic site in the Puuc "highlands" and, some believe, in all of Yucatan. Grouped as they are on a broad plateau, the buildings appear almost unreal.

Exquisitely proportioned structures extend over an area of about one-half mile in length and 600 yards in width. The site comprises seven known architectural groupings, three of which have been partially restored. Each of these has been placed in a highly precise fashion: The *Pyramid of the Magician* (sometimes called *Pyramid of the Dwarf*) in a vertical line, the *Quadrangle of the Nunnery* in a square and the *Governor's Palace* in a horizontal line.

Governor's Palace—Uxmal

The sound and light show dramatically highlights the intricate geometric patterns for which Uxmal is famous; but under any lighting conditions, this place is a marvel. A marvel? Miracle is more like it. There were no mines on the Yucatan peninsula, no metal tools used in construction, no dray animals and the wheel as a means of conveyance was unknown. Are the dwarf's fabled feats any more amazing than this?

The *Temple of the Magician* clearly dominates the site, stirring the imagination despite the forbidding, unapproachable aspect it presents from every angle. A flight of 118 steps leads to its two platforms. (A chain was added in 1865 to facilitate the Empress Carlota's climb and many are grateful for it today.) The pyramid is actually five superimposed temples, each embedded in the other–a synthesis in stone of centuries of continual occupation. Each of the succeeding sanctuaries buried the proceeding one, thereby altering its orientation.

Temple One, almost at ground level, was buried in rubble when the pyramid itself was built. Once it was uncovered, a fine facade was revealed decorated with Chac masks, astronomical symbols and human figures. Access to *Temple Two*, the walls of which were painted in a serpent motif, was by a stairway on the east side. *Temple Three*, embedded within the pyramid, is invisible from the outside.

One enters *Temple Four* through the stone jaws of the rain god Chac–a grim reminder of a sacred rite passage. According to Maya tradition, one must die in the jaws of the god in order to be reborn into a new life which followed initiation.

From *Temple Five* which is spread out over the summit of the pyramid, one has a plumed serpent's view of the entire site. For instance, the small ruined pyramid directly to the south is the *Pyramid of the Old Woman*, believed to be the former home of the dwarf's grandmother who didn't die at all and is believed to be alive and well and living with a pet snake at the bottom of a well somewhere not far away.

The biggest building is the *Governor's Palace.* If it looks that grand, it must have been the governor's palace — or so the Spaniards thought when they observed the abandoned structure 500 years after its abandonment.   Today we know that this is the place where Maya astronomer-priests once took measurements and consulted planetary charts as they watched Venus rise at dawn. Their calculations linked planting, harvesting and celebrating with propitious astronomical events.   One of the most awe inspiring of the latter occurred every eight years when the planet Venus rose on the horizon at a point aligned with with the center door of the palace.

The 318-foot long structure rests on three vast terraces overlooking the city. The effect is massive, grand, a little heartless. It's been called the most spectacular building in Pre-Columbian America and is frequently favorably compared with Greek architecture. The palace is made up of a central edifice and two side structures. It's main facade contains 11 entrances with vaulted passageways and lateral wings.

The stone frieze above it resembles nothing more than a bolt of shear lace. This exquisite construction is ten feet tall and surrounds the entire palace. The 2,200 square feet of surface bears mute testimony to the innumerable technical difficulties faced and surmounted by its creators. The theme of the cross vault, making up the motif of the frieze is composed of 20,000 identical carved stones, each weighing several pounds.   In addition to this there are also 150 Chac masks three feet long and almost two feet high, numerous

A portion of the Nunnery Quadrangle and the Soothsayer Pyramid.

stylized serpents and altogether more than 20,000 different carved stones placed tightly together. How did they do it?

Near the entrance to the site is the beautiful **Quadrangle of the Nunnery**. First let me tell you that no nuns ever lived there. It wasn't a pleasure palace where vestals enjoyed the wild life prior to their sacrifice to Chac either. Very probably the "nunnery" was once a kind of elitist boarding school. Its architecture is distinguished by edifices at the four cardinal points each of which opens onto the center courtyard.

The northern edifice with its 13 double rooms may have been reserved for the most prestigious of the young lords. It's the largest and most important structure in the quadrangle and is flanked by two diminutive temples, one being the **Temple of Venus**. Some of the lintels are original and the top of the door wall is a false front of intricately carved huts and Chacs.

The eastern edifice is the simplest and the best preserved. Here the lattice pattern flares elegantly upward toward the top of the building where the head of an owl—the omen of death—is inserted.

In the western edifice the ornamental motif is an imposing throne bearing a figure with the head of an old man and the body of a turtle. On the frieze, two plumed serpents reach out toward the corners of the facade with a human head in their open jaws. Other parts of the stone sculpture depicts men with tattooed genitals.

The southern edifice in the quadrangle has eight rooms. Above the door of each is a stone sculpture of a *na* or *Maya cottage* looking exactly as they look today but for the inevitable Chac mask on the roof. On the ceiling are red handprints similar to the one at Tulum.

Is there a link between the *House of the Turtles* and the stone figure of the man who's half man and half turtle in the quadrangle? The house, located "next door," gets its name from a row of turtles crawling across the facade. The understated elegance, economy of line and balanced proportions of this building call to mind a classic Greek temple.

There are other ruins to explore: the pretty *House of the Doves* which is laid out in a manner similar to the *Quadrangle* and gets its name from its undulating roof combs; the *Ball Court,* a small affair thought to be a kind of training camp for Chichen Itza Olympics; the *Cemetery Group* and the *Western Group,* both as yet barely touched by archaeologists.

Phalli are very big in Uxmal. I just had to say it! The Empress Carlota was so impressed she wrote home about it. There's very little eroticism in Maya art or architecture. Uxmal is an exception. Ornamenting the building ironically called the *"Nunnery,"* is a frieze of naked men and the *Governor's Palace* contains a phallus of proportions stupendous enough to embarrass some visitors while amusing others.

In the background, covered mound of ruins illustrate ongoing encroachment of the nature.

Following an obscure little path on a dutiful pilgrimage to the *House of the Old Woman* — unfortunately this shrine to the woman who started it all is in shambles — I passed a sacred grove of stone known as the *Phallus*

Collection. Some are erect, others fallen, a kind of petrified forest of fertility. And that's really what it's all about. Fertility was all important in this drought-ridden agricultural area.

Nearby is the **Temple of the Phalli**, named for its unusual representations of this symbol. They were even used as water spouts. One can imagine their effect during the rainy season.

Which brings me back to that all important subject of rain. The mask of Chac is every-

The petrified forest—Uxmal.

where in Uxmal. It reaches out from friezes, fills in corners, and clings to the spaces above doorways. The Chac features — the sneering, half-open mouth exposing jutting fangs, the horns, globular eyes and snout like nose — were designed to be awesome. And they are.

They also bear a striking similarity to the Chinese t'oa t'ie mask of the Chang period. How tempting to search for some form of relationship between them despite the geographic separation and a time gap of some 2000 years.

Nearly 1000 years has passed since Uxmal was abandoned but Chac remains very much alive. In a land of little rain, he continues to control the agricultural destiny of the Maya. Despite the, at times, forcible efforts of the clergy to destroy him, Chac is a god who will not die, a deity still venerated in secret ceremonies.

GETTING THERE & WHERE TO STAY_____

The breathtaking ruins of Uxmal are located in the Puuc (pook) hills 50 miles south of Merida on Highway 261.   Any number of tours will take you there or you can easily travel the distance by car or bus.   There are five buses a day which leave the main bus station in Merida, the price nominal.

One night and two days at Uxmal are a must, but two nights and three days would be still better. This is a fascinating site surrounded by other attractions.

The closest hotel to the ruins is the **Villa Arqueologica**, another in the Club Med run chain.   If you're looking for typical Club Med "action," you won't find it here—the bar closes at 10; but, as at the other hotels in the chain, the ambience is attractive, the food and amenities adequate.   (Tel: 800 555 8842)

A tourist taking the safer descent down the Temple of the Magician.

Hacienda Uxmal remains my favorite. It has something to do with vibes. The place was originally built as a headquarters for the archaeologist excavating Uxmal more than eighty years ago and has been well maintained. Many of the large, airy rooms with their blocky 1930s furniture and ceiling fans are built around an expansive courtyard, an Edenlike abstraction from the sur-rounding jungle. Call 1-800-258-2633 for reservations.

The *Lodge at Uxmal* across from the ruins entrance has pleasant rooms and two swimming pools. (1-800) 235-4079; www.mayaland.com

A pleasant choice for the budget minded is *Hotel Mision Uxmal*, a bit farther from the ruins, but not too far. This one, too, has a pool and restaurant. (Tel: 800 451 8017)

The most delightful option of all is the *Hacienda Temozon*, a 30 minute drive between Hacienda Temozon and Uxmal (a pleasant place to stop) north on Carretera Merida-Uxmal. (Phone (01 800 021-7526 or 99/4443-637; fax 99/448-484.

The *Hacienda Temozon* is so special that presidents Clinton and Zedillo met there in 1999. Its 29 rooms are all in the original buildings and in homage to the past come equipped with Maya hammocks as well as beds, soothing ceiling fans as well as AC. The grounds are gorgeous with a spectacular pool.

The road between Hacienda Temozon and Uxmal is well maintained, its an easy drive, but an option would be to have the hotel van pick you up at the Merida airport. Once at the Hacienda, you could select from a smorgasbord of day trips that include Uxmal, Loltun caves, the Puuc ruins, a working sisal factory the colonial town of Izamal, Mayapan and private cenote swimming.

A pleasant place to stop for a bite between Hacienda Temozon and Uxmal is *Hacienda Ochil*. The lovely old hacienda dating from the 17th century, built on the ruins of a Maya settlement, has been turned into a delightful restau-rant.   The menu offers a wide variety of Yucatecan favorites cooked in exciting new ways. You'll also enjoy a museum and craft shop with working displays.

Uxmal may be a bit short on nightlife — the one attraction is the slightly inane, but still spectacular sound and light show — unless you count, as I do, the appeal of spending the night in a Maya ghost town. Anyway, the day time potential is dazzling.

The Arch of Labna.

The cave of Loltun with the two ladders. See lower right hand corner.

THE PUUC HILL COUNTRY
(pook)

. . . the road unrolls like a ribbon offering a comparatively effortless opportunity to experience a whole new dimension of Maya life and architecture. Like Uxmal, the cities of Kabah, El Sayil, Labna and Zlapak belong to the late Classic period and feature such Puuc elements as decorative clusters of columns and hallways of columns which once supported temple roofs.

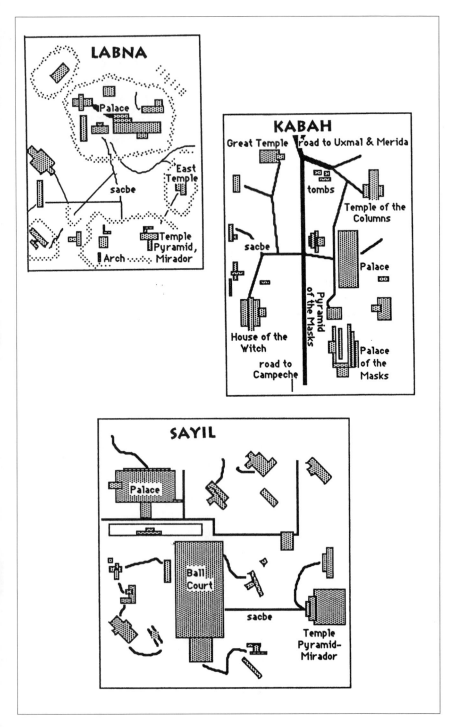

Thirty years ago I set off into the Puuc hinterlands with a jeep and driver. To me, it was a grand adventure. The driver was a Poncho Villa clone who packed a rifle and a machete. The machete came in very handy for the road was an overgrown track and the driver stopped many times to hack our way through the seemingly impenetrable walls of dense, brushy woodland.

Later as we shared a picnic lunch outside the temple at Zlapak, I tried to convey some of the excitement I felt. He grimaced, for him it was a hard way to make a living. A few weeks before he'd taken a party of anthropologists out to the site. As they'd climbed into the jeep for the return trip, a woman newly arrived to the area spoke up. "Okay, you've shown us how rough it can be, you've given us the jungle tour. Now take us back on the real road."

The wonder was still apparent in his eyes as he recalled the incident. After a weary sigh of resignation, he asked. "Do you imagine that I'd work so hard if there was any other way?"

It wasn't until 1978 that a real road was constructed linking this "new" network of Maya cities with their big sister Uxmal. Today the road unrolls like a ribbon offering a comparatively effortless opportunity to experience a whole new dimension of Maya life and architecture. Like Uxmal, the cities of **Kabah, Sayil, Labna** and **Zlapak** belong to the late Classic period and feature such Puuc elements as decorative clusters of columns and hallways of columns which once supported temple roofs.

Puuc, incidentally, refers to the late Classic period and to the slightly hilly country where this style of architecture flourished. These hill towns are still out of the way enough not to be crowded with tourists. They're intimate, less intimidating than Uxmal.

The surrounding jungle, though not of the "Tarzan" variety with tall trees blotting out the sun, has undergrowth so dense that it actually chokes out trees before they can grow tall. Trails lead past mounds of overgrown rubble, the remains of one-time Maya dwellings and temples where fallen idols wear spring bonnets of orchids. Climb to the top of one of these mysterious mounds and a vast chunk of southern Yucatan is yours for the viewing.

KABAH

Kabah—located 19 miles south of Uxmal—straddles Highway 261 The name, "He with a strong hand," is derived from a monumental stone figure of a naked man with a serpent in his hand which was found among the ruins. As is usually the case, the name was applied to the site long after the inhabitants had vanished.

Perhaps settlement here was an impressive experiment, one that proved useless in the long run. The ubiquitous Chac masks bear witness to the fervent prayers that were offered up to the rain god. The magnificent facade of the *Codz-Pop,* or **Temple of the Masks**, decorated as it is by row upon row of identical masks–250 of them–set so close together that there's hardly a gap between them seems to represent a colossal effort to bring the forces of nature under control.

This amazing structure which dominates the large temple complex on the east side of the site may have been placed there in gratitude. Before the temple is something more precious than gold or jewels– an ancient well still filled with life-giving water. This treasure was unique in Puuc country. Other settlements had to depend on choltunes, or man-made cisterns with their often inadequate supply of rainwater.

Where Uxmal exemplifies the essential simplicity and uncluttered lines of the Puuc style, some of the Chenes look of Chichen Itza seems apparent in the rich facade of the *Codz-Pop;* but, Chenes or Puuc, there's simply nothing like this anywhere in Mayadom.

Parts of the building, which once consisted of ten large rooms, have fallen away to betray the builder's technical secrets. The structure of the corbel or "false "arch is laid bare here. For all their architectural achievements, the Maya never discovered the principle of the true arch made with a keystone and many smaller fitted stones. Instead, they improvised with the corbel arch which consisted of a systematic placement in which each stone was cut longer than the one below it, so that a heavier weight above would press down and hold the lower stone in place. The longer stones, arching toward each other, formed a kind of vault.

Once you've seen *Codz-Pop* which means in Maya "rolled mat" or "Lord of the Mat" possibly for Chac's elephant snout, you've seen the highlight of Kabah, but there are still other things to explore. Close by the Temple of the Masks an overgrown path leads off into the jungle to more partially restored buildings and mounds covering temples waiting to be "discovered." A walk along this path will give you a sense of the way it used to be and the way it could be again–any time the highway department stopped cutting back the intrusive growth which creeps back almost before your eyes.

Another Kabah attraction is located across the highway. It's an impressive arch which once marked the beginning of a *sacbe* extending all the way to Uxmal. The 19th century explorer, John Stephens likened it to a triumphant Roman arch. What legions marched this way and when?

SAYIL

Sayil—Continue south 3 miles on Highway 261 to the new side road, Highway 184, Sayil is less than 3 miles further—partially restored, the 100-room *Palace* presents a completely new aspect of Maya architecture which reminds everyone of something different. Some say a Greek temple, others a Renaissance palazzo, still others a Babylonian ziggurat. To me, it has a distinctly Minoan feeling until I confront the extended Chac masks at corners of the frieze. Inside we meet an old friend, the Descending God — Spaceman whose likeness was first encountered hundreds of miles away in Tulum.

Palace of Sayil.

Off in the jungle behind the *Palace* is *El Mirador,* "the lookout." The pretty temple with its vaulted ceiling and slotted roofcomb is situated on the highest point of the highest pyramid.

Beyond El Mirador is a *stela* bearing a phallic figure of monumental proportions. The guides keep telling me that the Maya didn't go in for this sort of thing. Perhaps it's unique in more ways than one.

ZLAPAK

Zlapak (Shlah-pawk)—3 miles down the road–the name means "old walls" and they are. Despite the new road, this tumble down temple doesn't seem to have changed a bit since I saw it twenty-five years ago—or probably John Stephens' visit in the early 1840s.

Once again one sees tier upon tier of masks, collonettes and Chac noses. Nearby is the old jeep track, almost overgrown but still offering access to abundant bird and bug life and an opportunity to explore further.

LABNA

Labna—3 miles farther down 184—is believed to be the architectural prototype of Uxmal. The lavishly ornamented *Arch of Labna*, a far grander structure than the better known *Kabah arch*, was once a passageway leading to a courtyard surrounded—as in Uxmal's Nunnery Quadrangle—by edifices that no longer exist. This is the largest and most ornate archway known to have been built by the Maya.

Other Labna structures include *El Mirador*, another "lookout" on top of a pyramid. This one has rounded corners at its base similar to those at the Temple of the Magician. A closer look at the pretty, airy building reveals a macabre touch—a row of death heads carved into the roofcomb

The *Palace* is distinguished by a *chaltune* built into its second story. Thus far, 60 chaltunes have been located here indicating that this abandoned site once had a sizable population.

LOLTUN

Loltun— A little over 18 miles past Labna on the way to Oxkutzcab (that's ohsh-kootz-kahb) are the *Loltun caves*, the largest known network of caverns on the Yucatan Peninsula.

A visit to Loltun, which means "stone flower," is a kind of time trip. Each step of the ascent is a shift backward toward a primordial past. Along the way there are artifacts such as *choltunes* placed strategically about for catching rain water and metates or corn grinders.

Myriad formations of *stalactites* and *stalagmites* bear striking resemblance to any number of things from the Virgin of Guadalupe to a phallus. One cavern is a Hugh Hefner extravaganza comprised of thousands of mammaries. Searching for all the possibilities adds to the "guided fantasy" feeling about this excursion.

When tapped, giant floor to ceiling columns give out a resonant hum: "Lolltuuuuuuuuuun." There are *carvings* in the natural stone walls and handprints thought to date from 2000 BC are outlined in black. A complete set of *mastodon bones* has been discovered here and a large stone head. There's also a cave with *two ladders,* one leading out of the cave complex and another leading to a ledge with a small doorway leading to a ritual chamber.

These caves have twice sheltered the Maya; first in ancient times and later as a fortress and refuge during the *War of the Castes.* Its intriguing to speculate about the lives of the cave dwellers while walking through what must have been their very living rooms; but the most exciting aspect of the tour is yet to come.

There is light at the end of the tunnel! Finally the passageway emerges into a two-story high cavern open to the sky at the top. Ancient, towering trees thrust their way up through the sunny opening and dust-flecked shafts of sunbeams light up the black recesses of the cave. Leafy green vines twine their way down into the immense chamber from above, often wrapping themselves about the exposed roots of the trees. The sense of having emerged from a time capsule into a prehistoric era is a mystical experience not soon to be forgotten.

But there's more, yet another puzzle to ponder. Two American researchers, anthropologist Michael d' Obrenovic and archeologist Manson Valentine, decided to explore the vast uncharted areas of the cave system. Both had an unexplainable sense of danger. D'Obrenovic took photographs. Despite his previous success in photographing caves, only one out of nine shots turned out. The ninth picture revealed a swirling mass of glowing energy that illuminated the entire passage.

D'Obrenovic had no explanation for the phenomenon "unless the old legends are true and we somehow succeeded in photographing an energy force left by the old priests to guard the sacred area." Scientists endeavoring to X-ray the Great Pyramid of Egypt encountered this same mysterious force field.

The jungle encroaches on Palenque.

PALENQUE
(pa-len-kay)

Only partially redeemed from the jungle, Palenque remains a magnificent sight which rivals the sanctuary of Apollo at Delphi. Gleaming like alabaster, it lies upon the dark flanks of the Tumbala Mountains in the midst of a rain forest.

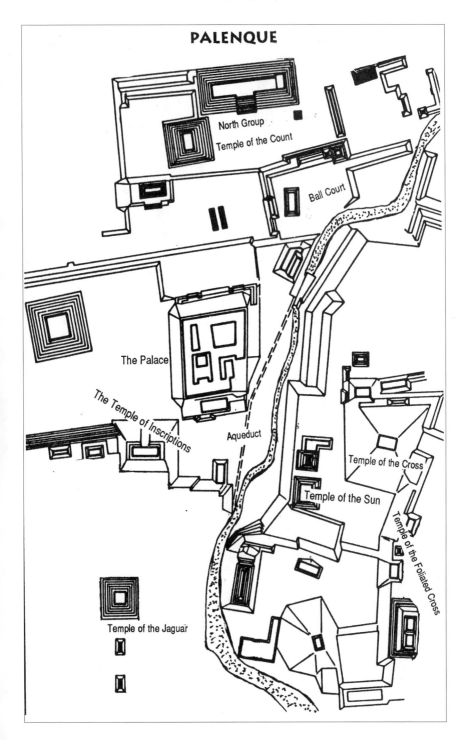

PALENQUE

In 1773 a bored priest heard a wild story that made his day.

A passing Indian told of an abandoned city deep in the jungle–a city far different, grander, more beautiful than anything he'd ever seen or heard about. The city, he explained, was located in the jungle near the village of Santo Domingo del Palenque.

Father Ramon de Ordonez y Aguilar, canon of Cuidad Real (now San Cristobal de las Casas), could scarcely believe the tale. A little more than 200 years before the great Cortes himself must have marched right by the place and somehow missed it. Impossible as it all sounded, the idea of being the official discoverer of such a relic was titillating. He decided to mount an expedition to discover the truth for himself.

Father Ordonez's dutiful parishioners carried him the sixty miles to Santo Domingo del Palenque in a sedan chair. Presumably after a brief rest, they picked him back up and hiked another eight miles into the dense jungle.

The sight that awaited was stunning. Here was the most beautiful Maya city of all, each building a work of art, intricately carved stone with the elegance of marble against a backdrop of emerald green.

As Father Ordonez studied the ruins — surely the most lovely in all of Mexico, if not the world — he recalled a legend about a charismatic leader named Votan who'd come to the area many hundreds of years before from across the Atlantic Ocean. The story was said to have been recorded by Votan himself in the Quiche dialect which the mysterious stranger had learned. The chronicle told of how he had come with his followers, introducing ideas and customs to the natives who offered their daughters in marriage. Ordonez's predecessor had burned this remarkable manuscript along with everything else pagan in an *auto de fe* very like that of Bishop de Landa. Fortunately a few sections had been copied for the select eyes of those deemed devout enough to read without fear of corruption. Ordonez had been one of these.

Puzzling over the account that had so fascinated him in his youth, Ordonez remembered that Votan had written of a sea journey from his far away homeland, Chivim, via the "Dwelling of the Thirteen." After reaching the Yucatan Peninsula, he'd journeyed up the Usumacinta River and founded a great city.

This must have been the city, Ordonez decided, surveying the magnificent ruins before him. He later theorized that Chivim was Tripoli in Phoenicia and the "Dwelling of Thirteen" must have been the Canary Islands. Since Votan's symbol was the snake, Ordonez named his find the "Great City of Serpents." Maya archaeology began with his preliminary investigation.

Ordonez's story piqued the curiosity of King Charles III of Spain who, in 1787, ordered a systematic exploration of the ruins.   The assignment fell to an unlikely candidate.   Don Antonio del Rio, later recalled as "wafting through the jungles of Palenque an aroma of the latest fashionable scent," was a true dandy refusing to forsake his three cornered hat and powdered wig.

Despite his dress sense, Del Rio was a man of action.   Maybe too much action.   He very quickly hired 200 Indians who hacked away at the ruins with their axes and machetes. As his proud reports states, "By dint of perseverance I effected all that was necessary to be done so that ultimately there remained neither a window nor a doorway blocked up; a partition that was not thrown down, nor a room, a corridor, court, tower, nor subterranean passage in which excavations were not effected from two or three yards in depth." Imagine the reaction of today's painstaking archaeologist.

Del Rio's account, which found its way into print 25 years later, was the first published book on Maya archaeology. He concluded that the ruins   at Palenque were probably made by early Roman colonizers, but didn't rule out a Phoenician connection.

The next adventurer to appear on the scene was by far and away the most colorful.   Jean-Frederic, Count de Waldeck, had been the student of artist Jacques Louis David, the friend of Lord Byron, Beau Brummel and Marie Antoinette (whom he'd visited in prison shortly before her execution), had campaigned with Napoleon in Egypt, then become a pirate preying on British shipping in the Indian Ocean.

Now at a time when others might have looked forward to a quiet, comfortable retirement, de Waldeck determined to explore and sketch the ruins of Palenque. Many would have thought sixty-four a bit old for a jungle expedition into an area of hostile natives and incredibly difficult terrain but surely not de Waldeck who would—in his nineties—turn down a handsome cash settlement in favor of an annuity.

Reaching Palenque at last, de Waldeck selected the prettiest ruin and the most nubile of the village ladies and set up housekeeping. (The ruin is still referred to as the "Count's Temple.") From this vantage point he produced ninety extraordinary drawings.

John Stephens, the next adventurer on the scene, happened upon de Waldeck's name scribbled on the wall of the Palace beside the drawing of a woman, (probably the mestizo mistress) with the date 1832. De Waldeck's drawings were incorporated into a book in which he concluded that the Chaldeans and Hindus were responsible for the construction of Palenque. The book was eventually published in 1866 when the incomparable count was 100 years old.

So many theories, so much conjecture, this much is known today: Palenque, uninhabited since the ninth century, but still pulsating with a curious

vitality, dates from the Classic period. Its rise from minor ceremonial center to metropolitan city came relatively late and owes much to one remarkable ruler, Pacal (A.D. 603-83), and his successors, Bahlum and Kuk. These three seem to have formulated the official Palenque mythology based on a divine origin for the royal dynasty and on the supernatural passage of power from one ruler to the next.

Unlike every other Classic site, Palenque has no carved stelae. Dated inscriptions are incorporated into the bas-reliefs and the high-relief stucco decorations. Many of the motifs are strikingly similar to those found in Buddhist countries.

A sculpture in the Palace courtyard.

According to tradition, the Buddha's third week of meditation was spent under a sacred tree. It was during this time that a serpent spread his hood to shield the divine meditator from the heat of the sun. For this reason, the sun, the tree, and the serpent are three of the most sacred symbols of the Buddhist. They are equally sacred to the Maya. The similarities don't end here. Both Buddhists and Maya believe that the world has been destroyed four times with a fifth destruction yet to come.

Only partially redeemed from the jungle, Palenque remains a magnificent sight which rivals the sanctuary of Apollo at Delphi. Gleaming like alabaster, it lies upon the dark flanks of the Tumbala Mountains in the midst of a rain forest.

The approach is from the west. The *Palace* comes first into view, and then, to the right is the *Temple of the Inscriptions*. Various little temples lie to the east including the *Temples of the Sun*, the *Cross*, and the *Foliated Cross*. The *North Group*, a series of edifices (to the north of the Palace) includes the *Temple of the Count*. A pre-Columbian aqueduct directs the waters of the Otulun, a stream, to the center of the city, the only example of this kind of construction in Maya civilization. In addition to these ruins there are literally hundreds more in the surrounding bush. The exposed part of the site is at most a half mile in extent while more ruins are known to extend for another six miles.

The *Palace* is a rectangular complex of broad stairways and numerous rooms, long corridors and a three-story tower, grouped around four large inner courtyards. This stunning building with its pagoda-like feeling contains 176 separate items of painting, stone carvings and stucco sculpture that have been called the finest examples of this ancient art in the world today. Themes of accession and death, divinity and royalty are never out of view.

This building, like so many others in Mayaland, is a kind of time machine. When the great Pacal died, it was arranged in such a way that from any vantage point in the Palace Complex, the sun at winter solstice appears to set into the earth at his tomb and the great temple constructed above it. Not only art and architecture, but the whole order of the universe were called forth to reinforce his religious and political ideology.

It used to be that no one thought that Maya pyramids were used for tombs but that was pre-Alberto Ruz Lhuiller. One day in 1948 this Mexican archaeologist was staring at the floor of the *Temple of the Inscriptions*. The floor differed from the others by reason of its flagstones which were beautifully worked and fitted together almost perfectly. Some were particularly large. One slab had a double row of holes bored into it, so that the heavy stone could be lifted. When Lhuiller investigated, he found that the floor appeared higher in places than the bottom of the walls.

The Temple of the Sun on the left and the Palace on the right—Palenque.

Realizing that another hidden room must lie below, he had the heavy flagstone lifted. Below was a passage blocked by sand and rocks. It took four field seasons before they reached the foot of the stairs. The concealed staircase led down into the interior of the pyramid. At the foot of the stairs the archaeologists found sacrificial offerings consisting of jade earplugs and beads, red shells and a perfect tear shaped pearl.

Another wall was removed and behind it were the skeletons of six young men. Eighty-two feet below the floor of the temple and six and a half feet below the base of the pyramid the passage ended. Or did it?

A closer scrutiny revealed that it was blocked by a triangular stone slab. On June 15, 1952 Lhuiller and his patient, hard working crew were rewarded when the last obstacle was removed and they saw before them the tomb of a Maya king–with all its priceless array of funerary gifts–completely intact.

This, they soon realized, was the tomb of Pacal himself. The great ruler and the attendants who'd accompanied him on his journey into the after-life, were buried with a splendor unique in the entire Maya civilization.

The tomb chamber itself was a large vaulted room containing nine great figures in stucco relief, slightly larger than life-size, forming a procession around the walls. In the center lay a sarcophagus with a huge elaborately carved stone lid. The skeleton inside was lavishly arrayed with jade jewelry which included a headdress, a necklace of beads in many forms, and elaborate, delicately incised jade earplugs.

At the time of burial Pacal, had been wearing a jade mosaic mask with inlaid eyes of shell and obsidian. In his hands he held great jade beads and in his mouth was another jade bead. Even more jade objects were twined about his feet. Red cinnabar had been sprinkled over the body, the jade ornaments and the interior sides of the sarcophagus. The color red was associated with the east and the rising sun and may have been symbolic of rebirth.

Today the treasures repose at the National Museum of Archaeology in Mexico City, but one can still descend into the tomb. Many find the covering of the sarcophagus particularly interesting, seeing in the intricate design the image of a man at the controls of a space ship.

Beyond this temple a narrow path leads off into the jungle. It's only a short walk to the *Temple of the Jaguar*, but once away from the sight and sound of the main cluster of buildings one finds a lost world of contemplation. The wall carving inside the temple shows a man seated with one leg in a lotus position while the other dangles from a splendid throne which is supported by the legs of a jaguar. Jaguar heads protrude from either side of the throne. The over all effect is decidedly oriental.

One of the most distant temples is possibly the most architecturally intriguing. The relief work in the *Temple of the Foliated Cross* is identical to a temple found in Angkor Wat in Cambodia. Add to this mystery the preponderance of lotus flowers in the wall designs throughout Palenque—a flower that did not exist in Mexico at the time the city was constructed. Puzzles and more puzzles. Latter day skeptics call Count de Waldeck's conclusions "fanciful," yet the striking similarities between two far distant cultures are difficult to explain away.

In this temple the constructural elements are exposed. Its layout is similar to the *Temple of the Sun* and the *Temple of the Cross* nearby. The central tryptich panel is in place depicting two priests, one tall and one short, worshipping a central figure thought to be a stylized version of the all important maize god.

The *Temple of the Count* still contains some excellent hieroglyphic panels by the central doorway. Inside the temple, three graves were discovered in a row, all sealed with slabs and lime. Upon investigation, each grave was found to contain a cache of rich funerary objects but no human remains.

Temple of Inscriptions—Palenque.

It's easy to understand how the Count de Waldeck came to select his "house," angled as it is in a manner that provides both natural air conditioning and a breathtaking view of the entire site. A fresh mountain stream flows close by; beyond it, ruins glisten like jewels against emerald velvet.

It's fun to sit on the count's front steps, alabaster stairs leading to his temple hideaway, and try to imagine the daily life of that amazing man and his woman friend. Perhaps this is where they sat at day's end watching the sun turn the old stones to burnished gold. Maybe while he sketched, she regaled him with local legends. It's possible that he offered her cognac; more likely, she introduced him to *balche*.

All we can know today is that they lived here together for two years . When Count Waldeck returned to Europe it was because he was gravely ill and may well have thought he was dying; but once back in Europe he made an amazing recovery. There were more adventures, amorous and otherwise. The count decided he was ready for marriage at 102. He died five years later in Paris, struck by a passing carriage as he paused to admire a pretty young woman.

GETTING THERE

The easiest way to reach Palenque is to fly into Villahermosa (a lively boomtown with a fabulous museum park filled with Olmec treasures). From here, you can catch a bus or rent a car. Palenque is less than an hour's drive on a good road. Once there, a car's not essential. Colectivos, little minibuses or vans, shuttle back and forth between town and ruins every 15 or 20 minutes literally for pennies.

The ruins are open from 8 to 5 daily, the price is nominal. If possible, go first thing in the morning, then return toward late afternoon. Or go for the whole day and take your bathing suit. There's a hidden pool near the tiny museum.

WHERE TO STAY & EAT

You'll love *Chan Kah Resort*   (tel: 916 34 511 00; website: chan-kah@palenque.com.mx) out on the "ruins" road — I surely did.   Each charming bungalow has a veranda overlooking a jungle stream.   Shallow, stone-lined pools in the large, leafy garden offer cooling relaxation. The food's good and so are the drinks — try the pollo pibil (chicken marinated in achiote wrapped in banana leaves and cooked on hot coals under the ground. Birding is great here, and a few guests have even claimed to have seen the elusive Quetzal bird. Chan Kah is located 3 km from the ruins. Colectivos headed to and from the site pass by regularly.

Hotel Palenque Nututun (Phone: 800 868 9718) on the Agua Azul road is an exotic alternative. The setting, on the *Rio Tulija,* is lovely. You'll find a dip in the river refreshing after a day of clambering up and down pyramids. The palm thatched dining room has a pretty river view. Be sure and insist on one of the newer rooms

The *Hotel Mision Palenque,* at the far eastern end of town on Avenida Hidalgo (Phone: 800 359 5672), one of a chain, is predictably adequate.

Rooms are clean and comfortable; there's a pleasant restaurant and pool. A mini van goes to and from the ruins four times a day.

Have heard good things about the *Howard Johnson D'Marco Palenque* (Phone: 800) 500-5020

Santo Domingo de Palenque— also known as *Palenque Village*—is located 8

A bas-relief from the Temple of the Foliated Cross—Palenque.

km from the archaeological site. It's a pleasant, friendly place to people watch. Enjoy the shopping possibilities, beginning with the *Casa de Artesanias Chiapeneca,* about a block from the square on Avenue Juarez. Then check out *Virgo* for a traditional Mexican dinner. A second floor restaurant at Calle Hidalgo 5, Virgo has a good view of the passing scene. A marimba band plays in the evening. Another possibility is *La Selva* on the "ruins" road — about a 10 minute walk from the colossal Maya statue in the town's center. Groups play tipico music and the palapa atmosphere is cool and inviting.

A mural at Bonapak

BONAMPAK
(bow-nam-pawk)

The figures depicted on these extraordinary paintings–the equals of any to be found in Crete, China or India—radiate aggression. Intellectual the Mayas most certainly were, but they were also just as implacable, just as ruthless, just as savage, just as human as any of the other tribes of the western hemisphere. Here at last was the full interplay of life forces only hinted at by the sculptured monuments of other Mayan cities.

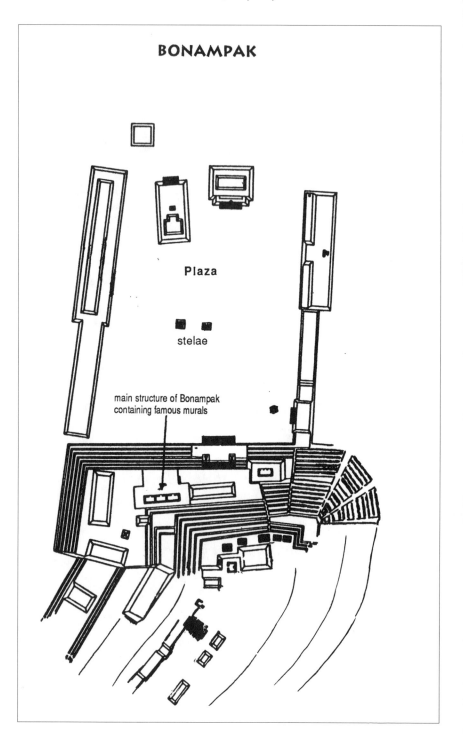

BONAMPAK

Plaza

stelae

main structure of Bonampak
containing famous murals

The jungle trail seemed to go on forever, aimless, constricted, morning steam rising from compacted vegetation. I paused, pushed back my straw hat and thought of Saturday matinees. Tarzan. King Solomon's Mines. Green Mansions. The African Queen.

Indiana Jones, where are you? I wondered. Didn't he know that it was me out here?

This was the stuff of daydreams surely, but I was too weary to indulge myself. The guide had disappeared around the bend and I hurried on, realizing that Bonampak was still a long way away.

It was a rough trail over grown with roots. Once I stumbled and found myself at eye level with a caravan of leaf cutters each carrying a parasol of green. Above me tiny monkeys no bigger than fists pirouetted, chattering derisively at my clumsy intrusion. Shafts of light pierced the canopy of trees as high as redwoods. Here and there a toucan with a banana yellow beak beat through the still leaves. The branches that closed in about me seemed black against the filtered sunlight.

The two ornithologists in our small party seemed to spend most of their time walking with their necks thrown back, heads cocked straight up, field glasses at the ready. They spotted numerous eagles, but it was I who pointed out the sacred quetzel bird—a flash of living jade.

I pushed on, and on and on, trying hard to keep pace with the others. For me, it was a kind of endurance test, every step an effort. Then suddenly dead ahead, an improbable looking tower of massive stones appeared. Emerging from a chicle forest of potential chewing gum, I confronted the incredible city of Bonampak.

This is more or less what must have happened in early 1946 when a group of chicleteros stumbled on the ruins by accident. Hearing their stories of a city with "painted walls," photographer Giles G. Healy prevailed on the United Fruit Company to mount a mini expedition. He reached the site on May 21, 1946.

The first thing that Healy discovered was that the city wasn't really "lost" at all. The Lacandon Maya had known of its existence for centuries and were still using the ceremonial center as a place of worship. God pots, censors and copal placed before the numerous altars bore mute testimony to recent devotions.

Approach to Bonampak.

Healy photographed all the standing buildings except one, which he didn't see because of the dense vegetation even though it was at the very heart of the site. Later that same year when the building was discovered, it literally made history.

Up until this time, the Maya had been considered not only the intellectuals of the new world but its pacifists. It had been pleasant to imagine them living in splendid isolation in their remote jungle retreats peacefully star gazing or working on their complicated calendric system oblivious or possibly immune to war.

One look inside the remaining building blew that notion forever. The walls and ceilings of the three inner rooms were covered with murals. The figures depicted on these extraordinary paintings—the equals of any to be found in Crete, China or India—radiate aggression. Intellectual the Maya most certainly were, but they were also just as implacable, just as ruthless, just as savage, just as human as any of the other tribes of the western hemisphere. Here at last was the full interplay of life forces only hinted at by the sculptured monuments of other Maya cities.

Taken together these three rooms form a continuous narrative depicting a raid on enemy territory, a counsel of victorious chiefs, the judgment of prisoners, and finally a sacrificial ceremony and victory celebration.

Figures are close to life-size and possess a remarkable sense of motion only momentarily arrested. The colors — vibrant reds, greens and yellows, a black that seems to shine against a backdrop of the famous Maya blue — are spectacular.

This was a classic fresco in which cement was applied to the walls and the original drawing executed immediately before they could dry. Then the artist's

A rendition of part of a mural from the Temple of the Frescoes, Bonampak

assistants — and there must have been many — applied the colors. It's believed by the muralist who copied the work for the Museum of Anthropology in Mexico City that the entire mural was completed in forty-eight hours, a continuous effort of artists and plasterers working simultaneously. The result has been compared to the Sistine Chapel.

The 270 figures are rendered with remarkable naturalism, some characters discernible in more than one scene. The sacrificial victims show anguish, the battle scenes bristle with sound and fury, the presiding lord and his lady are so regal in their style and bearing, so realistic in their arrogance that one expects at any moment to see a cool nod of dismissal.

But remarkable as these murals are as art forms, the statement they make about the Maya is of far greater significance. Here is a kind of true confession. The marauding warriors attacking nude, defenseless farmers depicted on the walls of Bonampak are a far cry from the mellow star gazers of earlier conjecture. The treatment of the captives pictured on the temple walls belies the theory that ritual sacrifice was forced on the Maya by Toltec invaders. This revolutionary discovery altered the whole concept of Maya society. After more than forty years, literature is only just beginning to come to terms with this change.

In their book, The *Blood of Kings: Dynasty and Ritual in Maya Art,* (Kimbell Art Museum, Fort. Worth, Texas, 1986), art historians Linda Schele and Mary Ellen Miller wrote, "Blood was the mortar of ancient Maya ritual life. Rulers were viewed as descendants of the gods. It was considered their duty to bleed and mutilate themselves on ritual occasions (a scene depicted in the murals) to cement their divine lineage and sustain the universe. Before going to war, for example, a king would puncture his penis with a stingray spine or a lancet made of jade or obsidian, while his queen would run a thorn-encrusted rope through her tongue. The trauma of massive blood loss induced hallucinations in which royalty contacted the gods and dead ancestors."

Though exposure to light since their discovery has caused the murals to fade, they remain one of the world's great art treasures; and one can see an excellent reproduction of their original glory at the Anthropology Museum in Mexico City.

At the foot of the terraced hill below the temple is an enormous stela cele-brating the warrior king of the murals, Jalach Huinic. He holds a spear in his right hand and a religious mask in his left. Two representations of the maize god adorn the lowers sides of this carved stone.

The rest of the site is interesting, a remote jungle outpost with a variety of tumbling temples covered with curious red moss, stone idols wearing spring bonnets of orchids, and stelae which tell chilling stories of blood sacrifice. There are three ways to get to Bonampak: the exciting, grueling, you wonder why you did it way like I did, flying in from San Cristobal de las Casas by bush plane, or ordering a van to pick you up from your Palenque hotel   All these options and a trip to Yaxchilan can be arranged by calling 1-800-451-8017.

SIDE TRIP
to a remote Lacandon village

The side trip is a four hour journey over rough roads. From there it's a five-mile walk into the jungle. An excellent dinner of venison, tortillas, beans and beer was served in the village where we spent the night. It was a choice of hammocks or pup tents. The ground was hard without padding (I opted for the tent) and the night cold. It wasn't an easy experience, but I wouldn't have missed it.

The Lacandon Maya are a splinter group, descended from rebels who fled the conquistadores more than 400 years ago taking refuge deep in the jungle — where they still live. The Christian Maya in Yucatan call their heathen cousins "gentiles." The Lacandons ignore the distinction. The Yucatecs, they say, merely have "different saints."

A visit to a Lacandon village is a journey into another time. The compound where I stayed was made up of five chosas, palm-thatched roofs supported by poles but without sides. The largest one was the kitchen, the others were used for sleeping.

Life is primitive. The men still hunt with bows and arrows, the arrows tipped with parrot feathers. The women grind corn on stone metates and weave cloth on small back-strap, horizontal looms. The concept of unisex would be nothing new to these people. Both men and women wear only one garment, a loose, white, knee-length gown which hangs about the ankles. Men, women and children all wear their hair shoulder length, making gender determination difficult for a stranger.

Obviously they know who's who, for this is a strongly patriarchal society. It's the man's responsibility to propitiate the gods. One means of doing this is to feed them. Before the family begins to eat, the male head of the household places food and an occasional cigar before the statues of the family gods. This ritual is not simply a prelude to a particular meal, but a means of sustaining the gods so that they can continue to provide food for the family.

The Lacandon Maya pay homage to their gods with incense as well as food. After a time the "dead" incense burners are taken to a special burial ground when obsequities are transferred to new ones — just as Hindus do with their images when a term of service is over.

Entrance to the labyrinth—Yaxchilan.

YAXCHILAN

(yash-ee-lawn)

Yaxchilan has yet to be excavated. The Mexican Government guards the site's virginity carefully. No one goes far without a guide, though it's hard to imagine anyone wanting to. The jungle with its indefinable scent of ferns, leaf mold and green life is particularly dense here. Getting lost could be fatal.

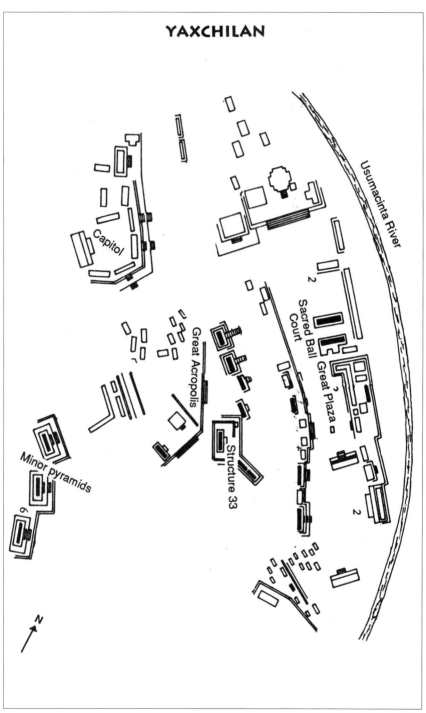

YAXCHILAN

Whether you fly in by bush plane or travel as I did by dugout canoe, the journey is a grand adventure.

The mighty Usamacinta River which divides Mexico from Guatemala is flanked on either side by the largest surviving rain forest in Northern America. Giant mahogany trees rising as high as 150 feet and sacred ceibas with tall straight trunks leafed at the top like umbrellas are silent sentinels guarding the banks. Orchids grow everywhere, begonias are waist high. This is truly the forest primeval.

A long, mahogany dugout with an outboard motor had taken me down river. Aided by the current it took just under three hours, a triumph of white water navigational skill. Varying depths and a jagged, uneven bottom make for dangerous pulsing currents and boiling rapids. There were exciting glimpses of bands of wild monkeys, of toucans and eagles. I watched for alligators–remembering that earlier explorers had written of hearing their teeth chomping at night. I didn't see any. Nor did I spot any Guatemalan guerrillas, though our progress was surely monitored from their side of the river. The Usumacinta traverses a tangled region, ecologically and politically. Aggressive Marxist forces have found the remoteness well suited to their survival. For centuries the name has been synonymous with trackless impenetrability.

At last the dugout headed for a sandy spit. Just above it was a small compound where the caretaker lives. Only a few yards beyond the jungle begins. Beyond that lies Yaxchilan, the "lost" city of my dreams.

Yaxchilan has yet to be excavated. The Mexican Government guards the site's virginity carefully. No one goes far without a guide, though it's hard to imagine anyone wanting to. The jungle with its indefinable scent of ferns, leaf mold and green life is particularly dense here. Getting lost could be fatal.

Despite the almost daily efforts of caretakers to keep the bush at bay, Yaxchilan lies uneasily before the jungle juggernaut. Tree-size roots extending down through roofs, walls and subterranean chambers, tear apart massive stones. Strangler vines creep over balustrades, through corbeled arches, binding statues of Chac, enshrouding figures of dead monarchs in leafy winding sheets.

Believed to have been a city of seers, Yaxchilan remains a place of brooding mystery. A narrow, rocky path leads through the jungle past the small airstrip emerging before two crumbling pyramids. Four pitch black entrances in the second structure lead into a labyrinth. The purpose of these inter-connecting chambers is unknown.

What we *do* know about Yaxchilan is that it was built during the Maya Golden Age, 200-900 AD, and reached its apogee during the 8th century under the governorship of Jaguar Shield and his son, Bird Jaguar. Their signatures are prominently placed throughout the site. (Jaguar Shield depicted by a jaguar profile, his son a slightly smaller jaguar with quetzal feathers exploding from his forehead.)

Emerging from the labyrinth, you're confronted by the grim specter of sacrificial stones and the grand vista of the central courtyard. The topography of Yaxchilan's riverside location ruled out the strict geometric configurations that characterize most Maya ceremonial centers. The effect here is more organic than monumental.

There are eighty-six known structures. Some are located on the hill near the river, others are found on still higher elevations. The labyrinth remains the most intriguing. Even today the Maya regard caves as entrances to the underworld and avenues of communication with the gods. During Yaxchilan's heyday this must certainly have been the heart of the peoples' religious devotions, magic rituals and secrets.

This is a ceremonial center filled with mystical symbolism. A reoccurring artistic theme throughout is one of blood letting–known to have induced altered states of consciousness. (A similar practice is still employed by the Hindu devotees of the deity Kali.) Near the labyrinth is the Jaguar Temple where one can see a carving of Jaguar Shield sitting in an eternal lotus position. Another remarkable stela depicts a woman serving a serpent, the serpent is thought to represent the beginning of new life.

Structure 33, considered by some to be the most interesting temple at Yaxchilan, is situated on a small rise overlooking the main plaza. Before the doorway is a headless statue of a humanized feline figure in a posture of worship. Many years ago mahogany cutters broke off the head- which can be seen a few feet away.

Lacandon Maya still frequent this holy city of their ancient culture burning copal and offering prayers to the time when the head and body will be reunited. They believe the sacred union will mark the destruction of this world and the beginning of a new one signaling the rebirth of the old gods and the final flowering of the ancient Maya culture.

Sitting in the central plaza of this forgotten city of seers almost anything seems possible. The angry roar of howler monkeys punctuates the incessant hum of cicadas. It's a long, long way from anywhere.

Typical of the baroque Colonial architecture of Campeche.

CAMPECHE
(kam-pech-ee)

A charming colonial town with narrow streets and baroque architecture, the city's landmark is its great seawall, part of the original fortress that bordered the entire town protecting its inhabitants from pirates.

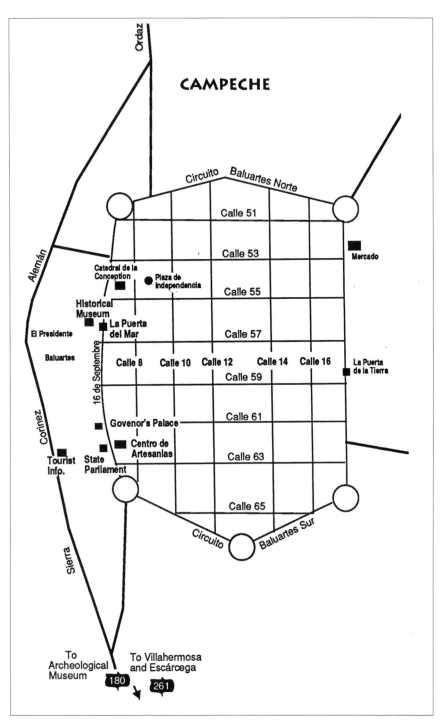

CAMPECHE

They tell an interesting tale in the old pirate town of Campeche. Perhaps it's true.

Campeche's always been a strategic port and a wealthy one. Everybody wanted the goodies inside. First came the Spaniards, then assorted pirates from France, Holland and England. Those who didn't come to steal wanted to trade. Ships arrived from all parts of the world and bars sprang up along the pier to accommodate sailors. The hastily improvised establishments could afford only copper spoons but these, when used to stir a drink, left an unpleasant taste.

Finally an enterprising bartender took to stirring his libations with a twig from a nearby tree. One day an English sailor, particularly pleased with his drink, asked its name. The Spanish bar tender, thinking he meant the tree's name, replied, "cola de gallo."

Translated into English this meant "cocktail." Only to think where it all began!

Campeche itself got its name from the Maya chief of the city, Ah-kin-pech. Such a tongue twister for the conquering Spaniards! Campeche was as close as they could come. A charming colonial town with narrow streets and baroque architecture, the city's landmark is its great seawall, part of the original fortress that bordered the entire town protecting its inhabitants from pirates.

All of the Gulf or Caribbean cities have a familiar litany of woes: invasions, occupations, rebellions, hurricanes, fires, etc., but in any contest Campeche would take the dubious prize in the Hard Times category. Conquered in 1540 by Francisco de Montejo, the younger, it quickly became a flourishing port. Too flourishing, it would seem. The city's wealth — and its isolation — made it a prime target for pirates.

Campeche was pillaged and burned, its inhabitants massacred not once but many times. It was the port of choice of every pirate who sailed the Spanish Main. In fact, on February 9, 1663 several actually joined forces, completely wiping out the city and killing everyone in sight.

If this essential port was to exist, something had to be done to protect it. Finally, on January 3, 1668, the cornerstone of a new walled city was layed.

The stout stone barricade, as high as a ship, had four gates strategically placed around the city, while also extending out into the water where other

gates permitted ships to sail into the fort. Only after the complex system of walls and barricades was finally completed in the latter part of the 17th century was the city relatively safe from marauders.

Luckily, Campeche kept its walls in good repair, because the War of the Castes in the 1840s brought yet another holocaust. With the uprising of the peninsula's Maya peasantry, Campeche was once again a besieged island of refuge for those of Spanish or mixed blood.

But times have changed. Now Campeche would like to be besieged — by visitors with a little money to spend. Isn't it time an outsider left some-

A remnant from pirate days.

thing behind? Well off the tourist track, Campeche remains with one foot in the past, the toe of the other edging into the present. The city of canons and cathedrals boasts a few modern touches with amusing nicknames, the Government Palace, for instance, known as "the jukebox" and the Legislative Palace or "flying saucer."

Campeche is a strolling town, somewhat reminiscent of Veracruz or New Orleans—there's even a lively carnival just before lent. Today, the most conspicuous relics of the pirate era are the remnants of the massive wall, studded with eight bastions that once sealed off the city. Inside *Baluarte* (bastion) *Soledad,* three blocks north of the sea gate on Calle 8, is an impressive collection of 1000-year old Maya stelae.

Baluarte San Carlos, south of the sea gate between Calle 8, the Progress Fountain and Avenue 16 de Septiembre, is now a government craft center. Don't miss the underground passageway in the San Carlos basement. It doesn't take much imagination to picture the hundreds of frightened women and children huddled in the dark, dank tunnel while above the shouts of the men, the boom of cannons and the smell of cordite signaled yet another battle in progress.

Much of Campeche is honeycombed with caves and tunnels, some natural, some man-made. Originally used as hiding places by the Maya, they were later employed by the Spaniards to escape the pirates. A principal emergency entrance located beneath the main altar of the Cathedral Concepcion leads to openings in many old houses as well as the various fortresses where those who were not taken by surprise sought refuge until the danger passed.

Baluarte San Miguel, with its drawbridge and moat (once said to have been filled with alligators) is the handsomest of the bastions. To reach the bularte, now a museum displaying pirate arms and portraits of the most infamous marauders, take the coast road S west until you come to a large statue of a man with a raised arm, a work called "The Resurgence of Campeche."

Archeologically speaking, Campeche's main attraction is *Isla Jaina,* north of the city and close to the coast. According to Sylvanus Morley, who discovered the site in 1943, Jaina was used by the Maya elite as an elaborate burial ground. It's here that the most beautiful Maya ceramics have been found along with vast quantities of jade. Small wonder the island has, until recently, been out of bounds to tourists.

Campeche has excellent handicrafts—including outstanding replicas of pieces found at Jaina—at enticing prices. But possibly the most pleasant pastime is sunset watching from the breakwater.

The food's good too. Known as the "Shrimp Capital" of Mexico, Campeche has many excellent restaurants. Besides the famous shrimp, local specialties include pan de cazon (baby shark) and *pescado empapelado* (wrapped fish)

.

____PEOPLE WHO KNOW THEIR PRIORITIES____

The Mexican Ministry of Ecology and Natural Resources rejected a proposal by an American developer to build a 131-house retirement village on the gulf coast in Campeche because the proposed project would threaten the nesting grounds of sea turtles.

WHERE TO STAY_____

Ramada Inn overlooks the sea on Avenue Ruiz Cortinez. The rooms are well appointed, the grounds charming and the food good. Reservations: 1-800-272-6232.

Baluartes, also on Avenue Ruiz Cortinez, is a personal favorite, possibly because it contains the elegant *El Olones* bar, named for one of the most notorious buccaneers. *L'Olonois* was a man who enjoyed combining business with pleasure, returning to Campeche again and again—first to pillage and then to dally with his beautiful Creole mistress. Reservations: 6-30-11.

The Colonial, a two-star alternative to the top two five-stars, was once the "Casa del Teniente del Rey"--the king's lieutenant or territorial governor. Today it's spotlessly clean, a great bargain. Located at Calle 14, #122. Reservations: 6-22-22.

Hotel Bulartes, Avenue 16 de Septiembre #128, has sea views and is close to the cathedral and town square. Phone: 981/6-39-11; Faz: 981/6-24-10.

Hacienda Blanca Flor (white flower) is an exquisitely restored 17th century estate. The hacienda occupies a special place in Yucatecan lore. Built originally as a Franciscan estate and monastic retreat, most of the high ceilinged rooms and Moorish gateways remain in tact. During the Caste War in 1848, defenders of the hacienda successfully fought of Maya rebels, stemming their advance toward Merida and possibly saving the capital from being overrun.

Then again, during the Mexican Revolution, Blanca Flor was the government of Yucatan's last defense in 1915 as it fought against the integrationist politics of the Federalistas. In 1915, in defiance of federal authority, hastily assembled militias drawn from Merida's middle class made a heroic stand at Blanca Flor. Surprising the advancing army, the ill-trained recruits held off the hardened Mexican troops for twelve hours, firing volleys from machine guns mounted on the chapel roof.

The hacienda's ancient church still shows vestiges of the fight. Blanca Flor was captured. Its defenders were all killed with the exception of one young man who somehow survived a "coup de grace."

Now restored, the 16-room inn recalls such events as the state visit of the Empress Carlota in 1865. The hotel offers an excellent restaurant, tropical gardens, a swimming pool, horses and bicycles. Sight seeing trips may be arranged. Located 75 kms from the City of Campeche and 88 kms from the Merida. Phone: 800 451-8017; local phone: 999 925 9655; e-mail: hblancaf@prodigy.net.mx

Another with a pretty sea view is *Hotel America*, Calle 10 #252. Phone: 981 1-25-94.

In my opinion, the most delightful of all is *Hacienda Uayamon*, built on the site of a ruined Maya pyramid. Two suites are in the Palladian style former workers hospital. Located at km 20 Uayamon-China/Edzna Highway. Phone 52 981 90-335: fax: 52 981 90-336.

WHERE TO EAT

The town has several excellent restaurants, all obviously specializing in shrimp. A favorite is the *Miramar* which also features a refreshingly unsweet margarita. (Corner of calles 8 and 61) The *Balneario Popular* on the beach is indeed popular and for good reason. *Cocteleria Morgan*, (Avenue Universidad #1) has atmosphere and an appealing menu that fulfills its promise.

GETTING THERE

Campeche is located on the Gulf coast, 190 km. southwest of Merida and 444 km northeast of Villahermosa (across the Tabasco border) on highway 180. It can also be reached by flying Mexicana Airlines from Mexico City.

Deer roam free among the Olmec statues.

VILLAHERMOSA
(vee–a–hair–mosa)

The heads, full lipped, round-cheeked and sensual, were found in the coastal swamps by oilmen and moved to Villahermosa.

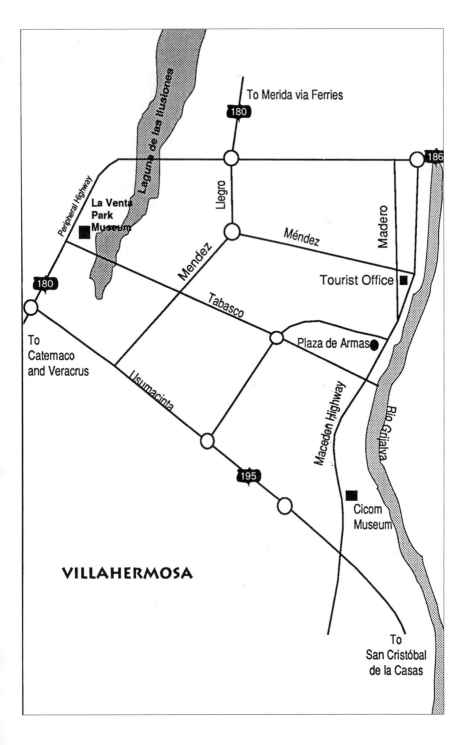

If travelers stop at all in Villahermosa, it's to see the "big heads." The town is known primarily as the gateway to Palenque. Most drive in, refuel and drive out; or fly in, rent a car, hop a bus, and take off. The lure of Palenque, surely the most gorgeous ruin in Mexico — if not the world — is that potent.

Sometimes, particularly if this is a second trip, one finds time for the colossal stone mega-faces carved by the Olmecs, often called the "Mother culture of Mesoamerica," who thrived here from 800 to 200 B.C.

The heads, full lipped, round-cheeked and sensual, were found in the coastal swamps by oilmen and moved to Villahermosa, where they are exhibited in an outdoor museum, *Parque La Venta*. Inside this mini-jungle — part zoo, part open air museum, part park, pathways wind past nature exhibits, carvings and the famous heads, 20-ton monoliths brought by the park's founder, the late poet and anthropologist, Dr. Carlos Pellicer. The original Olmec site of La Venta, some 140 km. down the Coatzacoalcos — Villahermosa Highway, has only a few small pyramids.

Before each exhibit a bench has been placed for viewing and contemplating. There are 28 dramatic sculptures including a 30-ton altar with the face of a monkey sculpted in basalt somehow transported by its Olmec creators for more than 100 miles. There are several other stone altars with human figures emerging from niches, some of them holding struggling children. Grim possibilities to ponder.

Nearby two jaguars prowl, their golden eyes watching every move of passersby just outside their large enclosure. Many other wild animals roam free, such as coatimundis spotted feeding behind a stela or an agouti sniffing among the trees.

But what of the city of the "big heads"? What of Villahermosa herself?

Capital of the state of Tabasco, the city appears to have been born under the sign of change and progress in the lowlands along the Grijalva and Usumacinta rivers. Mexico's largest rivers, they discharge an annual volume of 100 billion cubic meters of water.

The economic drive of the region stems from pre-Columbian times. The abundance of cocoa then prized as money and later recognized by the Spaniards as an exchange commodity enabled the Maya-Chontals to become both successful merchants and experienced navigators. In their enormous log vessels that held up to 40 men and all their merchandise, they sailed to what is now Central America, Cuba and Columbia.

This huge Olmec head measures over 8 feet tall.

Then along came Cortes.

Following his victory over the natives in 1519, the conquistador commemorated the event by hacking gashes in the trunk of a sacred ceiba tree before laying out the town with four districts around a central plaza and establishing Francisco de Montejo senior (later conqueror of Yucatan) as mayor. Leaving behind a statue of the Virgin Mary to "protect and enlighten the residents of the area for all the centuries to come," Cortes marched off in search of other cities to plunder.

At the center of Mexico's vast new oil fields, Villahermosa has recently been rediscovered. Since 1980, a village of 12,427 inhabitants has grown to a metropolis of more than 500,000 — a mini Mexico City smack in the midst of a jungle. One of the subsequent innovations is *Tabsco 2000*, a series of new buildings which includes a planetarium, theater, cultural center, convention center and a state-of-the-art shopping mall.

Second only to Parque La Venta in interest is **CICOM** (Centro de Investigaciones de las Culturas Olmeca y Maya), an investigation center for the Olmecs and Maya cultures. Its star attraction is the elegant *Museo Regional de Antropologia Carlos Pellicer Camara* with antiquities from the Maya, Olmec and Toltec cultures selected for their esthetic value.

WHERE TO STAY

Hyatt Villahermosa has undergone a 1.8 million renovation of all guestrooms as well as the Snob Discotheque. Rooms were completely refurbished using natural woods and native weavings. The effect is harmonious and lovely. The hotel, at Avenue Juarez, is located in the business district close to Parque La Venta. The restaurant is most probably the best in town, but also the priciest. Reservations: 1-800-233-1234.

The *Camino Real Villahermosa* (993 316 4400), Hyatt Villahermosa (993 320 1234) and Best Western Villahermosa (993 314 4466) come highly recommended.

GETTING THERE

Considered the gateway to central Mexico, it's hard to avoid Villahermosa if traveling by car. Highways from all directions converge there. Coming from either Vera Cruz or Campeche take the coastal road, Highway 180. There is also an inland road, Highway 186, that links Villahermosa with Campeche. From San Cristobal de las Casas and points south, take Highway 190.

Two bus lines, the ADO (first class) and Central de Autobuses de Tabasco (second class) offer transportation to and from any part of Mexico.

The busy airport links Villahermosa not only with Mexico City, but other major Mexican centers.

The church at Chamula. Photo by Vern Appleby.

SAN CRISTOBAL
DE LAS CASAS

(san cris–to–ball day–las cah–sahs)

*Over the years, San Cristobal
de las Casas has quietly become a mecca
for discriminating travelers.*

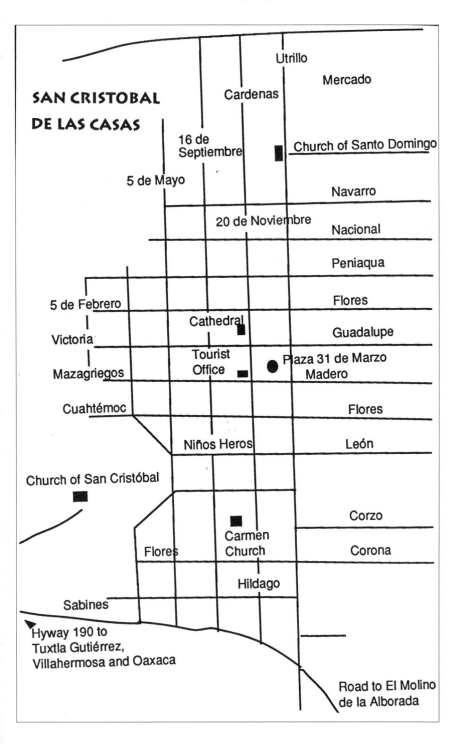

SAN CRISTOBAL
DE LAS CASAS

Utrillo

Mercado

Cardenas

Church of Santo Domingo

16 de
Septiembre

5 de Mayo

Navarro

20 de Noviembre

Nacional

Peniaqua

5 de Febrero

Flores

Cathedral

Guadalupe

Victoria

Tourist
Office

Plaza 31 de Marzo
Madero

Mazagriegos

Cuahtémoc

Flores

Niños Heros

León

Church of San Cristóbal

Corzo

Carmen
Church

Corona

Flores

Hildago

Sabines

Hyway 190 to
Tuxtla Gutiérrez,
Villahermosa and Oaxaca

Road to El Molino
de la Alborada

San Cristobal de la Casas is a strange town, brooding, cold, yet at times flamboyantly beautiful. It's also very macho.

Hiding as it does in the remote highlands of Chiapas, the southern most state in Mexico, San Cristobal de las Casas might well resemble Santa Fe one hundred years ago. There's still a strong frontier town flavor about the place. Indians stroll the streets like extras in Hollywood westerns. People watching is the main event, but don't stare too hard and never take pictures without permission.

What do you see? Sometimes a rare Lacandon, men and women like ghostly wraiths in long white sheets, black hair hanging to their shoulders. Only their walk betrays gender. These are the last Maya holdouts, still worshipping the old gods deep in the jungle despite the ruthless interference of Christian evangelists.

There are also Huistecos, the men wearing a curious costume consisting of a wide piece of cotton material placed waist-level at the back, and then crossed between the legs in numerous folds, diaper-fashion. The ends are brought up and fastened with a braided sash which dangles on either side. Their shirts are heavy cotton embroidered in geometric designs.

The Chamula Indian men wear white calf-length pants with black or white tunics, the color of the sleeves identifies the wearer's village. All wear goat horns suspended from their waists in which salt is carried to be used as a food additive or for barter.

But clearly it's the Zincantecan men who dominate the scene. They wear very short shorts intended to show off their well-formed, muscular legs. Zincantecans believe themselves to have the best legs in the world. Vying with this attraction are their pink tunics, vibrant with embroidery and tassels. As if this weren't enough, they flaunt wide, flat hats bedecked with beautiful ribbons. Married men wear their ribbons tied, while bachelors let their colorful silk streamers fly freely in the wind.

And a word of warning: though the hats, available in native markets, are a charming souvenir, wait until you get home to wear them. Zincantecans resent strangers, particularly women, wearing their finery.

As for the Indian women, their costumes are subdued. Whatever their tribe, they wear huipals, a straight, shapeless garment reaching to midcalf, in black or white and embroidered.

Over the years, San Cristobal de las Casas has quietly become a mecca for discriminating travelers. The colonial influence is immediately apparent.

The village appears to have changed little since the Spanish occupation. Two churches, carefully and somewhat threateningly placed by the conquistadors on two opposite hills, dominate the buildings that lie between, mostly one-story stucco houses painted in pastels.

The city gets its present name from Bishop Bartolome de las Casas who arrived on the scene in 1545. Conditions were so bad that the former capital of Chiapas was called Villaviciosa—"Vicious City." A humanitarian born out of his time, the bishop appears to have been the only Spaniard to champion the cause of the beleaguered Indians, chronicling the injustices of both the governor and the conquistadors to the very king himself in a series of blistering letters.

Market day at Chamula. Photo by Vern Appleby.

It was a most unpopular position, placing not only the bishop's career, but his very life in jeopardy, yet eventually his efforts bore fruit. It took twenty years--and even then the proclamation was largely ignored--but eventually the king did recognize the Indians as "humans." Once independence was finally achieved in the 19th century, the grateful natives, who possessed very long memories indeed, renamed the city in honor of their benefactor.

The good bishop has a modern-day successor in Sergio Castro, who maintains a private museum. Every evening at six, Castro opens the simple metal door of his residence at 32 Avenida 16 de Septiembre.

Inside, the dim lights and row upon row of coal-blackened staring statues make the initial effect slightly sinister. Castro quickly dispels that notion. Half pirate, half cowboy in his red bandana, boots and jeans, he's a warm and lively host welcoming all comers to view his amazing collections of costumes and rare native artifacts. A little posh, a very strong local cane liquor, distributed in paper cups is a warm up in more ways than one.

Castro's museum tours, conducted in Spanish, English, French and Italian (he speaks three Maya dialects as well) are free, though donations are accepted. One finds not only cash but pens, candy, gum even aspirin inside the donation box. All are used to improve the lot of the Indians of the surrounding area. A transplant from the rich northern city of Chihuahua, Castro has spent more than forty years helping them to build schools and grow better crops. He also treats burns, colds and epilepsy, even performs minor surgery — never charging a penny. Instead, the Indians show their appreciation with handiwork, mostly costumes, which fill three large rooms of his house.

Castro's museum tour is a splendid prelude to a side trip to the village of San Juan Chamula, a twenty minute ride from town. This visit is a must and should be timed for attendance at the Sunday market. Weavings are bright and beautiful, but the most fascinating sale items are terra-cotta candlesticks and incense burners, generally in the form of sacred bulls or horsemen. You will see their twins in use inside the famous chapel.

This nameless church that, from the outside, looks so innocent, so innocuous, so similar to hundreds of other Catholic churches in Mexico, is unlike any anywhere. Inside the white stucco facade with its faded aqua trim, is another world as primitive, as pagan as voodoo. There are no pews, the floor is strewn with aromatic pine needles. Against this lush green carpet hundreds of candles flicker eerily. In the background, the chanting goes on endlessly, incantation after incantation droning on and on seemingly into infinity.

It is here that the curanderos or shamen cast their spells. Priests and ministers seek to convert souls, curanderos attempt contact with an invisible, cosmic energy. By engaging this energy, they effect cures and ritual cleansings The cleansings (limpias) are to remove the individual's negative energy or what we might call depression. The outward, ostensible tools of their trade are Cokes, chickens, posh — the liquor a holy symbolic substance as wine is to a priest.

I watched while a chanting shaman, seemingly in a trance, ran eggs over a woman's body to absorb her bad energy. Then he sprayed posh, from his mouth onto her head, passed a live chicken over the candles and ended by

A Maya screen at Sergio Castro's Museum. Photo by Vern Appleby.

sharing a spiked Coke with his client. The idea was to burp up the problem. Limpias are a lot cheaper than conventional therapy and certainly more fun.

Back in San Cristobal the colorful kaleidoscope of daily life continues. One can see Indians from every major village at the market, open every morning but Sunday. Stands, manned by Indians with tawny chapped faces and glittering gold teeth, contain everything from foodstuffs to candles to pottery. Quartz-like copal incense ("the crystal tears of the copal tree") provides a pungent aroma that seems to pervade not only the market but the entire town.

The delights of the market spill into the surrounding streets. The nearby plaza around Santo Domingo and La Varidad is a visual feast, weavings flooding the stones. On the street of the artesanias, Real de Guadalupe, you'll find embroidered vests, blouses, skirts, woven sashes, patchwork duffle bags in brilliant splashes of purples and pinks.

Rich embroideries and weavings will assault you, amber will beguile you. There are many opportunities to buy strings of beads on the streets. Are they "real"? Does it matter? They are beautiful and cost so little. Be certain to visit the amber museum and workshop at Plaza Sivan, Avenue General Utrilla No. 10 near the market. It is here that artists, using the crudest equipment, carve amber into exquisite jewelry and miniatures. Besides honey-toned earrings, necklaces, pendants and charms, one sees replicas of slinking jaguars and Maya gods.

The most unique item, an amber spider with a real incarnation of itself frozen inside, is almost a metaphor for the city itself. For all its brilliant beauty, there's a dark, brooding quality to San Cristobal. The historic mountain stronghold is magic, but the color is black.

GETTING THERE & WHERE TO STAY

Getting there: From Mexico City, Mexicana flies to Tuxtla Gutirrez where first class buses make the two-hour trip several times a day.

When to Go: Because of its mountain setting, San Cristobal is usually cold in winter and cool at night even in summer. Pack warm clothes if you're going between October and March and at least a heavy sweater any other time.

HOTELS— Staying at *Na Balom* is like staying in a museum. The common rooms and gardens are show places and each bedroom a mini-treasure trove. Other guests may well include journalists, archaeologists, anthropologists from around the world as well as artists in residence and Lacandons. For reservations, write: Na Balom, Vincente Guerrero 33, San Cristobal, Chiapas. Telephone: 967 678 1418.

Posada Diego de Mazariegos, formerly an elegant mansion, is now a charming hotel with many gardens. Most rooms have fireplaces, much appreciated on cold nights. 5 de Febrero No. 1. Telephone: 967 678 0833; fax: 967 678 0827.

Hotel Santa Clara is conveniently located on the main square. Avda. Insurgentes No 1. Telephone 967-678 1140. Fax: 967 678 1041.

Hotel Ciudad Real, also on the plaza, has a very pleasant restaurant. Plaza 31 de Marzo No. 10. 916 345 1285.

RESTAURANTS— A personal favorite is *La Langosta* specializing in seafood and regional dishes (Francisco I. Madero No. 9). La Galeria (Calle Miguel Hidalgo No. 3) serves an excellent chicken baked in honey and soy sauce. *Fulano's* (Francisco Madero No. 12) has an enterprising menu that lives up to its promise as does the upstairs restaurant, *Cafe del Teatro* (1 de Marzo No. 8) which specializes in crepes.

El Castillo dominates Xunantunich. Photo by Vern Appleby.

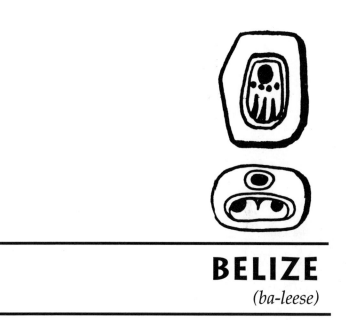

BELIZE
(ba-leese)

Expect a country tailormade for the adventure traveler, an unspoiled land of rich breathtaking beauty where humans are merely guests.

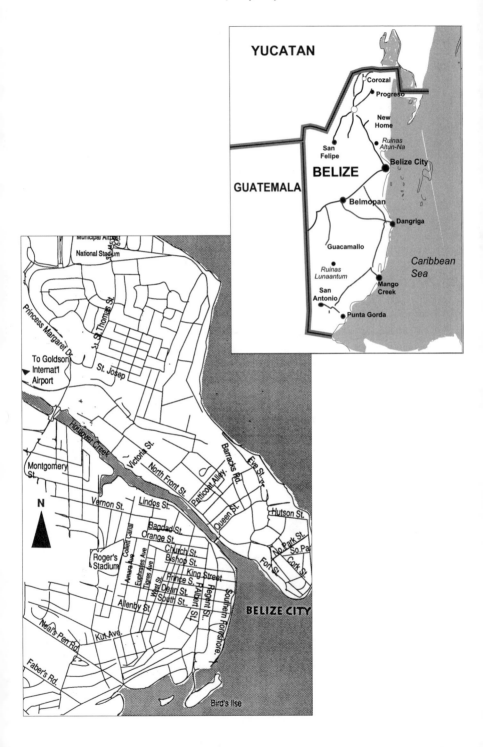

Travel Advisory: WALK SOFTLY AND CARRY A BIG LENS

In Belize they've learned that it's nice not to fool with Mother Nature — not only nice, but profitable too.   If you can't pinpoint Belize on your mental map—or even if you've never heard of it before, don't fret.   Many haven't. This tiny nibble between the borders of Mexico to the north, Honduras to the south and Guatemala to the west is a country that welcomes a new breed of tourist—one who happily goes on safari knowing that the only trophies will be memories.

The country now known as Belize was an early, highly advanced Maya culture center, its population in 700 A.D. eight times the current 262,000 census.   Why they chose to migrate north in 1000 A.D., no one knows. Europeans arriving some six hundred years later found only ruins. Before long the area was the haunt of pirates and slavers, later becoming a refuge for runaways and Confederate gun-runners.   Formerly British Honduras, Belize achieved independence in 1981, and today is the last fragment of the British Commonwealth in Central America, the smallest sovereign state on the continent.

Forget glamour.   Forget glittering casinos, tuxedoed waiters or duty free shopping.   Expect instead a country tailormade for the adventure traveler, an unspoiled land of rich breathtaking beauty where humans are merely guests. Much of the jungle owes its survival in part to the small population, but good intentions also figure in the grand design.   This is one of the few Latin American nations truly committed to controlled development.   A well conceived developmental plan calls for nature tourism—ecotourism. With almost nothing to export, Belize is well aware that its economic future, possibly even survival, lies with the three R's: rainforest, ruins, and reef.

In contrast to its Spanish speaking neighbors, the Belizean language is English—Creole English.   Expect to see Guatemalans vibrating to reggae rhythms, Haitians and Jamaicans munching tortillas. Talk about fusion! Its democratically elected parliamentary government, has a British clone judicial system in which judges wear the same white wigs and black robes found in English courts.   The only other remaining British tie is a very low profile army garrison. If a cultural tug of war exists for Belize, it lies between Latin America and Caribbean influences.   Blacks, descended from slaves brought from Africa in the 1700s, joined by more recent Caribbean arrivals, make up 60 percent of the population, a cultural melting pot that also includes Maya Indians, mestizos, Mennonites, Mexicans and numerous expatriates, primarily from the United States and Britain.

Belize City, home to one-fourth of the country's population, is the gateway to the rest of the country. For visitors, that includes the barrier islands, called cays (pronounced "keys"), a junglelike interior, a northern coast lightly

dotted with farms, a somnolent south coast. Not many linger in Belize City, though the town does have a crazy quilt charm uniquely its own: tin-roofed wooden shacks on stilts hung with bright potted flowers and fish nets, clapboard bungalows trimmed in gingerbread interspersed with a few colonial mansions. The pirate gene pool makes for aggressive hustlers and few visitors care to walk alone after dark. Part Bogart movie, part *Miami Vice*, Belize City is a one or two night town. Most visitors are eager to be off on inland safaris or to island dive resorts.

Mopan river excursion.

WHERE TO STAY IN BELIZE CITY_____

Tourists have discovered Belize. Can ramshackle chic be far behind? In the meantime, there are several charming, well appointed hotels.

At the **Radisson Fort George**, 2 Marine Parade, (Phone: 1-800-333-3333; fax: 027/3820 www.raddison.com) porters in pith helmets, faux-leopard carpets, rattan furniture and hardwood antiques recreate the British Raj feeling of the 1880s. The food and bar are excellent and the rooms are delightful.

The **Belize Biltmore Plaza**, 3 mile, northern highway, (Phone: 1-800-327-3573; fax: 023-2301, www.belizebiltmore.com) is another favorite. The décor has a charmingly Victorian feeling, accommodations are fresh and airy, with cool verandah views of lush tropic gardens. The food is good and if your time is limited, the hotel shop has some of the best buys in town.

The *Hotel*, a small family operated hotel popular with researchers and study groups. Located a block from St. John's Cathedral, and the Governor's General residence. Built in the early 1800s and three blocks from the city center, it offers private baths and good food. Website: www.hotelmopan.com.

The *Fort Street Guest House*, 4 Fort Street, (Phone: 023-0116; fax: 027-8808) is reasonable, atmospheric, kid friendly and has one of the best restaurants in town. Breakfasts are especially good here, so check it out.

No stay in Belize would be complete without a visit to the *Belize Zoo*, 30 miles from town on the Western Highway. The zoo was started in 1983 with 17 animals left from the filming of a natural history documentary. Since then the enclave has grown to include more than 100 animals all indigenous to Belize, many of them endangered.

Belize City

Visitors follow a forest path through habitat areas and observe animals in their natural environment. Guides offer personalized tours and, where it's safe, will even allow you to step into the cages to take photos or pet the animals. Yes, you really can scratch behind the ears of a 300 lb. Baird's Tapir or caress a friendly boa. Open daily 8:30am to 5pm. Entrance, $8 US. The zoo is located at Mile 30 on the Western Highway.

WHERE TO EAT

Don't leave town without having dinner at the *Smoky Mermaid* across the street from the Raddison Fort George. (14 Cork St.) Whether you dine at the romantic "great house" or outside in a courtyard shaded by large trees the seafood is exceptional. Try the "naked" lobster. This is an elegant restaurant with an extensive wine list.

Mango, 164 Newtown Barracks, seems to be everyone's favorite. The spicy conch ceviche is fantastic, so's the shrimp wrapped in coconut. Top it off with the dessert Ecstasy.

Macy's Café, 18 Bishop St., is not for the faint hearted. Stewed armadillo and iguana are featured choices on the menu. Harrison Ford professed to love it when he was making *The Mosquito Coast*. There's a happy, smiling photo of him posted alongside with a congratulatory note from the Bishop of Belize.

Don't miss the **Walkingstick Fine Art & Sculpture Gallery.** Despite the formidable sounding address(3 1/2 miles Northern Highway), it's right down town in Belize City, 1 block from the sea, catty-cornered from the Biltmore, and a few blocks south of the Flag Monument. Not only is the sculpture impressive, but so are the wood carving and other craft items.

AMBERGRIS CAYE & the "two" Belizes_____

San Pedro.

Actually there are "two" Belizes: the coastal section, long a well guarded secret of serious anglers and divers and the lush rain forests, known primarily to archaeologists, ornithologists and anthropologists.

The best known of the hundred or so cays and islets that fringe the coast is *Ambergris Caye*, a long, skinny island just minutes by plane from Belize City. The country's principal dive spot, it graces the northern end of Belize's famous barrier reef which stretches 175 miles—the entire length of the country.

Ambergris Caye has one town, *San Pedro*. Stroll down to the water's edge, ideally at sundown when the sun sinks low and orange. Watch the charter boats slide into port and know that big game fish lie in abundance just below the reef where the depth of the water drops quickly, and the sea turns from a tropical turquoise to dark cobalt blue. One hears lots of fish stories—all with happy endings. None of that "the one that got away stuff" from these sunkissed fishermen. Closeby are rows of marlin, barracuda, tarpon and shark waiting on the dock to be weighed and photographed while local taxidermists stand by, business cards in hand. No need to ask: "How's the fishing?"

Most divers and fishermen spend their days on or under the water off the caye and their nights in San Pedro, where bars are numerous and seafood supreme. Unlike Belize City, the aggression level in San Pedro is zero.

Nobody bothers you. A night on the town is a fish or lobster dinner at *The Hut* followed by a few beers at the *Tackle Box,* where the decor highlight is a tank of sting rays and sharks. As with most bars, the floor is sand.

San Pedro has developed into a delightfully arty town. *Art Unique* features the amazing work of Chris Emmanuel, *The Little Old Craft Shop* has marvelous masks and very pretty jewelry, *Ambergris RT Gallery* specializes exciting primitive art, *Ambergris Jade* is a jewel of a museum as well as a shop. They don't bother with street addresses but since the village itself consists of only four blocks, you aren't likely to miss any of the boutiques or galleries. These just happen to be my favorites.

Day time activities on Ambergris are decidedly more esthetic. Local guides take novice and experienced divers alike to their favorite spots where the magical mystery of the sea comes alive in fish, coral and colors of every description. A highlight is the *Hol Chan Marine Reserve.* The consideration in locating the first marine reserve there, rather than in a more remote and pristine part of the reef, was the existing community of conch and lobster fishermen. Taking snorkelers out to the reserve has become a profitable second use of the fishing fleet. The reserve was controversial at first, but by the next election the party in power was campaigning in San Pedro with the slogan, "Remember who brought you the marine reserve."

Perhaps you'll want to make a day trip to Belize's famous *Blue Hole,* considered one of the most outstanding dive sites in the world. Believed once to have been a land cave formed some 10,000 years ago by underground rivers, the Blue Hole cavern was transformed by the ocean crashing through its ceiling. The geological quirk, an almost perfect circular hole measuring 1000 feet in diameter and 480 feet deep, was made famous by Jacque Cousteau's crew in the 1970s.

A shaft drops from a ten-foot deep lagoon opening into a series of elaborate stalactite-filled caverns. The wall, carpeted in thick green vegetation, gradually slopes during the descent. At about 100 feet, a shelf juts back, exposing a series of 15 to 20-foot long, thumb-shaped stalactites. Before you is an awesome underwater cathedral with alcoves, archways and columns: eerie, majestic, dark, yet fascinating. Considered the jewel in the crown of Belize diving, the Blue Hole has remained the same for 10,000 years.

Ramon Nunez, a full blooded Maya, opened *Ramon's Village Resort* in 1981 on the very same day that Belize gained its independence from Britain. Since then the resort, which manages to be both lively and laid back, has become an institution on Ambergris Caye. People go there and return again and again for very good reason. The atmosphere's just right, the location perfect—everything you want within easy walking distance. The palm-shaded, thatched roof cabanas are rustically romantic. The excellent restaurant, with its Maya décor, serves Cajun dishes, fresh seafood and island specialties. I loved eating out on the verandah as well. You can't beat the ocean view. Guests and locals alike turn out for the beach cookout on Tuesdays and Fridays which also features live entertainment. Phone: (1-800) 624 4215; website: www. Ramons.com

The beach at Journey's End.

Journey's End, a self contained resort, ten minutes by water taxi from San Pedro, has been popular since the early 90s. Transportation into town is complimentary, but everything one might desire is located on the premises. Journey's End operates an excellent dive facility and state of the art deep sea fishing craft. Excursions to mainland sites can also be specially tailored and arranged. No wonder Harrison Ford, former president Jimmy Carter and members of the British nobility stay there. It can be fun to hang out with the "rich and famous" (yes, the club has been featured more than once), but the resort is also family-friendly and hosts "Eels on Wheels," a US. Diving group for the handicapped. 1-800-541-6796; fax: 713-780-1726; website: www.journey-sendresort.com)

Ramon's Reef Resort is an institution on Ambergris Caye. The atmosphere is comfortable and casual. Meals are tasty and portions plentiful. Dining is family style with an accompanying friendly, informal atmosphere. The individual palm-shaded, thatched roof cabanas with ceiling fans are rustically romantic. (Phone: 1-800-624-4315; fax: 026-2214)

Victoria House is a classy enclave that has the style and seclusion of a diplomatic residence. It's a dream retreat with a colonial style mansion, airy verandahs, leafy walkways—a romantic novel set to life. There's an excellent restaurant that serves the best Sunday brunch in town and has music and dancing Tuesday and Friday nights. (Phone: 1-800-247-5159; fax: 404-373-3885; www.victoria-house.com)

The *Sun Breeze Hotel* is lovely and inviting and has a great view restaurant (1-800) 688-0191; www.sunbreeze.net). The *Aqua Marina Suites* may be the prettiest hotel on the beach. (Phone: 1-800-641-2994; www,aquamarina-suites.com) *Captain Morgan's Retreat* is secluded and romantic (1-888-653-9090; website: www.belizevacation.com)

Wherever you stay, managers of hotels and restaurants seem to have the same idea: "No shirt, no shoes, no problem." It's all a part of the laid back ambience that's part of San Pedro's charm. But more importantly, keep in mind the fragile reef environment that is all important to both the beauty and the economy of this true tropical paradise. During your dives, remember another admonishment of Ambergris Caye villagers: "Take only pictures, leave only bubbles."

— PLACENCIA —

The Garifuna Indian culture and a pervasive Creole dialect give an Antillean cast to Placencia to the south. Set in a sheltered half-moon bay with crystal-clear green water and palm-dotted white sand, this layed back fishing village "founded " by pirates, is now peopled by a delightful melange of races.

Placencia is so small that it doesn't even have a main street—it has a concrete path, just big enough for two to walk side by side. Stroll the sidewalk and you've seen the town—everyones' backyard, houses on stilts, cottages festooned with laundry and bougainvillea.

"Diving into the lap of luxury" takes on a whole new meaning when you combine one of the world's top scuba diving locations with one of the Caribbean's finest beachfront resorts, the *Inn at Robert's Grove*.

Inn at Robert's Grove. Photo by Charles Herndon.

The Inn's state-of-the-art dive center is supervised by a PADI certified Divemaster with worldwide diving knowledge. The center is equipped with brand new, top-of-the-ranger Oceanic equipment and two dive boats including a 30 ft. dive boat with two Honda four-stroke 130 hp engines and a 28 foot dive boat with two Honda four-stroke 115 hp. Engines.

Diving from the Placencia Peninsula is considered some of the best in Belize since, as the edge of the barrier reef comes south along the coast, it separates further and further from the mainland. The result is a broad expanse of coral reef with channels going from 90 to 110 feet that rise abruptly into shoals and cays providing many scuba locations. At last count there were a minimum of 20 named dive sites in the southern waters of Belize off Placencia bursting with untouched coral and abundant fish life.

The Inn itself offers lovely sea views, a tennis court, rooftop Jacuzzis, and tours to animal preserves and Maya ruins.   Phone: 1-800-565-9757; www.robertsgrove.com.)

Another possibility is **Rum Point Inn** which offers comfortable cabanas within a few feet of the Caribbean, plus good food served in an intimate family setting, plus a library featuring information on the natural history of the area, Maya archaeology and mythology.

— RAINFOREST EXPLORATIONS —

So where is everybody? I wondered.   Base camp set up at the **Bermudian Landing Community Baboon Sanctuary Land,** an Englishman and I set off in the noon day sun to see the show. Rainforests, we reminded each other, are supposed to contain between forty and fifty percent of the planet species in less than two percent of its area. These statistics firmly in mind, we looked

around expecting to see wildlife lined up waiting to greet us. Instead, the jungle appeared empty, eerily empty.

In the bright sunlight, the rainforest was lifeless. Fortunately the stage setting was plenty dramatic — green, lush, exotic. But where were the players? The only sound was the metallic whir of the cicadas, a

The Belize rainforest.

steady drone. The only movement our own. Not so much as a leaf rustled. Yet nothing could displace the mysterious feeling about the place, a sense of hidden life waiting in the wings.

As the afternoon progressed, I began to realize what I, and most first time visitors to Belize, frequently miss. I was in the right place, but at the wrong time. Birds and animals come out early in the morning and late in the afternoon when the air is cooler. So much smarter than the average human.

Next morning, the sun was just starting to filter through the thick jungle canopy when I staked out my loge seat—a crumbling ruin—and settled in. The 5:30 concert was about to begin. This time I wasn't disappointed. Sunrise is that magical hour in the Belizan jungle when

Baird's tapir or "mountain cow"—Belize's national animals.

the nocturnal birds, insects, reptiles and animals try to get to bed and the daylight beasts try to eat them before they can get there.

A toucan—one of the star performers at Bermudian Landing.

The symphony began with a distant melody, almost flutelike, followed by a chorus of high caws from keel-billed toucans and aracaris with their bruised-banana-colored bellies. Laughing falcons with hysterical human sounding cackles picked up the tempo while woodpeckers pounded out the back beat on tall, swaying palms.

Suddenly a crashing sound was heard in the canopy above. Looking up I saw carelessly confident spider monkeys flinging themselves from tree to tree, some jumping up and down, breaking off branches to scare off intruding tourists. The crescendo came at daybreak when the principal sopranos

— howler monkeys — joined the cacophony with their incredibly loud, lionlike howls. Unlike the feisty spider monkeys, howlers—called baboons in Belize — are a rare sight. The jungle echoes with their deep, guttural roar but the monkeys generally remain hidden in the high canopy. Their larger size (up to three feet tall), coupled with the heavy lower jaws and a bulbous throat which enables them to make their fearsome growls, lend howlers a pugnacious appearance. That fierceness is all bluff. Territorial fights are rare. Howlers just howl a lot.

The *Sanctuary*—eighteen square miles of forest on the banks of the Belize River—is protected jointly by the *Belize Audubon Society,* the *Zoological Society of Milwaukee County, the World Wildlife Fund,* and the inhabitants themselves. Nearly every landowner in the eight villages of the sanctuary has signed a voluntary pledge to farm in ways compatible with "baboons" — the endangered howler monkeys — and the other wildlife on his property. He has promised to spare forest along the river, leave foodbearing trees when clearing land, and maintain corridors of forest around his fields.

A bus link to Belize City has been established. Camping or a nominally priced bed and breakfast can be arranged. A guide is advisable for orientation and protection.

The *Cockscomb Basin Wildlife Preserve,* located in southern Belize near the town of Dangriga, was declared a Forest Reserve in 1984. Two years later a portion—some 150 square miles—was set aside as a the world's first jaguar preserve to protect this exotic creature which heavily populates the Cockscomb Basin area. Largely through the efforts of New York Zoological Society researcher Alan Rabinowitz (author of *Jaguar*), it's now a crime to kill a jaguar unless it's a "problem cat." The third largest member of the cat family, jaguars can grow up to six feet in length, usually exceeding 200 pounds.

Besides the jaguar, Cockscomb Basin is home to other cats such as the puma, ocelot, and jaguarundi. Other local wildlife includes otter, brocket deer, peccary, agoti, paca, anteater, armadillo and the national animal of Belize— Baird's tapir or "Mountain Cow". The lush jungle of the Cockscomb Basin is a birder's paradise with more than 290 species which include the Scarlet Macaw, Great Curassow, Kill-billed Toucan and King Vulture.

With the exception of the nearly tame spotted large and conspicuous turkey, most birds remain hidden in the rainforest. It generally takes a guide to lure them out into the open with a whistled love song.

The rainforest itself is a magical place supporting up to 80 species of trees— compared to an acre in a temperate forest, where there are possibly four.

The sacred ceiba tree, the giant mahogany, the sopadilla or chicle tree are so awesome, you find yourself walking much of the time with head tipped backward—but there are interesting things underfoot as well. Swarms of army ants attract marauding woodcreepers and tanagers. The birds feast on insects scrambling to escape the advancing legions of omnivorous ants. Hawks in turn prey on those smaller birds, so that the army ants may trigger a promising chain of events for bird watchers. 48 km (30mi) southwest of Dangriga, take the Southern Highway where a dirt road leads into the reserve. Open daily from 8 to 5. Phone: (027-7369).

50 km. (31 miles) west of Belize City. Take Northern Highway and turn left on road to Burrell Boom. The visitor center has a few rooms to rent but you must reserve them well in advance. Open daylight hours. (Phone: 027-7369)

Xunantunich as seen from El Castillo. Photo by Vern Appleby.

— THE RUINS —

So long romanticized as peace-loving, visionary people, were the Maya in fact brought down by their addiction to war and violence? Certainly most of the new findings strongly indicate this. According to the late Linda Schele of the University of Texas, pioneers researcher, the ceremonial centers, far from being peaceful theocracies were constantly warring city states where blood rituals were the rule.

Victors tortured royal captives in displays that lasted for years before the unfortunates were finally executed. In other public ceremonies kings drew blood from their genitals, queens from their tongues with stingray spines and obsidian blades while using hallucinogenic drugs. The sacrificers drenched bark paper with their blood and burned it so the gods could consume the smoke as divine food.

It was Schele's belief, upheld by recent discovery, that blood was the mortar of ancient Maya life. Whatever the motivating philosophy, we now know they led urban lives in Central America and Mexico before Rome was built. New findings have revealed that Maya scholars were perfecting concepts of time, space and astronomy when Europeans were entering the Iron Age. The relevance of this is rendered all the more significant by the awareness that the drama was played out on the rainforest's ecological stage where the activities of human civilization were often near the limits of the environment's capacity to sustain them.

There are more than *600 known* archeological sites to explore. Few are maintained, many virtually inaccessible. Belize has some of the earliest and latest examples of the Maya civilization. Words alone can't convey the magic of experiencing the ancient cities rising from the jungle. . . . the *great temple of Xunantunich,* the splendor of *Caracol,* the treasure trove of *Altun Ha* and *Lubaantun,* home of the fabled *Crystal Skull.* Belizian archeology is only just beginning.

—XUNANTUNICH(Shu-nan-tu-NEECH)—
Belize's Skyscraper.

In 989 A.D. Maya may have scarcely glanced at the **great temple of Xunantunich** frowning down at them from a high hill. It was already a ruin. In that year, only the oldest of the old could dimly remember what their fathers

and grandfathers had told them about the way things used to be.

What happened to this wonderful society, thought to be one of the most advanced the world has ever known? There are as many theories as there are Maya scholars.

Bas relief depicts the sun god on El Castillo. Photo by Vern Appleby.

Some say epidemics destroyed the backbone of the population. Others believe a revolt of the masses against the establishment wiped out the leaders. Others still claim that wide-spread famine due to repeated crop failures finally rang down the curtain.

All that we know for certain is that the Maya lived in the area for thousands of years, that their golden age lasted from 150 A.D. to 900 A.D. and that it was during this time that Xunantunich was built. *El Castillo*, the great temple, stands like a stone crown atop a green, leveled hill some 130 feet above the plaza floor. From its summit, Belize and Guatemala are a patchwork quilt of gray rooftops, red and blue huts sewn on a background emerald green.

A remnant from the Classic period. Photo by Vern Appleby.

The site consists of three ceremonial plazas and a ball court enclosed by house mounds, pyramids and palaces. One shelters stelae found among the ruins. The most striking depicts a man wearing a feather headdress standing on a slave or captive, who crouches on his hands and knees.

Xunantunich, the first Maya ruin to be excavated in Belize, was first explored in the late1800s by, Thomas Gann, a young British medical officer. Nothing further was done until Gann returned in 1924, at which time he reportedly unearthed many Maya treasures. The recorded history of these items has been lost and, at present, no one knows of their whereabouts. It is possible that many museums and private collectors of Maya artifacts are displaying them, with no idea of their origin. The site was opened by Sir J. Eric

S. Thompson in 1938. In 1959, Evan Mackie, a Glasgow University archeologist, made a startling discovery when he uncovered evidence indicating that Xunantunich had been at least partially destroyed by an earthquake in the late Classic period of the Maya civilization. Mackie found signs that the Maya had partially repaired the area and continued to live there, but he believes that the catastrophe had caused the people to lose faith in their leader's ability to control the gods. Perhaps, they reasoned, the earthquake was a sign of heavenly displeasure.

At any rate, Xunantunich ceased being a religious center some years before the end of the Classic Period (900 A.D.)

The ceremonial center is located approximately 80 miles from Belize City, near the western border at San Jose Succotz. Every day between 9 a.m and 5 p.m. an old man cranks a hand-drawn ferry across the Mopan River. It is the only means of reaching the ruin and a voyage that traverses time as well as distance.

It's less than a mile farther (up a steep road) to the site. The ferry service is free. The entrance fee is BZ$ 5 for Belizeans and $10 for visitors.

The *Inn at Xunactunich* across from the ferry, overlooks the Mopan River and a series of small waterfalls, where women wash clothes on the rocks. (phone: 804-3739; www.discovercayo.com)

— ALTUN HA —

Altun Ha, the most extensively excavated of all the Maya centers in Belize, is located approximately 30 miles north of Belize City. It's believed to have been settled some 2000 years ago in Pre-Classic times, growing in wealth and significance with the emergence of the classic period as a link between inland centers and the Caribbean.

Two main ceremonial plazas have been cleared, but the site covers a much larger area. Many spectacular discoveries have been unearthed including the largest jade item in the entire Maya world—a spectacular head of the god *Kinich Ahau*, weighing nearly ten pounds and standing six inches in height. Also uncovered here was the *Temple of the Green Tomb*, a burial chamber containing human remains and a wealth of jade pieces.

The *"Jade Head"*, representing the Sun God, Kinich Ahau, was the most significant find during Dr. David Pendergast's excavations. At approximately six inches high and weighing nine and three-quarter pounds, it remains to this day the largest carved jade object found in Belize.

Altun Ha is located 31 miles north of Belize City near Rock Stone Pond Village. No regular public transportation is available, but local tour operators and taxi services can be of assistance. Simple but adequate accommodations are available near the ruins.

GETTING THERE

Private Vehicle—travel 28 miles on the New Northern Highway from Belize City until the road intersects the old Northern Highway. Turn right (sign marked Maskall and Orange Walk). Drive 11 miles on the old highway, then follow signs to Altun Ha. It's a narrow winding road so drive with caution.

Guided tours from San Pedro travel up the North River through mangrove channels for 30 to 40 minutes before arriving at the small village of Bomba. A short stop is taken to see local carvings made of mahogany and seracota, then the group boards a van, for a short ride to the site.

— CARACOL —

No one knows what the Maya called *Caracol.* The word means "snail" in Spanish. The city so named, possibly, because it lies at the end of a deeply rutted, corkscrew road through dense jungle. Located near the western boundary of Belize and 86 kilometers from the nearest town, it isn't easy to reach. Yet the site which was, until recently, a mere dot on the map of Mayadom is now known to be even larger than Guatemala's famous Tikal.

Today Caracol is yielding dramatic clues to the concept of Maya warfare and has raised provocative questions pointing to a much more prominent role by women in that society than has ever been suspected.

The city's myriad broad plazas, temples, acropoli, causeways and residential compounds were completely overrun by the lush growth of ceiba, allspice and cohune when a woodcutter, literally stumbled into it in 1938. It would be twelve years before the first archeologists arrived and even then the site got little attention.

The picture changed dramatically in 1985 with the arrival of Arien and Diane Chase, archeologists from the University of Central Florida. Their first discovery—a ball park marker—rewrote Maya history. The hieroglyphic carvings on the stone tell of successful wars fought by Lord Water of Caracol, first with neighboring Naranjo and then, in 562 A.D., with mighty Tikal.

It's not surprising that such an important document would have been set in the middle of a ball court; there was most certainly a gladiatorial aspect to the game. Closely related to death and the underworld, to war and religion, politics and dynastic change, the "game" was carried on by two teams sometimes using rubber balls, at other times human skulls.

Noble captives like Tikal's unfortunate Lord Double Bird, whose defeat by Caracol was followed by a 140 years of peace, were taken in hand-to-hand combat. It was imperative that a royal captive be brought alive to the captor's city for display in a demeaning public ceremony. Afterward, if not earmarked for the ball game, he was sacrificed in a bloodletting ritual. Though a personal disaster for the defeated ruler, this type of warfare spared the lives of the vast majority and preserved their cities and culture.

In other words, there were no draftees, no devastation. Imagine the possible consequences if today's disagreements were settled by hand-to-hand battles between heads of state. Perhaps there would be no more war.

Another archeological breakthrough at Caracol has revolutionized Maya scholarship. Over the years, figures wearing long, flowing garments have been discovered again and again on excavated ceramics, murals and carvings. Unable to conceive of women playing any significant role in the hierarchy, generations of Mayaists have interpreted these portrayals as male priests. Now, as a result of the discovery at Caracol of many elaborate tombs inscribed with royal symbols, but containing the skeletons of women, it is conceded that Maya women also ruled.

In tracing the tentacle-like causeways of Caracol, the Chases made yet another discovery. No one was prepared for the immensity of this forgotten Cinderella. In mapping the site, the archeologists have come to the realization that Caracol was far larger and more densely populated than the former jewel in the Maya crown —Tikal.

The Belizean government envisions Caracol as an archeological park, something comparable to Tikal or Chichen Itza, but at the present time there are no scheduled tours and no place to stay once you get there. However, there are several hotels and organizations that will form tours. Anyone wishing to go it on their own, should call the Belize Department of Archeology at 501-08-2106 for advice on road conditions.

—LUBAANTUN and BELIZE'S CRYSTAL SKULL —

In 1927, on her seventeenth birthday, Anna De Guillon Mitchell-Hedges, the adopted daughter of eccentric British adventurer F.A. Mitchell-Hedges, discovered an object beneath an ancient altar at the ceremonial center of Labaantun.

What she found was the top half of an almost life-sized *crystal skull*. Three months later, just a few feet away, she found its detachable lower jaw which had become separated from the rest of the head. The skull is an exquisitely detailed piece with no signs of tell-tale concentric circles, even at a microscopic level, that would be present if any type of machine had been used in its crafting. The eye holes have lenses in the rear which in terms of modern day optics, "channel" light from beneath the skull out the eye openings, producing a strange glow in the sockets.

Even though the solid crystal is clouded in some parts by tiny bubbles, when objects below are viewed from above, a slightly magnifying effect is evident. Hinge-like connectors at the joints enable the jaw to move—truly a remarkable feat for an ancient people who possessed no metal cutting tools.

Ground with meticulous care to the size and shape of a human skull, this enormous gem must rank in any record book or almanac of oddities as contender for the title of the world's strangest object.

In part because there is no scientific technique for dating crystal, controversy has centered around the skull from the beginning. Some say it's a remnant from the lost continent of Atlantis while others maintain the crystal is a kind of computer left by visitors from another planet. Mitchell-Hedges, a real life Indiana Jones who once rode with Pancho Villa, appears to be the only one who had no doubts about its origin. In his autobiography, *Danger is My Ally*, published in 1954, five years before his death, he wrote, "It is at least 3,600 years old and, according to legend, was used by the high priest of the Maya when performing esoteric rites. "

Anna Mitchell-Hedges laughs at those who believe the skull to be cursed. Her father lived for more than thirty years with the bizarre crystal in his possession during which time he survived eight bullet wounds and three knife attacks. She, herself, now keeps it on display in her home in Kitchener, Canada. Dismissing the more exotic theories, Mitchell-Hedges insists that the skull is as Maya as the city in which she found it.

Lubaantun is the largest Maya site in southern Belize. Eleven structures and three ball courts have thus far been uncovered. Structures in Plaza IV bear mute testimony to the enthusiasm of the site's first excavator, Thomas Gann. In 1903, explosive archaeology was de rigueur. Much of what's known today of Lubanantun brought to in the course of joint expeditions by Harvard and Cambridge universities.

The site's beauty lies in its form. Lubaantun's rounded corners and curves are like no other Maya site. No mortar was used in the limestone blocks which were chiseled—stone on stone—so precisely that buildings retain their graceful lines even when collapsed. Perhaps this is why the modern Maya gave the site its name, "place of fallen rocks."

Plaza XII, a small plaza in the eastern corner of the site, contains a covered altar where offerings are still found from time to time.

Though major construction lasted only 160 years, from 730 to 890 A.D.at Lubaantun, the city seems to have been a thriving commercial center. Jade and obsidian from the Guatemalan highlands have been uncovered along with the bones of deep water marine animals—indicating trade.

Lubaantun lies on a ridge above a valley cut by a tributary of the nearby Columbia River. Streams flow from the base of the ridge and below the site is an expanse of tropical forest. The site is not accessible by public transport but can be reached by following a 1.5 mile uphill trail from the village of San Pedro Columbia, one of the larger Maya communities in Toledo District. Lubaantun has restrooms and a picnic area but no drinking water.

The visitor center displays interesting ceramics found on the site. Caretakers have assisted with various excavations and make excellent guides, but visitors can also wander freely. Often you can have this wondrous place completely to yourself.

— THE PANTI MEDICINE TRAIL —

Courage, curiosity, callouses—all three enabled Dr. Rosita Arvigo to become possibly the world's strongest link between witch doctor's magic and test tubes in the advanced research laboratories of the National Cancer Institute in Washington, D.C.

Ix Chel Farm—named for the Maya goddess of medicine and childbirth — Arvigo's research center near the town of San Ignacio, is a place where the frontiers of medicine and the ancient knowledge of Maya curanderos or shaman converge in a search for drugs to combat AIDS and cancer.

Slender, olive-skinned, Arvigo looks at home in Belize, despite her Italian background and street smart American lingo. She's a doctor of Naprapathy (a system of manipulation of ligaments, muscles and bones to heal the connective tissue damage that may cause faulty circulation to the body's organs and systems) and taught nutrition as well as herbology in her native Chicago.

While traveling in Belize, Arvigo chanced to meet the late Don Elijio Panti, el primero, the first one, then the most esteemed bush doctor in Central

America. Fascinated by his skills—and concerned that they would die with him—Dr. Arvigo, through much effort, won Panti's confidence. Machete in hand, she assisted him for more than a year collecting material from the rainforest and then helping to carry the heavy sacks of roots, barks and vines back to his home. After that came the endless hours of chopping the materials into usable portions. It was another year before he would allow her to attend his "clinic."

Arvigo's ten year association with Panti, who died in 1996 at the age of 97, enabled her to learn the traditional uses of plants such as billyweb—for diabetes as well as hypoglycemia. Her background in both naprapathy and nutrition adds another dimension to the study of herbal remedies. In the case of billyweb, Arvigo suggests that the herb possibly corrects the sugar imbalance by mobilizing cellular sugar from other sources in the body.

Other Panti remedies are china root (red cocolmeoca) used for blood clotting, especially when parasites have been at work on the red blood cells, and a tea made from the ki bix vine which facilitates birth control by coating the uterus lining. The list goes on and on, the work underscoring a growing partnership between native healers and scientists, the latter racing worldwide deforestation to find medically useful plants before they become extinct. Currently twenty-five percent of all medicines used in the United States are made from tropical extracts.

Rosita Arvigo participated in the National Cancer Institutes's five-year program to scour the rainforests in search of medicinal plants to be used against cancer and AIDS and is also working with Dr. Michael Balik of the New York Botanical Gardens collecting plant material for testing. She's active too in a program funded by the United Nations to train lay people in remote villages throughout Belize to set up medical screening units to eliminate the need to go to distant hospitals for simple ailments. In the process, Dr. Arvigo has offered workshops in every district in Belize.

In addition, doctors, herbalists and nutritionists from all over the world now come to Ix Chel Farm to attend Dr. Arvigo's seminars.

To help visitors understand and appreciate these secrets of the rainforest, Dr. Arvigo has established the Panti Medicine Trail, a mile-long path which winds its way through a world of bush medicines still rooted in the earth. Trees and shrubs along the way are marked with signs and a guidebook explains the practical or medicinal use of each.

The Panti Trail begins at Ix Chel Farm, beyond San Ignacio, off the Western Highway. (Next door to Belize's primo jungle lodge, Chaa Creek Cottages.)

Anyone wishing to explore may drop by the farm during daylight hours any day of the week.   Those desiring an appointment or seminar information may write c/o General Delivery, San Ignacio Cayo, Belize or call (08)-23180.

JUNGLE LODGES

— CHAA CREEK COTTAGES —

Chaa Creek Cottages

When Mick and Lucy Fleming arrived in Belize in the late 1970s, their dream was to establish a dairy farm. Who would have imaged a jungle lodge? The only access to the outside world was by dugout canoe or horseback; besides, tourism to Belize's interior was unheard of.

Ecotourism?   What was that?

What the Flemings never anticipated was company. To their very great surprise, they suddenly found themselves playing host to a variety of friends from all over the world who were hungry for the wild beauty of their new home, a tapestry of rainforest spread over the Cayo hills above the meandering Macal River.

Suddenly, it seemed, they were running a hotel. Slowly, the farm was subordinated, eventually eliminated. By 1990, everyone knew about ecotourism and *Chaa Creek was declared a Private Reserve by Conservation International.*

The cottages, located in the Cayo District 20 minutes drive from the village of San Ignacio, overlook the river.   On the other side, a jungle waits to be explored. The remote setting creates a sense of seclusion while providing the perfect compromise between comfort and   adventure. There's a distinct African feeling to the architecture, a legacy from the Flemings earlier adventures in Kenya and Uganda. Each of the round thatch-roofed cottages has a tile floor, large mahogany beds, gorgeous hand-embroidered spreads and hangings. Oil lamps cast a soft warm glow in keeping with the natural ambience. The water is clear and safe, showers hot, toilets state-of-the-art.

In the evening, the often forgotten art of conversation is still enjoyed as instant friends compare notes on the day's adventures over cocktails and dinner—the latter an excellent blend of Belizean, Mexican, and American cuisine—served family style in a palm-thatched restaurant.

Birding is superb at Chaa Creek. On a recent field study, the Carnegie Ornothological Group identified more than 190 species within a five mile radius of the cottages. There are also opportunities for canoeing, horseback riding and exploration of the Panti Medicine Trail next door. Visits may also be arranged to the ruins of Xunantunich and to Tikal, across the Guatemalan border.

A forest stream on Antonio's property. Photo by Vern Appleby.

Certainly the most exciting adventure available from Chaa Creek is an overnight visit to a Maya ceremonial cave high in the mountains. The cave is mystical, its discovery pure magic. It began with Antonio and his wife, Leah. Antonio used to be a rubber tapper. Now he farms and manages his land as a private nature reserve, refusing to cut his mahogany trees, though he could sell them at a handsome profit. Antonio won't even kill the jaguars that sometimes raid his chicken pen and have even attacked his dogs—better to keep the dogs indoors.

The *Camp at Chaa Creek*, located a half-mile down the Macal River from the lodge, features ten fully-screened casitas, each with two beds and a private sheltered porch for jungle viewing.

Bas relief depicts the sun god on El Castillo. Photo by Vern Appleby.

But Antonio's not an impractical man—he can't afford to be. In the long run, he believes that he will make a better living from preserving the environment than by destroying it. He has turned a portion of land into a hostel where campers can experience life in the very center of the rainforest. Cabins are rustic but comfortable; swimming in jungle streams a delicious experience.

In 1987, while cutting thatch in the hills above his property, Antonio and his son, William—a gifted artist—discovered a cave containing a wealth of 1000-year-old Maya artifacts. In keeping with their preservationist principles, they left everything as they found it, installing an iron gate to forestall looters. Now the cave is part of their mountain retreat itinerary.

Antonio's waterfall. Photo by Vern Appleby.

One can spend hours in the cave exploring its many chambers, each filled with ceremonial vessels — among them a number of large, lidded, spherical black pots — some as large as a man —which still contain seeds and grains of corn as though used only yesterday. In the deepest section of the cave, accessible only by shimmying down a rope, is what Antonio believes to have been the ceremonial chamber—a large, round room with a vaulted ceiling at least two stories high. A standing stone in the chamber's center was clearly an object of veneration.

Information regarding Chaa Creek Cottages, excursions and facilities, may be obtained by writing P.O. Box 53, San Ignacio, Cayo Belize, Central America. Phone: 092-2037. Fax: 092-2501.

—CHAN CHICH—

Some say Maya sites should be left to the archaeologists. I say a few should be reserved for the rest of us.

Cha Chich built within the ruins of a thousand-year-old plaza, is a compromise that delights everyone. Literally surrounded by burial mounds, the small enclave of twelve thatched cottages is a delicious departure point for the resort's three major activities—nature, ruins and nothing. Few spots on earth make it so easy to communicate with a dead civilization or the wilderness arising from its demise. This is the back of beyond, the ultimate nature fix.

A large bulletin board by the dining room lists sightings. Howler monkey above Temple Loop. Crocodile on Laguna Seca. Scarlet Macaw near Norman's Temple, jaguar in Plaza A. The lodge's resident ornithologist has recorded 260 species of birds. My friend and I spotted 17 in an afternoon— including a white crown parrot. Maybe that's not too surprising—Chan Chich means little bird—but we also saw spider monkeys and a portly peccary. Once I discovered a jaguar track. Looking over my shoulder, I wondered if his great yellow eyes weren't watching me.

Chan Chin.

Four massive ramparts, now covered with grass, hold the lodge in a loose embrace. Once they were the pyramids and temples of a Maya plaza. Slumbering undisturbed under a blanket of forest, they hint at dark and mysterious secrets.

One day an archaeologist excavating at Chan Chich took us to a looter's trench. Exposed was the cross section of a temple that had grown in stages spanning hundreds of years. Each successive structure taller and grander. When looters breached the innermost chamber, they revealed red-painted walls.

The lodge's existence protects the ruins from future would-be looters while offering guests an opportunity to experience the power and mystery of an ancient past. We walked through roofless passageways, peered into corbel-arched vaults all the while aware that the original inhabitants were entombed beneath us.

Close by in a mahogany cottage with jalousie shutters open to the jungle, we slept for three nights amid these ruins. Afternoons we relaxed on the wrap-around verandah and contemplated the Maya. From our his and her hammocks we watched deer nibble at the shrubbery and oscellated turkeys stroll the lawn. A couple of parrots knocked a squawk back and forth like a tennis ball while we lazed. The mystery of a staunchly elitist civilization remained, resisting our wish to probe its secrets. But one thing we knew for certain. The Maya had gracious living down cold.

Phone 1-800-451-8017; Fax: 027-6961. Chan Chich is (barely) accessible by Landrover. By far the best way to get there is a brief, gorgeous flight by bush plane. Call 1-800-4521-8017 for schedules and reservations.

Chan Chich Lodge caters to both scientific naturalists and the adventurously curious. Days in the bush are concluded with hot showers back at the lodge, excellent meals and plenty of lively conversation.

—MARUBA —

Yes, you can have it all. It is possible to play "Sheena, Queen of the Jungle" and Nicole Kidman at the same time. *Maruba*—surely the most unique of the jungle lodges—offers a full range of body and facial treatments, beauty salon services, exercise programs, herbal wraps, seaweed wraps, aromatherapy massages and mineral baths.

Located in dense jungle—many of the "Tarzan suites" are actually fitted up as bird blinds for better viewing—the state-of-the-art spa, offers a variety of photographic and nature safaris as well. Just thirty miles north of Belize City, Maruba is a departure point for the nearby ruins of Altun Ha or a boat trip to the 3000 year old ceremonial site of Lamani.

This is a place where you really can have elegant ambience and excellent cuisine in the midst of a lush rainforest.

Additional information maybe be obtained by writing P.O. Box 300703, Houston, TX 77230 or telephoning (713) 799-2031 or 1-800-620-8227; website: maruba@flash.net

— JAGUAR PAW —

Donna and Cy Young went to Belize on their honeymoon and remained to build a jungle resort. A stay there is a unique and delightful experience. Imagine yourself passing through one unspoiled cave after another, stalactites and stalagmites glistening like diamonds as you float by tube down river. Far above, bats whirl and circle, wings like lacy valentines. And that's only one option.

Jaguar Paw is located on 215 acres of jungle preserve skirted by the Caves Branch river and honeycombed by miles of underground caverns, once the habitat of Maya Indians. Named for the gorgeous creature sometimes spotted there—as well as for a 4th century Maya ruler—Jaguar Paw rests on an animal sanctuary. Guides are knowledgeable, thoughtful and humorous. Obvious in everything they say and do is a pride in the natural wonder and beauty of their country. Each of the one-of-a-kind cabana is decorated with artifacts culled from the great jungles of the world. This, plus air conditioning! There's also an excellent restaurant and lively, well stocked bar. It's fun to swap stories there in the evening after a day of tubing, caving, birding, canoeing, hiking, climbing or rappelling.

Later, a short walk under the jungle canopy leads to the river and the mouth of a small cave. Subtly illuminated, it provides a romantic setting for a late night dip. Easy to understand how Donna and Cy fell in love with the place and why they never left.

Jaguar Paw is an hour and a half from the Belize airport, which makes this jungle oasis a fine choice for a first or last night in the country. Phone: 1-800-451-8017; e-mail: cyyoung@btl.net.

— BLANCANEAUX LODGE —

Blancaneaux Lodge is the tropic of Coppola, staying there an opportunity to luxuriate in a film magnate's Shangri-La. Once the private preserve of Francis Ford Coppola, the posh resort with its cascading river and soaring pines combines stunning accommodations and barefoot chic with an exotic locale.

Situated on Mountain Pine Ridge, Blancaneaux's high country advantages-- moderate temperatures and few insects--lend themselves to airy, open construction. There's little distinction between inside and out. The living room spills onto the verandah--and surrounding forest--with no fourth wall. The effect of the lofty cathedral-like palm-thatched ceiling pitched atop thick bamboo poles is that of a glamorous tree house.

Whitewashed walls offset by chocolate mahogany floors accent museum quality furniture, fabrics, and artifacts. There are bright masks, woven rugs, carved and painted animals from Central America, Spanish colonial tables, chests and chairs from Mexico, and ceremonial kimonos from Japan.

The bathrooms, open-air yet totally private, have green marble sinks set in mahogany and oversize tub-showers.   Maybe you think that bathing beneath palm thatches while looking out over bamboo and tile into the rainforest isn't a peak experience. Maybe you haven't tried it.

It was hard to tear ourselves away from all that, yet another advantage to Blancaneaux is its close proximity to Caracol. Until recently almost inaccessible, the Maya ceremonial site, a fascinating complex of temples, plazas, acropoli and palaces, offers an opportunity to watch archaeologists in action.

Once far larger and more densely populated than Tikal--the former jewel in the Maya crown--Caracol is a popular destination.   But there's also Thousand Foot Waterfall or the rock pools at Rio Oro. Guests may even hop the twin-engine Islander, spend a day snorkeling at Ambergris Caye, and be back for a luxury dinner and vintage wine by nightfall. Writing your own fantasy script is the whole idea at Blancaneaux.

Phone: 1-800-746-3743; fax:029-3919; website: www.blancaneaux.com

—EK'TUN—

For two hours we followed the Western Highway through rugged countryside that changed from level surface to mountains. The road narrowed becoming more and more jagged before we turned off onto ten more miles of bumpy dirt. Finally the trail ended at the bank of the Macal River where a boat waited to take us on the final lap of the journey.

Phyllis Dart, owner of Ek'Tun waited for us on the opposite bank, a mile or so upstream. How had she come to this remote spot? It was, we learned, a case of love at first sight.   A native of Colorado, she went to Belize on a holiday and never left. A true pioneer, Phyllis and her former husband, Ken, carved a tiny, but exquisite resort out of dense jungle.

My cabana, tastefully decorated with antiques and Maya artifacts, had two double beds, one on the main floor and one in the loft. A sitting room looking out over river, valley and jungle, contained a small library of classics. The pretty bathroom was miraculous—hot water, flush toilet and walk-in shower. Remember, we're talking dense jungle here!

Phyllis cooked and served our meals, entertaining us with marvelous true adventure stories. It was elegant food—chilled papaya soup, barbecued shrimp, superlative salsa—served on smart stoneware with linen napkins and colorful place-mats. A dining room open to the stars, CD classics and croaking tree frogs provided background for endless philosophizing.

By day, we skinny dipped in jungle streams and explored trails—cool, moist and leafy green. We found a cave where our flashlight beams spotlighted large pots, unbroken and undisturbed. More than a thousand years ago Maya walked there carrying offerings to their gods. Now we followed in their footsteps through a maze of tunnels. Far inside was a cavern large as a cathedral. At its center, an altar. Legend has it that a high priest is buried there. Does his spirit watch?

Like the cave, Ek 'tun is awesome—a place for contemplation, for quiet nurturing, talking, reading, exploring. By night, it's dark, mysterious, lit only by stars and fireflies. By day it's Eden. Phone: 091-2002 in Belize; 303-442-6150 in the U.S. Website: www.ektun.com

—MOPAN RIVER LODGE—

Every minute at Mopan River Lodge (a mile up river from Xunactunich) seems better than the last. Really. This all-inclusive resort is a kind of working fantasy.

From the Belize City airport we set off for the two hour journey through the back country to the village of Benque Viejo del Carmen. The lodge van pulled up to a boat ramp where Jay Picon, owner of the lodge, come to welcome me himself. There are no roads into the resort, so I and my luggage were quickly loaded onto a little red boat and ferried across the Mopan River, a meandering sliver of emerald.

Jay's wife, "Ms. Pam" met us at the dock. My bags were whisked off to a waiting cabana while Jay and Pam led me to the lounge. A frosty Banana Velvet was placed in my hand. It was a wonderful—a blend of coconut, pineapple, orange and banana juices combined with rum. Lots of rum. I thought a lot about banana velvets in the days ahead. I visualized one waiting like the Holy Grail as I climbed pyramids, canoed through subterranean streams and explored ceremonial caves.

My cabana was delightful: sparkling hardwood floors, a thatched roof (accented by amber "mood lights"), mahogany furniture, a totally modern bathroom and shady veranda. There were ten acres of lush garden to explore, a swimming pool and bird-watching platform.

Around six, I heard marimba music and knew it was cocktail time. Pam introduced me the other guests, friendly, bonded by shared adventures.

At 7, we were called to the bright and colorful tables in the dining room. There's room for 24 people at the lodge, they sit together at two or three large tables. Pam, a world traveler, has a cache of fabulous recipes. Each night a team of excellent Belizean cooks prepare a dinner with a different theme: Greek moussaka, southern fried chicken, linguine carbonara. It's all good!

After dinner Jay announced the next day's activities with a brief explanation. Guests are advised that breakfast starts at 7, tour departures at 8:25. A schedule is set for each day and those wishing to participate have merely to show up. Lounging, swimming, kayaking or exploring the village are ready alternatives.

Now here's the nitty gritty. Although the location of Mopan River Resort may not be considered remote, it is very much at the jungle's doorstep. Expeditions scheduled during a week's stay include Tikal, the Chechem Hah pottery cave, the Green Hills Butterfly farm, Barton Creek Cave, Xunantunich, El Pilar, Chal Pech, the Aguacate Nature Preserve, San Ignacio market and sometimes Caracol.

There are government entrance fees for many of the sites and a border fee for the trip to Tikal, but everything else is included in the package rate: lodging, meals, drinks, guided expeditions, transfers, taxes and service. There are literally no bills and no tipping. Even the drinks in the cabana's mini-bar are free.

At the present time, the price for 7 days (a recommended stay) is under $1000. Phone: 501 823 2047; www.mopanriverresort.com

A GREAT PLACE TO STOP

In the center of the Cayo District is the town of San Ignacio—you can hardly miss going through it, no matter what your destination in Belize. By all means, stop at Eva's (22 Burns Ave.) This place is an institution that'll give you a true sense of what the interior of the country's all about. Chichen, rice, beans and slaw run about 6 $U.S. a person, burgers and fries around $4. Sometimes you'll find deer or more exotic items on the menu at market price. They serve a wickedly strong black tea that everyone loves. No one's in a hurry. This is the perfect place to people watch and write your postcards.

GETTING THERE

Belize City's international airport is served by Tan Sahsa Airlines from Miami, Houston and New Orleans (1-800-327-1225); Continental Airlines from Houston (1-800-231-0856); Taca International from Houston, New Orleans, Miami and Los Angeles (1-800-535-8780); American Airlines from Miami (1-800-433-7300).

U.S. and Canadian citizens need a valid passport and a return ticket for entry. A departure tax of US $10 is required. Children under twelve are exempt. The Belizean dollar, which is pegged to the U.S., is equivalent to 50 cents. U.S. money is accepted everywhere.

Belize is relatively free of endemic diseases. No inoculations are required for entry, but for extended stays in the mainland, a typhoid booster, a dose of immunoglobulin for protection against hepatitis and a malaria preventative, such as Aralen, are advisable. If planning to remain on the cays, forget the health precautions; just bring sun screen!

Buses, running north, west and south from Belize City, are cheap and comfortable. There are a variety of car rentals, which is the ideal way to see the country. Expect that the often unpaved roads are hard on vehicles, you'll want a four wheel drive. Be prepared to pay twice as much for gas—which must be imported—as you would in the United States.

Additional information may be obtained from the Belize Tourist Board, 415 Seventh Avenue; 18th Floor, New York, NY 10001. Telephone 1-800- 624-0686.

Pyramid Two. Photo by Vern Appleby.

TIKAL
(tee-call)

The largest and possibly oldest of the ancient Maya sites, breathtaking, awe-inspiring Tikal overwhelms the visitor with its temples that rise from the tops of towering pyramids.

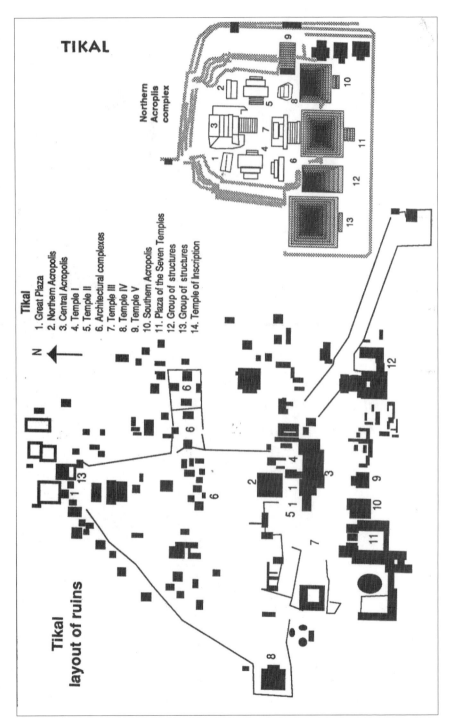

TIKAL

Northern Acropolis complex

Tikal
1. Great Plaza
2. Northern Acropolis
3. Central Acropolis
4. Temple I
5. Temple II
6. Architectural complexes
7. Temple III
8. Temple IV
9. Temple V
10. Southern Acropolis
11. Plaza of the Seven Temples
12. Group of structures
13. Group of structures
14. Temple of Inscription

N

Tikal layout of ruins

W ouldn't we be afraid to go inside there into a lordly house? Wouldn't we be just wide-eyed? Take pity on us! Wouldn't we look like mere dancers to them?

Don't be afraid. Don't be ashamed. Just dance this way. . . ..

Popol Vuh

Dancers? Translate that to tourists. No, not tourists. In the magical alchemy of Tikal, tourists are transformed to travelers. Tikal is the Big One. A pilgrimage there reminds us of the Popol Vuh, that mysterious Maya bible with its correspondence to more familiar origins, the garden of Eden, the forest primeval, the beginning of the world, creation itself.

The largest and possibly oldest of the ancient Maya sites, breathtaking, awe-inspiring Tikal overwhelms the visitor with its temples that rise from the tops of towering pyramids just as the site itself rises from the forest of Guatemala's Petén region. Tikal is the most impressive way to begin an acquaintance with the Maya world, but because of time, effort, distance, politics, it's frequently deferred. Yet this is the one journey that all Maya scholars must take in dream if not reality.

Approximately twenty-five hundred years ago, somehow, for some reason, a group of people settled on this low-lying hill in the midst of a dense jungle where their descendants would create by almost unfathomable means one of the most amazing civilizations the world has ever known. Today we call that hill and the surrounding area Tikal.

Pyramid I. Photo by Vern Appleby.

The prime city of the Maya people who populated the Yucatan Peninsula, Tikal is considered so important that it's been the object of the most extensive excavations ever undertaken in Central America. Archaeologists from the

Contemporary Maya doing their laundry in Lake Petén-Itza.

University of Pennsylvania have been working since 1956 to uncover and record the remains of this Maya site distinguished from all others by the height of its pyramids, the size and quantity of its constructions. Tikal includes the most ancient definitive date linked to a Maya site. The year A.D. 292 inscribed in the stone of Stela 29.

The central core of the city, covers an area of six square miles containing some 3000 structures. Beyond this, a peripheral city encompasses forty-eight square miles, roughly the size of San Francisco.

All the major features of a Maya site are represented: flat-topped step pyramids supporting temples decorated with tiled pediments known as "roof combs," realistic bas-reliefs, jutting corbeled arches, ball courts, steam baths, edifices built around large open public squares, tombs concealing polychrome ceramics, altars, stelae, and monoliths bearing sculpted portraits of awesome personages surrounded by hieroglyphic inscriptions

Once again the central buildings were apparently used for religious or ceremonial functions as well as markets. While the idea of a "city" implies a concentration of individuals living in close proximity, the arrangement of this and many other Maya sites leads scholars to doubt that these were ever urban settlements as we think of them today. Rather, it appears probable that only the elite lived there, while the rest of the Maya visited the centers for specific purposes only.

Though the discovery of Tikal dates back 150 years, it's doubtful that it was ever "lost." People living around Lake Petén-Itza must have been well aware of it, yet it wasn't until 1847 that an official expedition was begun. Since then the fascinating, life-consuming challenge of attempting to discover the cause and course of this civilization has continued unabated Once you've paused in a temple doorway high above the jungle that eventually conquered Tikal and its people, once you've observed the crumbling roof combs rising above an undulating rainforest ending at the shoreline of the distant Caribbean sea, it's easy to understand why.

Though the architectural achievement is phenomenal, the concept of city planning as we know it is clearly lacking. A map reveals structural anarchy, each grouping a disordered mass. One possible reason for the lack of vision may have had to do with the burial of city dignitaries in foundations of buildings that appear to have been demolished only to be reconstructed. It's easy to hypothesize that the death of an important personage in some way required the destruction of edifices standing during his lifetime. Tikal has more than a hundred such tombs; their furnishings revealing valuable information about various stages of Maya history.

The Guatemalan government has set aside a 222 square-mile area to preserve its Maya legacy.

A stela in the Central Plaza.

Ideally visitors should plan a three day stay to insure ample leisure to see "everything". If this is impossible, an overnight stay at least allows time for the Great Plaza and its surrounding area, a visit to a twin-pyramid group, as well as the almost obligatory climb to the top of *Temple 1V.*

The Great Plaza is a natural beginning. *Temple I,* is Tikal's trademark, the postcard impression millions have seen. To the side, the Central Acropolis, with its five main courts, contains some 500 years of building activity accomplished without benefit of wheel, beasts of burden or metal cutting tools. Much of Tikal is still covered by dense jungle, as one can see by a climb to the top of *Temple IV* (the best panoramic view of the city), but generations of

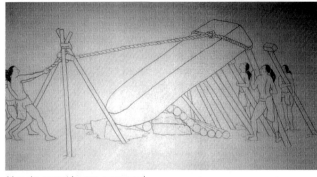

How the pyramids were constructed.

explorers and archeologists have left behind a legacy enabling visitors to enjoy a sense of the monumental grandeur that was Tikal.

Maps are inexpensive, readily available — a must. The **Tikal Museum,** which contains many excavated finds and a reconstruction of a tomb, shouldn't be missed.

Few would regret hiring a guide. Under the tutelage of Louis, Tikal came alive for me. With his history of political dissidence, Louis is not on the government's list of "approved" interpreters of the ruins, yet the benefit of both his knowledge and intensity of feeling was profound.

I knew that crossed eyes were considered a mark of beauty among the Maya and noted that Louis possessed this feature — as do many in the area. I'd heard the ancients had deliberately cultivated the look by placing a hanging pebble between their babies' eyes. Louis suggested a deeper meaning behind the practice. Focusing the eyes in this fashion, he said, was a form of meditation — a means of screening out the mundane world in order to concentrate on an interior reality, a practice very like Zen.

Louis also offered a solution to the greatest Maya mystery of them all — the great civilization's collapse. The Maya aristocrats, he theorizes, were devoted above all to their own spiritual development. For centuries they strove to attain some mysterious, psychic goal. Then around 900 A.D., they achieved it and simply vanished—perhaps disappearing to some higher plane of existence—leaving behind the simple, uneducated masses who could not possibly maintain the complex civilization on their own. One more fascinating theory to ponder.

So regal are the ruins, so totally compelling, that one may forget that Tikal National Park is to Guatemala what Banff is to Canada or Yellowstone to the United States. In fact, biologists say that tiny Guatemala has more species of birds than the United States and Canada combined. Long protected, the wildlife within the park's confines are both plentiful and oblivious to human intruders. Visitors can take guided tours to prime bird-watching and wild life areas; and the ruins, protruding as they do from dense jungle, provide great seats to watch the action.

One evening I sat atop *Temple IV* watching the moon come up—large, luminous, full. My companions were an eclectic lot: another American, a Guatemalan, a German couple, a Mexican family, three Frenchmen. Stunned to silence by the beauty, our reverie was suddenly shattered by two bat falcons—bright orange and slate gray—approaching through the twilight. Soon they were swooping and circling the temple top, their dinner quarry consisting of large tropical dragon flies.

Then, off in the distance, a sound like an angry jaguar distracted us from the colorful air show. It was the — by then — familiar cry of the howler monkey. Howlers rarely come down from their lofty perches. Why should they? Once this wily creature, threat-

Flores as it is today. Photo by Vern Apppleby.

ened now by extinction, was revered by the Maya as the god of writing.

Why a monkey for a god? Why indeed was the raucous howler credited with the benign bestowal of the most sophisticated written language native to the Americas?

As with many questions surrounding the Maya, no one has an answer. Yet.........

WHERE TO STAY

The Tikal Inn   (502/950-0065; e-mail: hoteltikalinn@internetdetelgua.gt) (Tikal Park Headquarters—no fax) is my favorite of the jungle lodges. With its thatched roof stucco walls and colorful Guatemalan fabrics, it looks like a jungle lodge ought to look. The food's good too.

The alternative is the somewhat larger and more *Spartan Jungle Lodge*. (502/477-0570). Neither takes credit cards. Both have pools.

But, really, for both these places, it's clearly location, location, location. They're in the midst of a vast jungle. At night you fall asleep to the sound of exotic bird and bug noises. In the morning you may look out your window to see ocellated turkeys, scarlet macaws or even howler monkeys.

We may think it all began in Tikal, but we know it ended in Flores only a few miles away.

The island town, tier upon tier of pastel buildings, rises from Lake Petén-Itza to the crest of a hill. In pre-Conquest days, the island was separated from the mainland by a stretch of open water two hundred yards in length. Now a causeway connects it with the mainland. Cobblestone streets circumscribe the island in ever decreasing spirals until they converge in a vortex at the highest point where a view of jungle and savanna extends farther than the eye can see.

Though located in the heartland thought to be the cradle of Maya civilization, *Tayasal* (which lies beneath *Flores*) was settled long after such great ceremonial centers as Tikal, Palenque, Yaxchilan, Coba and Copan had been abandoned. Its founders were the Itza, the once-powerful rulers of Chichen Itza forced to flee to Petén after their city fell to Mayapan. (Remember the tale of Princess Sac-Nicte who fled with her lover, Canek, ruler of Chichen Itza? Tayasal was their love nest.) Canek's people, fearing reprisals from Sac-Nicte's father, the mighty Hunac Ceel, followed.

The Itza flourished in their new home, developing a city that rivaled any city in Middle America, and was occupied at the time of the Conquest. When Herando Cortes, first Spaniard to visit the city, arrived in 1524, he was impressed. Twelve of its twenty-one temples were capable of holding at least a thousand people.

Canek, the ruler (the name, like czar or kaiser, designated supreme authority) received the conquistador cordially, professed a sincere interest in the new religion espoused by the Spaniard, but persuaded him that the time was not quite right for conversion. Canek explained that prophets had already predicted that the old gods would be forsaken, but not yet. The Spanish god's ascendancy was to begin in the Katun 8 Ahau, and as the present Katun was only 3 Ahau he respectfully suggested that Cortes continue with his expedition and return at a more propitious date.

Prompted by tales of even vaster treasures, Cortes moved on leaving behind an injured horse. The Itzas, who'd never seen such a creature before, were so impressed that they adopted the animal into their pantheon of gods. Daily

—a park as well as a ceremonial site.

tributes of flowers and poultry were offered, the diet eventually proving fatal to the poor horse. Horrified, the Maya quickly raised a temple to house a stone statue of the animal.

In 1618, two Franciscan friars arrived. They, too, were received by the ruling chieftain of the Tayasal dynasty. This Canek, too, assured them that the time was not quite right. When one of the friars expressed his disappointment by desecrating the sacred horse statue, only the direct intervention of Canek himself prevented a massacre Later missionaries were not so fortunate.

Eventually Don Martin Ursua mounted a massive campaign against this last stronghold of the Maya. Arrows were no match for muskets. The town was quickly secured. Soldiers, urged on by zealous priests

Pyramid I rising from the surrounding jungle.

undertook the systematic destruction of everything in sight.   The last
vestiges of a monumental civilization were destroyed in a single day. That
day was March 13, 1697 just four months short of the Katun 8 Ahau.

GETTING THERE & more WHERE TO STAY_____

One may reach Tikal by land from Belize or by air from either Guatemala
City or Cancun.   Both flights land in Flores where buses or rental cars are
readily available. Take time for at least a brief visit to Flores, the town that
time forgot.

For the budget minded, Flores is an excellent place to stay. The *Maya
International* (502-8136 e-mail: stpvillas@pronet.net.gt) has lovely water
views and gregarious jungle fowl who stroll the grounds in hopes of sharing
dinner.

Another option offers the best of two worlds.   The *Hotel Camino Real-Tikal*
(Phone 1-800-228-3000) is a fantasy come true. Somehow in the midst of the
jungle a world class hotel has risen, the state-of-the-art quality of its appointments rivaling the ingenuity of the Maya themselves.   Not only is it
gorgeous — all the exquisitely decorated rooms look out over the crystal

clear waters of Lake Petén-Itza — but comfortable. Yes, it is nice to drink the tap water, yes it does add to the enjoyment of the gourmet food to know that surgery could be safely performed on the kitchen floor. Buses or rental cars speed you to the nearby ruins, an excursion boat takes you to Flores and any number of other excursions can be arranged. If what you want is a romantic getaway, the Camino Real is perfect. Or, if you've been roughing it in the ruins, possibly camping in jungle preserves, perhaps you owe yourself a long soak in a real tub, a cool drink on a private balcony, a exquisitely prepared meal in an elegant dining room.

The Camino Real—Tikal.

The ball court at Copan. Photo by Charles Herndon.

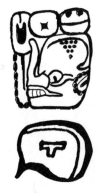

HONDURAS/COPAN
(hun-door-az/coh-pahn)

*Copan may have been the starting point
of the Maya civilization.*

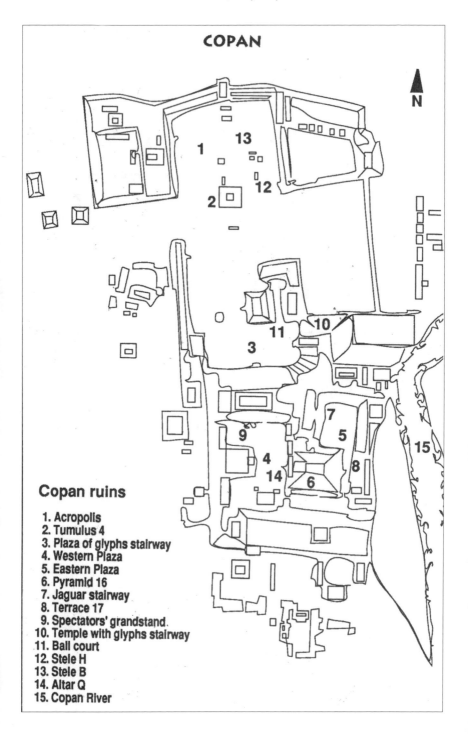

COPAN

N

13

1

12

2

11   10

3

7

9   5

4

14   8

6

15

Copan ruins

1. Acropolis
2. Tumulus 4
3. Plaza of glyphs stairway
4. Western Plaza
5. Eastern Plaza
6. Pyramid 16
7. Jaguar stairway
8. Terrace 17
9. Spectators' grandstand
10. Temple with glyphs stairway
11. Ball court
12. Stele H
13. Stele B
14. Altar Q
15. Copan River

L ocated on the Central American Isthmus, Honduras, with a total land area of 43,277 square miles, borders three countries: Guatemala to the west, El Salvador to the south and Nicaragua to the west and has a coast line on both the Caribbean Sea and the Pacific Ocean. Honduras's past is a finely woven web of history, myth and legend. Though the history could be said to begin with the Maya, when the Spaniards arrived the glories of that vast civilization already lay in ruins.

Christopher Columbus discovered what was to be Honduras on his fourth and last voyage to the New World on July 30, 1502. His brother, continuing the expedition, arrived at Punta Caxinas on August 14 and celebrated the first mass to be held on the American continent. Legend has it that the admiral, having just survived a devastating storm at sea, was heard to exclaim: "Gracias a dios que hemos salido de esas honduras!" (Thank God we have cleared those depths.) That line would eventually christen a province and a country.

A series of rival expeditions followed, everyone seeking a slice of the glory. Hernando Cortes, commander-in-chief of the New World, sent Cristobal de Olid to check out the theoretical leader Gil Gonzales de Vila. Then, doubting Olid's loyalty, he sent Francisco de las Casas to check on him. Soon others got into the act; the ruthless Pedro de Alvarado came from Guatemala while Hernando de Soto arrived from Nicaragua. Now the conquistadores were not only fighting Indians but each other. The situation got so out of hand that Cortes himself had to intervene.

Order was finally restored when Diego Lopez de Salcedo, the first royal governor, arrived in October 1526. He succeeded in appeasing the ambitions of the conquerors but made bitter enemies of the Indians. By 1537, the Indian population was in full revolt. Under the leadership of Cacique Lempira, they came very close to overcoming their Spanish oppressors but eventually Honduras was incorporated into the Kingdom of Guatemala. At the time the key economic activity was gold and silver mining. With the depleted ranks in the Indian population, African slaves were brought in to work the mines.

The country declared itself independent from Spain in 1821 and immediately joined the newly forged Mexican Empire. When the latter collapsed, Honduras became a member of the United Provinces of Central America, a union which was dissolved on May 31, 1838. From then on the country has been fully independent. Today Honduras has a population of more than five million, approximately ninety percent of which are mestizo, a blend of European, Black and Indian.

A democracy headed by a popularly elected president, its constitution allows for three governing branches: the legislative represented by a national congress of eighty-two elected deputies, the executive consisting of a president and his thirteen member cabinet of ministers, and the judicial making up the country's supreme court in which the nine judges are appointed by the congress and the president. All of these officials are elected for four year terms. The president and his cabinet appoint the governors of Honduras's eighteen departments or states.

Currently a great boom is taking place in the north with San Pedro Sula, leading the way as the country's most industrialized city. In its efforts to diversify the economy, the government has attracted international companies anxious to take advantage of the incentives currently being offered to foreign visitors.

The lempira (named for Cacique Lempira) is the currency of exchange — pegged now at 18.20 to the dollar. A seven percent sales tax is added to bills at hotels, restaurants and shops, a ten to fifteen percent tip customary when dining out. Prices are extremely reasonable by North American or European standards.

Honduras has two seasons: rainy from June to October and dry from November to May. Temperatures during the rainy season range from 59 degrees fahrenheit in the highlands to 86 degrees in the lowlands. During the dry months, temperatures are slightly higher in both zones. Visitors can count on wearing light clothing throughout the year. Men usually wear suits or the traditional guayabera, a loose shirt worn without a tie. Women wear dresses. Shorts are definitely out of place in the cities.

Honduras is serviced by SAHSA, the Honduran national airline; TACA, the Salvadorian national airline; Continental and American airlines. There is a city tax o2 $2 and an airport tax of $24 to be paid on departure.

— COPAN —
(coh-pahn)

One morning archeologist William Fash was awakened by a longtime employee.

"What's the matter?" he asked the Honduran workman, whose name happened to be Napoleon.

"It's bad, boss," Napoleon replied, obviously agitated. "I had this dream last night. The mighty ruler, 18 Rabbit, came to me and said, 'You'd better tell those archeologists that 18 Rabbit is not my real name." Napoleon paused, then added ominously, "He was really pissed."

Fash, a leader of the Copan Acropolis Archaeological Project from Northern Illinois University, understood Napoleon's concern. Maya Indians consider dreams direct communica-

Copan art among the ruins.
Photos by Charles Herndon.

tions from their ancestors. In the days when Copan was a mighty city, its kings conversed with gods in dreams and trances then emerged from lofty pyramid temples to share their revelations with the waiting populace.

He admits the translation of the name could be wrong, since there are 2,000 or more carved signs each with its own phonetic value. The 18 comes from a carving with three dots, each representing the number 1, and three bars, each standing for the number 5, in conjunction with a carved head that might as easily be that of a gopher or possibly even a jaguar as a rabbit.

"If his name wasn't 18 Rabbit, what was it?" Fash eagerly asked.

Napoleon's answer was disappointing. "He said that was for you to discover."

Whatever his precise name, the king known as 18 Rabbit was the greatest patron of the arts the Maya ever produced and the carvings at Copan created during his reign are considered the best in Pre-Columbian America.

Copan ruins.

Southernmost of the great lowland Maya centers, Copan lies in the western part of the Central American country of Honduras, adjacent to the Guatemalan border and some 250 miles from Tikal. Its geological and climatic conditions, so different from Petén, make it a unique site. Though still mountainous, the surrounding land is more fertile and the climate milder. Human settlement and civilization might be expected to flourish in such an area, causing some scholars to speculate that Copan may have been the starting point of the Maya civilization. Yet, for whatever reason, the site had been abandoned for 800 years when Diego de Palacio discovered the ruins in 1570.

It remained for the famed American traveler John Lloyd Stephens and his companion, English artist-architect Frederick Catherwood to rediscover the site and introduce it to the world. The intrepid pair literally stumbled into the ruin deep in the forest one rainy winter day in 1839:

> "It lay before us like a shattered bark in the midst of the ocean, her masts gone, her name effaced, her crew perished, and none to tell where she came, to whom she belonged. . .or what caused her destruction."

In the more than 150 years that followed, generations of scientists have endeavored to solve the riddle posed by Stephens. Today the 15-square mile site with its known 3450 buildings is a mecca for biggest names of the archeological world: Bill and Barbara Fash, Richard Williamson, Rebbeca Storey, David Stewart, Gordon Willey. The list grows daily for this is a working site, excavation and discovery constantly in progress.

Ongoing archeological work at Copan.
Photo by Charles Herndon.

What they have learned thus far is that Copan reaches back more than 3000 years and flowered during the Classic Period (A.D. 300 to 900). Originally a ceremonial center, it expanded over the years to include a large bustling city of possibly 30,000 inhabitants. Today Copan's outstanding feature is the soaring *Acropolis*, whose ornate buildings and sculptures, even in ruin, make it one of the greatest treasuries of art and architecture in all the Americas.

Known as the Main Group, the Acropolis with its platforms, pyramids, stairways, and plazas, contains a marvelous series of carved stelae, or monoliths—the true glory of Copan. A celebration of rulership frozen in stone, these proud figures—larger than life portraits of the city's greatest rulers—are sculptured almost in the full round, each replica laden with the symbols of ancient power politics and its accompanying complex ideology.

Stelae at Copan.

Close examination of the stelae—Linda Schele's *Forest of Kings*— reveals great technical prowess, but what does it mean? The sculptors of Copan knew how to represent their figures entirely with the face — oddly contemplative faces, with a surprisingly eastern feeling about them — while the shapes of the bodies disappear under vestments. Enigmatic, sphinx-like, the purpose of these giant monoliths must certainly have been more than commemoration. Clues may be found in the hieroglyphics that lavishly cover each monolith, but many remain indecipherable.

Stela H, for instance, depicts a female figure. Opposite is the stela of a man covered by hieroglyphs that speak of controversy thought to surround her. The stela of 18 Rabbit shows the ruler as an old man, but there is another face carved into the figure as well—the likeness of the same man as a youth. Besides the bittersweet, sunrise/sunset message of passing time there are also hieroglyphic inscriptions hinting of impending disaster.

At the heart of the plaza, the oddly-shaped stone ball-court, a flat aisle flanked by two sloping side walls, was designed for a game a bit like soccer except that the small rubber ball was not allowed to touch the ground. The use of hands was out of bounds, the ball instead propelled by hips, thighs or shoulders. As in other Maya ceremonial sites, it was winner take all—the losers forfeited their heads. Some theorists believe that wars were fought this way with the fate of a city state riding on the prowess of its team.

One of the most interesting areas in the complex is the residential suburb known as *Las Sepulturas.*   Some of the rooms are obviously bedrooms, others servants' quarters. Beneath the patio floors, within earshot of adults at work and children at play, deceased ancestors slumbered happily—it was hoped—in the Otherworld.   It must certainly have been a comfort to the family patriarch as he stood on the patio parapet conducting his ritual blood-letting to know that his ancestors were beneath his feet, close at hand should he wish to summon them forth.

In addition to a wealth of jewels and artifacts, the tombs have yielded a variety of information regarding the belief system of the Maya. Among the finds were small bottles of poison standing within easy reach of the bodies, the assumption being that if the individual awakened and found earth not quite to his liking, he might take a sip and try again. Also among the ruins were the remains of a brujo or shaman surrounded by the tools of his trade. These may be seen in the marvelous museum that adjoins the site.

Many of the discernible hieroglyphs found at Copan indicate that this was a scientific center with particular emphasis on astronomy.   A relatively high altitude of 2000 feet within a wide open valley permitted regular and precise astronomical observations. Though the Maya had no optical instruments for such observations, they did use jade tubes to assist in concentrating their vision. In this manner they were able to calculate the revolutions of Venus and to predict eclipses with amazing precision.

For centuries the Maya made rigorous astronomical observations. Very possibly to record both these calculations and the passage of time, they invented mathematical techniques and writing methods. Their elaborate calendars were more precise than those used today. Every period of time—day, month, year, or cycle was apparently represented by a god set on the shoulders of another god, a chain stretching from one end of the horizon to the other. Time moved tirelessly in the oriented space of the Maya universe. No people in the world have ever appeared so preoccupied with time.

COPAN Museum

Museum entrance. Photo by Charles Herndon.

Copan now has an exciting museum, one of the most imaginative this writer has seen. You enter through a serpent's mouth. Remember caves were considered the secret connections to the underworld—often symbolized by a snake's mouth. Inside are two floors of original stela that have been removed from the site for safe keeping, priceless jewels, artifacts, and frescos. A highlight is the fascinating reproduction of the Rosalila Temple in its original colors. This temple was discovered inside a major pyramid.

The reproduction of the Rosalila Temple.

Don't miss the museum shop. The sculpture and hand carvings are phenomenal.

Copan is located one hundred miles west of San Pedro Sula. The paved road winds through coffee plantations, banana groves, fields of maize, growing more and more beautiful as

Museum artifacts. Realism is the dominant feature of Copan art—note wrinkle on face of head at left.

one ascends into the foothills. The small village of Copan Ruinas adjoins the site. It's a charming town that sprang up around the turn of the century to accommodate the archaeologists working at the

nearby ruins. Today it has a colonial feeling with its cobblestone streets and tile roofs. The shopping just gets better and better. I particularly liked the weavings at *Souvinir Yax K'ukmo* at No. 1, El Centro. *Tipicos Balxe* is a lively place to eat featuring local specialties. If you're really daring, try the balxe (or balche) a very strong Maya drink that tastes too much like vinegar to suit me.

A must see while in Copan is **Macaw Mountain,** a bird park and nature preserve. The multi-faceted ecotourism project on ten heavily forested acres is home to a multitude of rescued and donated parrots, macaws and toucans from the surrounding areas.

Large flight aviaries and an open encounter area allow personal interaction with birds in their habitat. There are trails through the natural botanical garden—an incredible variety of tropical plants—flourishing in the cool micro-climate of a stream-cut valley and observation decks for wild bird watching. The preserve has a pleasant stream-sized restaurant. The preserve is located six minutes by taxi from Copan Ruinas's Central Plaza. It's open from 9 to 5 throughout the year for a nominal price. Phone: (505) 651-4245; www.macawmountain.com

Massive turtle dominates Copan site.

WHERE TO STAY

The **Marina Copan Hotel** with its inviting swimming pool is justifiably popular. The staff is thoughtful, rooms clean, food good. Telephone: (505) 652 4070; reservations: (505) 651 4477.

An alternative is **Hacienda San Lucas,** a 100 year old family farmhouse turned into a charming nine-room inn nestled in the hill above the ruins. Horses are available. The grounds are fun to ride or hike. An added treat is a visit to Los Sapos ("the toads") a sacred spot where Maya women went to give birth. The hand-built, solar powered, adobe hacienda has an excellent restaurant frequented by town people as well as hotel guests.

The owner, Flavia Cueva, is a delightful hostess. Her family has been associated with the archaeological dig for more than one hundred years and he has many tales to tell—in perfect English. (Cueva lived for a number of years in the United States.) Today she's busy collecting authentic local recipes as well as recreating food enjoyed in ancient times. Cueva and her master chef, Carlos Rivera—who received his training in Italy and France—hope to make Hacienda San Lucas a culinary destination. Their signature sauce is the delicious adobo. Phone: 504-651-4106; www.haciendasanlucas.com

> www.mayancaribbean.hn offers a smorgasbord of
> information about Honduras.

One generally enters Honduras by flying into San Pedro Sula, a modern, industrialized city of 300,000, centered between the country's main attractions, Copan and the resort island of Roatan. Because of plane connections, it's generally necessary to spend at least one night there. San Pedro Sula has two excellent hotels, both modern and air conditioned. The *Gran Hotel Sula* is centrally located by the cathedral, plaza and pedestrian shopping streets. (Reservations: 800 359-5672) The pretty pink *Copantl Hotel* on the edge of town has a resort atmosphere with impressive views of the city and surrounding mountains.   Reservations: (504) 556-6030; fax: 512-341-7942; website: www.hotelcopantl.com.

An excellent way to take advantage of a lay over in San Pedro Sula is to have clothing made there. This is the bargain that Hong Kong used to be.

Bring a photo or have a favorite dress or suit copied at a fraction of home prices.   Measurements can be taken before leaving for Copan and the finished garment will be waiting on your return. Carracchi, at 3 calle, 4 y 5 avenues., #23, is a shopper's dream come true. Telephone: 52-88-85.

Honduras's greatest buy is woodwork. A trip to the woodworking factory in the outlying village of El Progreso (Boulevard salida a Tela) is fascinating; but, if time is limited, visit "La Careeta" on Avenida Circunvalacion, Calle 1 in the central district.

Particularly lovely native crafts of all kinds may be found at *Galeria del Arte* on the Centro Commercial (the down town plaza kitty cornered from the Gran Hotel Sula.)

Most agree that the best food in town may be enjoyed at *Don Udo's* located on the continuation of the Boulevard Morazan off Avenida Circunvalacion, three blocks from the Fountain Bella Vista.   Phone: 553-3106. The menu is varied, you

Wood working factory. Photo by Charles Herndon.

can select your own live lobster, but for a personal recommendation: try the porkchops in whiskey sauce. Don Udo's also serves a divine martini—rum drinks are fun, but after awhile......

— ROATAN —

Many people on the lovely island of Roatan claim to know the whereabouts of buried treasure, but no one will dig it up. If they do, the "duppies," or ghosts will get them.

A history like Roatan's makes the duppie theory easy to buy. Roatan, the largest and most accessible of Honduras' Bay Islands, lies on the Spanish Main, the route that gold-laden galleons took from Panama to Havana, then on to Europe. With its plentiful fresh water, oak for repairs and hidden coves and inlets, the island made a perfect pirate hide-out. Small wonder that the likes of Sir Henry Morgan and John Coxen hung out there. Morgan prepared for his famous attack on Panama at Roatan and an estimated 200 sunken ships lie beneath the clear, warm waters.

Until recently, about the only people who had discovered anything on the island were scuba divers venturing beyond the coral reef of Belize, about 100 miles to the west. Though the island might be shaped like a crocodile, divers liked liked Roatan's friendly, laid-back, English-speaking locals, its low prices, clear waters and the pristine reef that is second in size only to Australia's Great Barrier Reef.

Roatan is inhabited by approximately 20,000 people. English is widely spoken (part of the English heritage) although Spanish is the official language of Honduras. Traveling around the island by car is easy. The majority of roads are paved.

But now Roatan, a mountainous island 45 miles long and less than 4 miles at its widest point, is beginning to change. The traditional wooden stilted buildings are gradually giving way to more modern construction, though locals are attempting to regulate rapid development and to insure that the natural beauty of the island is preserved. One of their demands is that no building be higher than a palm tree.

Coxen's Hole, named for the pirate captain John Coxen, is the capital and official port of entry. Several hotels and some very good restaurants make this the liveliest spot on the island. Surrounded by the Caribbean, there's an abundance of seafood simply prepared and delicious to eat.

Eagle Ray's Bar & Grill— Roatan. Photo by Chrales Herndon.

The island is home to more than 50 species of coral and boasts the richest selection of parrot coral in the Caribbean. Divers will also find an incredible variety of sponges including candlestick sponges, red, purple and buff rope sponges and fabulous sea fans.

On land you're bound to glimpse some of the 22 species of birds found there, including snowy egrets and brightly colored parrots. You'll also find deer, possum and iguana—some over four feet long—and an odd little critter called an agouti, a rabbit-like rodent unique to the island. The green turtles once so plentiful are now a rare and beautiful sight.

Surely one of the loveliest hotels is **Fantasy Island,** a peachy pink confection with an elegant plantation feeling.   The decor is charming and the restaurant excellent—key lime pie is a special feature not to be missed. Each room looks out on the private palm-studded beach.   Beyond lies the resort's gorgeous sea garden with every species of coral and an endless variety of sponges and schools of bright fish of all colors.   Further still, the challenge of the deep and the mightiest sport fish of the Caribbean: marlin, tarpin, king mackerel, sailfish, barracuda and wahoo. Boats can be chartered and quality guidance is available for beginning and intermediary divers. Reservations: (800) 676-2826 USA, fax: (813) 251-0301; (888) 357-0811 Canada.

Three alternatives are *Coco View Resort,* reached by shuttle boat from a bridge near Fantasy Island. US and Canada telephone: (800) 535-3483 and wbesite: roatancocoview.com. *Anthony's Key Resort,* which has 55 lovely water front casitas and a little museum.(1-800-277-3483)

With an abundance of fresh fish and lobster, restaurant fare is almost uniformly good, but I particularly enjoyed the conch soup, broiled lobster and delicious Honduran fried chicken at the funky *Hotel El Paso* in Coxen's Hole. But don't forget *A Bite On the Beach* on the layed back West End for unforgettable barbecued lobster.

The West End is the quaintest, least developed part of the island. It has the longest stretch of white sandy beaches on the island, the sea is calm and clear—perfect for all water activities. West End village, on the northwest side of the island, 13 klm. from the airport, is one small street running parallel to a few dive shops, gift shops and restaurants. Once there, everything is within walking distance.

Lost Paradise Inn at the edge of the village is Roatan's hidden treasure. Eighteen charming units overlook the sandy beach of a bay fringed by coconut trees. Phone: (505) 445-1306. e-mail: front desk@lost-paradise.com

Though Lost Paradise Inn has a pleasant restaurant, there are two other goodies. *Rudy's* and *Eagle Ray's Bar & Grill.* Rudy of Rudy's has a wonderful face that invites artists. His simple food is an art form too. *Eagle Bay's Bar & Grill*, a ramshackle Victorian built out on a pier, was made for romance.

Crystal Symphony cruise liner stops at Progreso, Cozumel, Belize and Roatan, as well as Ocho Rios and Grand Caymen.

Once a vociferous part of the rain forest, the howler monkey has almost disappeared.

ECOTOURISM

What is the essence of an environmentally sensitive traveler?

Such tranquil sites may be lost forever.

L OOK BUT DON'T TOUCH: ECOTOURISM

Now Mexico, like Belize, Guatemala and Honduras, faces an even more serious dilemma—one common in tropical countries: how to maintain the environment while harvesting its valuable energy resources.

Today in tropical rain forests one is more likely to hear the whine of a chain saw than the cry of a monkey or jaguar. In Central America, tropical forests the size of Norway have fallen since 1962—sentencing the black howler monkey to the endangered species list. Political, economic and population pressures are destroying the culture and natural resources of an area where, merely to survive, people must cut down the forest trees. In Guatemala, for instance, the average agricultural worker earns $2 a day, while a gallon of milk costs $1.60 and a gallon of gas $2. Not surprisingly, one of the hottest selling items in the area is a chain saw. Besides logging, the primary industries are killing animals for their pelts and illegal pet trade in jungle creatures.

At the same time acid rain falling on the Yucatan Peninsula and much of southern Mexico is fast bringing destruction to the temples, murals and haunting megaliths of the ancient Maya civilization.

Evidence of widespread damage to the Maya ruins is the most telling example yet that acid rain, which can blight forests and lakes as well as damage stone structures, is not confined to the world's northern industrial regions. It's a clear warning signal that this form of "chemical weathering" is threatening the millions of acres of tropical rain forests in southern Mexico and Central America. The damage to Maya treasures is greatest, the experts say, in the exquisite temples of Palenque, where paint is flaking off and stucco surfaces and stone inscriptions are corroding and crumbling. A black crust of acid deposit coats one wall of the Great Ball Court at Chichen Itza. Archeological treasures at Coba and Uxmal are also showing acid's devastating effects.

In a three-year study, supported by the National Geographic Society, Dr. Merle Greene Robertson, then an art historian and director of the Pre-Columbian Art Research Institute in San Francisco, not only documented that "the sculpture and architecture of the Maya civilization are being destroyed by acidic precipitation," but warned that surrounding forests "are now subject to increasing levels of acidic rainfall."

In her studies Robertson explained that researchers used meteorological observations to trace the source of the Yucatan's acid rain to emissions from

Heliconia

uncapped Mexican oil wells and oil field smokestacks near Coatzacoaleos and Ciudad del Carmen on the Gulf of Mexico.

The wells are operated by Pemex, the government owned petroleum company. The nearest oil field is 75 miles from Palenque and 250 miles from Chichen Itza. The burning of petroleum produces oxides of nitrogen and sulfur that rise into the upper atmosphere where they are borne by wind and undergo chemical reactions from sunlight and moisture. After a few days, the sulfuric acid and nitric acid particles fall as acid rain or as dry acidic debris.

Acid rain eats into stone surfaces at once. The dry particles settle into crevices, ledges and molding. The damage they create comes later when rain falls on the deposits and creates corrosive chemical reactions. One of the ugliest manifestations of accumulated acid fallout takes the form of a "black scab." Even if deposits are removed with extreme care, Robertson said, underlying paint and stucco usually flakes off in

How long will jaguars continue to inhabit the rain forest.

the process. Some of the stucco walls that used to be painted red or blue are now virtually white from the acid-caused flaking and moldings and inscriptions are severely eroded.

The interior of the Temple of the Paintings at Coba is an example. Once decorated with vividly colored murals, the walls are "in such a devastated condition that there is very little one can see inside this shrine except the black scab, bacteria and mold

that covers everything." Black scab was painstakingly removed from a stone carving at Palenque in the early 1980s. Today it is already recoated.

Despite this evidence, the Mexican government has officially acknowledged acid rain as a problem confined only to the Mexico City area. The threat is obvious, yet the issue is a politically explosive one. How could it be otherwise when Pemex is the beleaguered nation's No. 1 earner of hard currency?

— "SEA, SUN, SAND, SEX" VS. ECOTOURISM —

The solution could come, many believe, through enticement and re-education of tourists. According to Bill Garrett, former editor of National Geographic, speaking at the World Congress on Adventure Traveling and Eco-Tourism held in Colorado Springs, 77 percent of a group from Liverpool, England vacationing in Cancun, when surveyed didn't know what country they were in.

What most of the 1.5 million annual visitors to Cancun also don't know, Garrett said, is that just a few miles away are more ancient ruins than can be found in Egypt—built by a culture that lasted six times longer than the Roman Empire and was in full flower when Europe was in the Dark Ages.

Garrett is an activist in the Virginia-based La Ruta de Maya Conservation Foundation aimed at fostering "rational and sustainable" tourism development in the ecologically and archeologically rich areas of Mexico and Central America.

"We have to make the environmental and cultural aspects too valuable to be destroyed, too valuable to the local people to destroy. Ecotourists," he says, "have been found to spend twice as much money as the 'sea, sun, sand and sex' crowd—and may even have twice as much fun."

Tourism to natural areas is indeed booming. Worldwide, tourism is expanding at a rate of four percent per year. Industry watchers predict that developing countries will double their share of the receipts of personal travel spending in the near future, capturing up to a third ($750 million) of the world total.

A natural response to all this is Mundo Maya, a cultural travel concept linking the Maya sites in Southeastern Mexico, including the states of Yucatan, Quintana Roo, Tabasco, Campeche and Chiapas, all of Guatemala and Belize, Northern Honduras and half of El Salvador. It parallels the longest coral reef in the Western Hemisphere, follows 250 miles of the original Pan American Highway and passes within easy reach of thousands of Maya ruins as well as eight international airports.

Eventually it's hoped that a single tourist visa and quality bus service with a Eurail-type pass will allow passengers to come and go conveniently stopping at areas seldom visited now. A cable way or monorail through environmentally sensitive areas would provide access to wildlife and Maya ruins while preventing the uncontrolled settlement and the forest destruction that typically follows new roads.

Enthusiasm for the project runs high. Recent studies by the World Wildlife Fund show that the nature-oriented tourist is an especially valuable prize, prone to stay longer and spend more than the beach resort crowd and be more tolerant of modest accommodations.   Green is very trendy now. Growing interest in natural areas and competition for tourist dollars naturally spawned the promoter's dream: ecotourism.

But is it the rainforest's dream? The prospect of wildlife-watching tourists taking only pictures and leaving only dollars is a fantasy scenario, but can it work?   Money from tourism seldom "trickles down" to environmental protection. In fact, the most popular sites already suffer negative impact from too many visitors.

According to the previously quoted Merle Greene Robertson, the rapid deterioration of painted walls at the Temple of the Frescoes at Tulum— the most frequently visited of all the Maya sites—was caused by the exhaust from tour buses that stand for hours with their motors running in front of the stone structures.   Other archaeologists speculate that the one reason that Guatemalan ruins have largely escaped similar damage is because they're less accessible to tourists. Also the more remote sites have not been cleared of overarching vegetation, which acts as a screen protecting the stones against much of the acid rain fallout.

Only a few miles from main roads are villages that, for better or worse, stand as monuments from another time. Centuries of isolation has preserved attitudes, architecture and crafts long lost to wealthier, more industrialized societies. How will these indigenous peoples and their cultures be affected by increased contact with affluent visitors?

What is the essence of an environmentally sensitive traveler? In an effort to prevent ecotourism from becoming eco-terrorism, the International Wilderness Leadership Foundation lists the following:

GUIDELINES_____

- PROTECT WILD LIFE AND WILD LANDS—Respect the animals' space and privacy and watch from a distance comfortable for them and you. Move lightly to prevent damage to delicate vegetation. Consider not only your impact, but also the total impact of all those who have had or will share the same experience.

- RESPECT THE HOST CULTURE—Local customs, beliefs, social systems, art work and artifacts are as important to your nature adventure as are the wildlife and wild lands.

- SUPPORT LOCAL PEOPLE—Use local services and purchase locally made goods for a fair price. The best nature tour companies employ as many indigenous people as possible and provide advancement opportunities for them. Steady livelihood, adequate education and appropriate training for local people are key elements in sustaining wildlife and wild lands.

- ENHANCE YOUR PERSONAL UNDERSTANDING—The essence of the wilderness is a unique combination of the inner person with the outer world, of the human soul with the spirit of the land. Allow it to happen and allow yourself to change.

- INVOLVE YOURSELF IN CONSERVATION—Translate the adventure and excitement into a personal commitment to nature conservation. Find out what you can do to protect wildlife, wild lands and local cultures—and then act.

For nearly one hundred years—the last half of the 19th century to the first half of the 20th— henequen (sisal hemp) was king in Yucatan. To accommodate production some 4,500 kms. of tramway track was installed running throughout the plantations and linking them to train stations and the port of Progreso. It was a colossal network unequaled anywhere in the world. In 1916, Yucatan produced 90% of the world's twine, but with the advent of synthetics in the 1940s the demand dwindled. Today the grand old plantation houses are being turned into hotels, jungle has reclaimed the land. Only a handful of plantations remain, growing fiber for locally produced hammocks, mats and baskets.

Henequen fibers drying. Photo courtesy of Marian Sanders.

TRAVEL TIPS

- Getting around
- Maya meals
- What to do until the curandero comes?

The best way to enjoy
Mexican food is simply to relax.

GETTING AROUND_____

• PLANES—*Aeromexico* has direct flights to Cancun, Cozumel and Merida from Houston, Los Angeles, Miami, New Orleans, New York, Phoenix, San Diego and Tuscon. *American Airlines* has Dallas and Miami departures for Cancun. *Continental Airlines* services Cancun, Cozumel and Merida as well as Belize, Guatamala, and Honduras from Anchorage, Cleveland, Denver, Houston, Los Angeles, Newark and San Francisco. *Mexicana* has flights from Chicago, Denver, Los Angeles, Miami, New York, San Antonio, San Jose, San Francisco fro Cancun, Guatamala and Merida. *Sahsa* services Belize, Guatamala and San Pedro Sula from Houston, Miami and New Orleans. *TACA Airlines* services Belize, Guatamala and San Pedro Sula from Houston, Miami, Los Angeles, New Orleans and San Francisco.

• TRAINS—There's very little that I can say about taking trains on the Yucatan Peninsula other than don't. At one time there was an excellent sleeper car that left Merida around midnight and reached Palenque the next morning. Unfortunately, this service was discontinued in early 1987. Yes, there's still a night train. I was told the trip would take 12 hours. In reality, it was 17.

Yes, it was an opportunity to experience the real Mexico: snoring passengers, wailing babies, loud music, etc. There are other, easier ways. Besides being a long, hard trip, it can also be dangerous. I've known people who've been robbed.

• BUSES—the bus system in Mexico is relatively efficient and seems to go everywhere. This really is a good way to meet all kinds of people. If you're traveling light, are in reasonably good physical condition, possess a sense of humor and an adaptable nature, traveling by bus can be fun. Sometimes bus seats can be reserved, try to arrange this whenever possible. Check and re-check everything.

• CARS—there are two very different kinds of people who don't like traveling by car in Mexico. One kind feels that car travel tends to "isolate" them from the real Mexico. In a way, it does; but after my numerous bus and train experiences, I find there's something to be said for isolation.

The other kind of person avoids car travel out of fear. There's always somebody who knows somebody who heard this horror story from someone else. As far as I'm concerned, driving a car in Mexico is no different from driving one anywhere.

Whether you drive your own car or rent one, insurance is essential. Rental cars are highly competitive, so do comparison shop. When you leave town be sure you have a full tank of gas. Service stations aren't as prevalent in Mexico as they are in the United States. Roads in Yucatan, Quintana Roo and most of Chiapas are excellent, but I don't suggest night driving in remote areas. (I wouldn't suggest it in remote areas of the United States either.)

Recently a car I'd rented broke down in the middle of a tiny village–fortunately in broad daylight. People emerged out of nowhere and pushed the car over to the side. There were offers to help, but the car appeared beyond help. There was no phone, but a bus came by. My companion hopped on and the driver detoured to take him to the very door of a garage.

I waited with the car practicing my Spanish on the children who appeared out of nowhere to admire my red fingernails and jewelry. By the time my friend returned with the mechanic I'd met all twenty residents of the town. Before long the car was drivable and we were on our way, but the next day as we were about to leave Valladolid it acted up again.

This time we called the rental office in Cancun. Within two hours a representative was there with a new car. All repair connected bills were matter of factly subtracted from the final rental fee when we turned in the second car at the Merida airport. I've had cars breakdown in Lisbon, on the island of Crete and the Hollywood freeway. It can happen anywhere.

That relatively remote possibility is scarcely worth the loss of mobility and independence that car travel offers.

MAYA MEALS

The best way to enjoy Mexican food is simply to relax. Speed is not a quality on which Mexican waiters pride themselves. Additionally, they consider it tacky to present the bill without being asked for it. This lifestyle offers a splendid behavior modification opportunity for Type A's.

Forget who you are and where you came from and think instead about the reasons why you needed this vacation. While you're contemplating, you can also practice a little Spanish. La cuenta, por favor (the bill, please) for instance.

Separated from most of Mexico by water and jungle, the Yucatan Peninsula has a character all its own. The early colonists had far more in common with Europe and Cuba than they had with Mexico. This and the Maya influence accounts for the area's independent spirit and unique cuisine.

The *frijol negro*, a rich black bean, is popular throughout Yucatan as well as in the Caribbean islands. Banana leaves are used for wrapping tamales, meats, and fowl while steaming, baking, and grilling--open-fire cooking is common in Yucatan. The bitter Seville orange and sour lime are peculiar to the peninsula, adding a tangy touch to sauced dishes.

The Yucatan has several specialties which you'll see often on menus. Once away from Cancun, the English explanations will be omitted. A few to remember are:

Sopa de Lima—chicken broth, lime juice, onion, corn, chips and small pieces of chicken.

Cochinita Pibil–baked pig with sour orange juice, salt, and banana leaves served with relish made of onion, coriander leaves, hot pepper and salt.

Sac-kol de Jambali—Wild boar with sauce made of corn flour, tomato and peppermints leaves.

Pok-chuc—broiled pork meat, tomato, onion, coriander leaves and sour orange served with black beans. This dish was originally introduced to Yucatan more than 100 years ago by Chinese immigrants but has become a staple found everywhere in Yucatan.

Tzic de Venado—baked venison, shredded and mixed with coriander leaves, radish, mint leaves and sour orange juice.

Pavo en Relleno Negro—turkey with tomato, achiote, epazote, salt, vinegar, hot peppers and pork meat stuffing.

WHAT TO DO UNTIL THE CURANDERO COMES _____

Turista isn't inevitable. After more than 30 trips to Mexico, I've yet to experience it–though I've gotten "ze trots" twice in France.

A government seeking tourists is going to do everything in its power to keep them carefree and comfortable. Many Mexican hotels and restaurants have their own water purification systems. As a travel writer I've inspected many. The possibility of picking up the nasty E. Coli bacteria in such pristine places is probably less than in your kitchen or mine. Of course, if you plan to venture off the tourist circuit, the odds change. Though Mexico often seems like an exotic annex to California, it's still a Third World country with a few potential hazards.

The best way to avoid the need for a curandero or healer is to practice preventative medicine. The day before leaving for Mexico, I zap my immune system with a gamma globulin shot. This virtually guarantees immunity to Hepatitis A which is transmitted the same way as travelers diarrhea, via water and food that's been contaminated with sewage. A common source of hepatitis A is eating raw shellfish that was caught in polluted water. In other words, you can get it at home as easy or easier than in Mexico.

Though developed primarily for hepatitis A, gamma globulin seems to strengthen the body's resistance in other, as yet, undefined ways. In addition to this shot, I take a sulfatrim tablet on the day I leave and on every day of my trip. This combination continues to sustain me in some highly primitive areas.

Whenever possible I drink bottled water, beer, soft drinks, etc. I also purify my own drinking water by dissolving halizone tablets in the carafes left in my hotel room. I carry this water with me in a plastic flask and also brush my teeth with it. Besides halizone, my medicine bag contains Pepto Bismol tablets–just in case.

Friends who prefer to "wait and see" rather than take medication before the fact swear by lomotil. Lomotil is available at any farmacia in Mexico without a prescription, as are two other standbys: streptomagnum and mexaform. However, since each of us reacts differently to medication, it's a good idea to check with your doctor.

ABOUT THE AUTHOR

A writer who has traveled extensively all over the world, Antoinette May is repeatedly drawn to Mexico. As a psychic researcher whose work has been the subject of such TV documentaries as *In Search Of* and *The World of People* and *Unsolved Mysteries*, she's particularly intrigued by the mysteries of this remarkable land.

May is a travel writer, a biographer, former newspaper editor, and the founder and publisher of a women's magazine. She writes a weekly column for the San Francisco Chronicle and lectures on parapsychology at universities and colleges. She is currently writing a novel about first century Rome.

May is the recipient of the prestigious *Pluma de Plata* award from the Mexican government.